THE WORLD OF  ULYSSES S. GRANT

SERIES EDITORS

John F. Marszalek & Timothy B. Smith

INTERRUPTED ODYSSEY

Ulysses S. Grant and the American Indians

Mary Stockwell

Southern Illinois University Press • Carbondale

Southern Illinois University Press
www.siupress.com

Copyright © 2018 by the Board of Trustees
Southern Illinois University
All rights reserved
Printed in the United States of America

21 20 19 18 4 3 2 1

Jacket illustration: "Let Us Have Peace," drawn by C. S. Reinhart and published in *Harper's Weekly*, June 18, 1870, showing Ulysses S. Grant greeting Red Cloud, Spotted Tail, and Swift Bear during the visit of an Indian delegation with the secretary of war, William Belknap; LIBRARY OF CONGRESS.

Library of Congress Cataloging-in-Publication Data
Names: Stockwell, Mary, author.
Title: Interrupted Odyssey : Ulysses S. Grant and the American Indians / Mary Stockwell.
Description: Carbondale : Southern Illinois University Press, [2018] | Series: The world of Ulysses S. Grant | Includes bibliographical references and index.
Identifiers: LCCN 2017048174 | ISBN 9780809336708 (hardback) | ISBN 9780809336715 (ebook)
Subjects: LCSH: Grant, Ulysses S. (Ulysses Simpson), 1822–1885—Relations with Indians. | Indians of North America—Government relations. | BISAC: HISTORY / Native American. | BIOGRAPHY & AUTOBIOGRAPHY / Presidents & Heads of State. | HISTORY / United States / 19th Century.
Classification: LCC E93 .S87 2018 | DDC 323.1197—dc23 LC record available at https://lccn.loc.gov/2017048174

Printed on recycled paper. ♻

This paper meets the requirements of ANSI/NISO Z39.48-1992 (Permanence of Paper) ∞

To Adam

Contents

List of Illustrations — ix

Ulysses S. Grant: A New Perspective — 1
Prelude — 4
1. One Man's Journey — 15
2. Parallel Lives — 29
3. A Better World Ahead — 50
4. The Dawn of a Revolt — 69
5. Interrupted Odyssey — 86
6. A Sea of Change — 115
7. War on the Far Horizon — 134
8. The Web of Corruption — 155
9. A Forgotten Legacy — 180

Acknowledgments — 195
Appendixes
A: Army Officers Appointed to the Indian Service, 1869 — 197
B: Christian Missionaries Appointed to the Indian Service, 1871–72 — 202
Notes — 207
Bibliography — 233
Index — 247

Illustrations

Portrait of Ulysses S. Grant	6
Painting by Cadet Grant	26
Major Indian Tribes (1860s)	30
Ulysses Grant and Ely Parker	37
Ely Parker at Grant's headquarters	39
Treaty of Fort Laramie (1868)	60
Red Cloud's first visit to the White House	75
William Welsh	97
General Norton Chipman	100
Shooting buffalo on the line of the Kansas Pacific Railroad	129
Modoc War (1873)	137
General Edward Canby	142
Captain Jack and his followers	144
Quanah Parker	147
Red River War (1874)	149
Red Cloud's second visit to the White House	163
Sitting Bull	168
Custer's Last Stand	175
Great Sioux War (1876)	177
Savagery to "Civilization"	188

Interrupted Odyssey

Ulysses S. Grant:
A New Perspective

Contrary to what previous historians and biographers have written about America's eighteenth president, *Interrupted Odyssey: Ulysses S. Grant and the American Indians* makes the case that Grant never recommended a "peace" or "Quaker" policy toward the Indians. Instead, even before he assumed his nation's highest office, he developed an Indian policy with the help of his friend and military secretary, Ely S. Parker, who was himself a Seneca Indian, that placed the president and the army in charge of Indian affairs.

More specifically, against those who called for the extermination of the Indians, Grant proposed moving the tribes to reservations where they would be protected from the onrush of settlers. Here, under the watchful eye of American soldiers, and not Christian missionaries, the Indians would come to realize that their traditional way of life could no longer sustain them in the modern world. Over a generation or two, they would learn new ways to support themselves, mainly as farmers or ranchers, and be welcomed into the American mainstream as citizens of the United States. In the process, the executive branch would reassert its traditional control over Indian policy, which had been lost in the aftermath of Andrew Jackson's removal of the eastern tribes.

Interrupted Odyssey follows the struggle of Grant, along with Parker, his first commissioner of Indian affairs, to implement this new policy in the opening years of his presidency. Opposition arose from the start, especially from Congress, which resented the fact that Grant excluded the Indian service from political patronage by placing army officers in charge of reservations, and from the Board of Indian Commissioners, a ten-man committee of wealthy Americans that Grant and Parker established to advise the administration and audit the Indian service.

The two friends soon found themselves caught in a power struggle with Congress and the board, both of which wished to strip the executive branch of all power over Indian affairs. They succeeded early in Grant's presidency by disallowing army officers' service in civil posts, making the Board of Indian

Commissioners the supervisors of the Indian service, and eventually abandoning the treaty system. Grant responded by placing missionaries in charge of reservations, primarily to prevent a return to the political corruption of the past in the Indian service.

The heart of *Interrupted Odyssey* tells the story of the ousting of Commissioner Parker from his post by way of unwarranted accusations of political corruption, which were brought to Congress by William Welsh, the first chairman of the Board of Indian Commissioners. A noted reformer on behalf of the Indians, but a man of deep-seated prejudices, he despised the "savage" Seneca Indian whom Grant had placed in charge of the Office of Indian Affairs. Unlike other works on Grant, *Interrupted Odyssey* describes in detail the public trial that Parker was forced to undergo before the House of Representatives. The attacks on the Seneca in charge of the Indian service eventually led to Parker's resignation, as well as to the ruination of Grant's Indian policy, which was helped along by the continuing resistance of Congress, the ever more powerful Board of Indian Commissioners, the press, reformers, the American public, and the tribes themselves.

Interrupted Odyssey follows Grant in his second term as he loses faith in many of his original ideas, especially after the uprising of the Modoc in 1873, the Red River War in 1874, and the conflict between greedy miners and the Sioux that led to the Great Sioux War in 1876. But no matter how much he comes to doubt his plans, he never surrenders the belief that all Indians must one day become citizens of the United States. Sadly, once Grant left office, historians ignored all this and instead spent most of the nineteenth and twentieth centuries discussing whether his "peace policy," as the press nicknamed his plan, ever had anything to do with peace or ridiculing him as a clueless administrator who stumbled into reforms of the Indian service with no real concern for the tribes. Now in the twenty-first century, there is a movement under way among several historians to reevaluate Grant's Indian policy in terms of his Civil War experience and within the context of the wider events of the Reconstruction. These scholars see Grant as having taken the same interest in the well-being of the many far western tribes as he did in the condition of the freedmen in the South. However, for most of them, their starting point remains the erroneous claim that Grant intended to put Quaker missionaries, rather than the army, in charge of reservations from the start of his presidency.[1]

In telling a remarkable and forgotten tale, *Interrupted Odyssey* succeeds not just in revealing Ulysses Grant's true Indian policy but also in placing him at the forefront of the wider story of the relationship between the United States and the Indians. In its pages, Grant emerges as the one key figure who, in between

Andrew Jackson, the president who pushed the tribes out of the American experience, and Franklin D. Roosevelt, the president who welcomed them back in, was brave enough to say that the Indians must be saved, not exterminated, and made citizens of the United States.

Finally, it should be noted that to bring Grant's forgotten Indian policy to life, the language in this book follows the language used at the time of Grant's military service and his presidency. This includes the use of the term Indians rather than Native Americans, natives, indigenous people, or the people; white people rather than European Americans, Euro-Americans, or Anglo-Americans; and Americans for citizens of the United States.

Prelude

As Ulysses Grant prepared his inaugural address early in 1869, many Americans wondered what he planned to say about the continuing crisis in the former Confederate states. Although the Civil War had ended four years previously, the violence in the South had not. White Southerners, who had grudgingly accepted the dissolution of slavery, could hardly stomach the fact that the men and women they once owned were now their equals. The very idea that the people they had bought and sold like livestock could enjoy the full benefits of citizenship, including owning businesses and holding political office, was more than most could bear. Attacks on freedmen became a regular occurrence throughout the South. Race riots in places like Memphis and New Orleans were so violent that only the federal army, made up of the same soldiers who had finally brought the Confederacy to its knees, seemed capable of stopping the murder of blacks and the destruction of their property. No wonder so many people in the North and South waited anxiously for what the former head of the Union army and now the newly elected president of the United States would say and, even more important, what he would do to stop the nation's descent into what appeared to be a second Civil War.

Grant had come down on both sides of the question of how best to handle the recalcitrant Southerners. His compassionate treatment of Robert E. Lee at the home of Judge McLean in April 1865 was already the stuff of legend. After four years of bloodshed, with a million soldiers killed or wounded and much of the South in ruins, the man who had defeated the rebels at Vicksburg, Chattanooga, and finally Appomattox told the Confederate commander to have his soldiers leave their artillery and small arms behind but take whatever horses and mules they owned, along with their sidearms, and go home. A stunned General Lee would always remember how Grant, who had first worked the land as a boy in Ohio, knew that most of the Confederates were small farmers. "It is doubtful whether they will be able to put in a crop," said the general through the haze of smoke from his cigar, "without the aid of horses they are now riding."[1] Would this forgiving man be the same person sworn in as the nation's eighteenth president? Would the words he chose to address the American people for the first time echo the final poetic ones spoken by Lincoln just weeks before his assassination? Would he bind up the nation's wounds, care for the widows and orphans, and build a lasting peace for "ourselves and with all nations?"[2]

One thing was certain: Grant would not tolerate any continuing prejudice against black people. He had demonstrated this after the war while serving in his new post as the general of the Army of the United States. In 1866, he reluctantly joined Johnson on his campaign swing across the nation to defeat the passage of the Fourteenth Amendment, which granted American citizenship to black people. He left the tour early, disgusted with Johnson's diatribes against the freedmen and their Radical Republican supporters. The strain between the two men grew even stronger when Grant openly supported the Fourteenth Amendment and the Reconstruction Acts, which divided the South into five military districts. He became the acting secretary of war after the departure of Edwin Stanton and decided which generals would govern these districts. Grant had already issued General Order 44, which gave the army the right to step in and keep the peace if local authorities could not maintain it. Did all this mean he had lost his compassion for the former Confederates since Appomattox? Would he keep the Union army in the field forever?

He gave the first clue that he would not assume the role of an avenger when he stepped out of his house on I Street in Washington, DC, and into a waiting carriage on the morning of March 4, 1869. Instead of wearing a military uniform, as most people expected, he was dressed in a simple black suit just purchased from Brooks Brothers. The only color in his outfit came from the yellow kid gloves he wore. Instead of being escorted by the generals who had helped him defeat the South, Grant sat behind the coachman with his friend John Rawlins, his former adjutant and the future secretary of war, at his side. They stopped at his headquarters, where other members of his military family joined them. One of these men was Ely S. Parker, a Seneca Indian who had served as his secretary from Chattanooga to Appomattox. Together they proceeded to the White House, where they learned that President Johnson was too busy to attend the inauguration.

Grant made his way to the Capitol, where a large crowd of black citizens waited to greet him. He smiled as he walked past them up the steps into the Senate Chamber. Here generals and admirals bedecked in their medals and ribbons, ambassadors in their formal attire, and the justices of the Supreme Court in their long black robes quickly surrounded him. After listening to a short speech by Schuyler Colfax, who had just been sworn in as his vice president,

Prelude

Portrait of Ulysses S. Grant. One of the many portraits of Ulysses Grant taken by a photographer, probably during his presidency.
COURTESY OF THE LIBRARY OF CONGRESS.

Grant walked out onto the eastern portico of the Capitol. Chief Justice Salmon P. Chase escorted him toward the podium where he would be sworn in as president. The outer calm he had maintained throughout the day broke when he heard the twenty-two-gun salute given in his honor. Even after all the battles he had fought, he still could not bear the sound of cannon fire. When the gun blast was finally over, he regained his composure, placed his right hand on a Bible, and recited the oath of office as prescribed by the Constitution.

Taking the speech that he had written from his breast pocket, Grant turned toward the thousands gathered before him and began reading in a voice so low that only those near the podium could hear him. As he continued, he grew ever quieter, until finally no one could hear him. The spectators did not grow restless, however, since they kept their eyes on Grant's little daughter, Nellie, who came forward and stood by her father until a chair was finally brought for her to sit next to him. They also remained at attention because the speech was so short. At just over eleven hundred words, it was only a few paragraphs longer than Lincoln's now famous Second Inaugural. After Grant finished speaking, the dignitaries near the podium roundly congratulated him as the crowd cheered, but to learn exactly what he had said, they would have to wait until they read their newspapers the following day.

When transcripts of the speech were finally printed, the president's words appeared as simple and direct as the man who spoke them. Grant reminded everyone that the nation's highest office had come to him without his asking for it. When he had accepted the Republican nomination for president, he had vowed, if elected, to govern "with the view of giving peace, quiet and protection everywhere," and this sentiment echoed throughout his inaugural address. He promised to work "calmly" for the "greatest good to the greatest number of people," no matter their politics or religion or the section of the country where they lived. Making a veiled reference to Andrew Johnson, without ever mentioning his name, Grant promised to restore peace between the White House and Congress. Though he might propose legislation, he would always uphold the laws passed by the House and Senate.³

Speaking as clearly as Lincoln had about leaving the past behind, but without the soaring heights of his grand poetry, Grant turned toward what he believed was the greatest problem facing America's future. The massive debt built up during the Civil War must be paid, he explained, preferably with the gold that was pouring out of the Rocky Mountains, a sure sign of God's continuing providence for the United States. He called on the young men of the country, who would lead the nation in the next twenty-five years, to make sure the debt was finally paid. As to any further specifics, he had only one. He supported the passage of the Fifteenth Amendment, which would guarantee the right of black men to vote.⁴

The one surprise in Grant's speech came when he looked beyond the aftermath of the Civil War to another problem that had haunted the nation since its founding: "the proper treatment of the original occupants of this land—the Indians," he said, "one deserving of careful study." He added, "I will favor any course toward them which tends to their civilization and ultimate citizenship."⁵ His words, so uneven in their grammar, brought to mind the Indian Wars, which had plagued the West even as fighting raged at Shiloh, Antietam, and Gettysburg back east. The list of conflicts across the Mississippi River went on and on: the Santee Sioux War in Minnesota; the Long Walk of the Navajo to Bosque Redondo; the Sand Creek Massacre in Colorado; the revolt of the Cheyenne,

Arapaho, and Comanche along the Washita River; and finally, the Powder River War of the Oglala Sioux in Montana. At a time when many Americans, in both the North and the South, agreed with General Philip Sheridan that the only good Indians were dead ones, Grant was determined to respect the hated savages as the first owners of the land, educate them in the ways of the modern world, and make them citizens of the nation that had long opposed them.[6]

What made this all the more surprising was the fact that no American president had mentioned the Indians in an inaugural address for forty years. Before that, all the way back to George Washington and continuing up to Andrew Jackson, the subject of the Indians came up regularly in the speeches of the presidents, especially in their State of the Union addresses. During this time, the American presidents considered themselves the primary shapers of the nation's Indian policy. But once Jackson had set in motion the removal of the eastern tribes to the country west of the Mississippi River, the nation's chief executives no longer considered this job solely their own. Instead, a patchwork of authorities from the federal to the local level managed Indian affairs. The fact that Grant mentioned the "original occupants of this land" in his inaugural address showed that he meant to put the president back in charge. He would assume the role that every president from Washington to Jackson had accepted and every president serving after the removal of the eastern Indians had rejected.

Washington set the nation's first Indian policy under the Constitution by recognizing the tribes as the true owners of the land. He believed this approach would prove to the Indians that the United States respected them, unlike European nations that had simply taken their land. But even with this attitude, Washington remained determined to win as much Indian land as possible and open it for settlement. He planned to accomplish this by negotiating treaties in which the tribes surrendered their land to the United States in exchange for annuities, yearly payments of money and goods to the chiefs. These annuities would tie the Indians to the United States, as would government trading houses established throughout the western country, where the tribes could exchange furs for even more goods.

Over time, Washington believed, the two peoples, red and white, would merge into one, especially once the Indians realized that the days of the warrior and hunter were over and must give way to the habits of the commercial farmer. They would become "civilized," meaning they would live just like the settlers coming their way. While hoping to avoid war, Washington was prepared to send armies against the Indians if they refused to sell their land or continued attacking frontier settlements. Even if they rose up against the United States, they would be forgiven, once they were defeated, and brought into the negotiating process again. If all went as Washington planned, even with a few interruptions like General Anthony Wayne's campaign against the Ohio Indians in the early 1790s, which led to the Battle of Fallen Timbers, the United States would grow peacefully west to the Mississippi River, the boundary set for his nation at the end of the American Revolution.[7]

For all the rationality of Washington's original policy, which was consciously implemented by his successors, resistance to it erupted in the persons of the Shawnee leader Tecumseh and his younger brother Tenskwatawa, better known as the Prophet. Early in Thomas Jefferson's second term and continuing through James Madison's first term, the two Shawnee brothers organized the largest confederation to date to resist the United States. Traveling in secret to avoid the watchful eye of frontier officials, Tecumseh, a warrior and gifted orator, visited tribes near the Great Lakes, convincing them that they should unite on the twin principles that the Indians were one people who owned the land in common, and therefore no one tribe or chief could sell it to the Americans. Through either negotiations with the government or a bloody war on the frontier, he promised to win a homeland for all the Indians in the old Ohio Country. The Prophet, a holy man whose visions convinced him that the Great Spirit would protect the Indians if they rejected the white man's ways, preached openly to the Indians who gathered around him first near Greenville, Ohio, and later along the Tippecanoe Creek.[8]

In the summer of 1810, William Henry Harrison, governor of the Indiana Territory, discovered the plans of Tecumseh and openly confronted him, setting off a chain of events that led to the Battle of Tippecanoe in November 1811. The skirmish, fought between Harrison's soldiers and the Prophet's warriors, temporarily dispersed Tecumseh's followers. But the American victory did not bring peace to the West. Tecumseh rebuilt his confederation among the northern tribes while also recruiting Alabama's Upper Creek to his cause. By the spring of 1812, the growing Indian revolt in the western country became a rallying cry for Americans who favored a war against Great Britain. Politicians known as War Hawks, like Henry Clay of Kentucky and John C. Calhoun of South Carolina, blamed the British for inspiring and directing Tecumseh's confederation. They called for the conquest of Canada to break the tie between the redcoats and the Indians. Not once did any War Hawk look to his own nation's Indian policy as the cause of the troubles on the frontier.[9]

During the War of 1812, President Madison and his secretary of state, James Monroe, twice witnessed the near total loss of the western country to the Indians: once on the battlefield when Tecumseh's followers and British regulars took frontier outposts from Detroit to Michilimackinac and again at the negotiating

Prelude

table in Ghent, Belgium, when the British demanded a separate Indian homeland on American soil north of the Ohio River. The British finally relented but insisted on adding Article IX to the Treaty of Ghent, which mandated that their nation, the Americans, and the Indians live in peace forever. In the summer of 1815, with the war finally over, Madison and Monroe implemented Article IX by negotiating treaties promising lasting peace with the Indians at Springwells near Detroit and at Portage des Sioux in the Missouri Territory.[10]

When Monroe became president, he worked to make the peace a lasting one by refining the nation's Indian policy handed down from Washington. He set aside specific reserves within territory surrendered by the tribes where the Indians would have a permanent homeland. He also advocated the eventual allotment of these reserves to specific individuals within the tribes, a plan the Senate overturned, fearing that land so divided would be sold off to white people, leaving the Indians homeless. Monroe went further than any previous president in winning funds for projects meant to "civilize" the tribes. With his support, Congress passed the Civilization Act, which provided $10,000 annually to run mission schools, build churches, and buy farm equipment for Indians living on reserves in the East.[11]

While he refined Washington's policy, Monroe made no change to its overall purpose. The tribes still had to sign treaties, giving up most of their land in the East, and eventually assimilate into the wider American society. But even as Monroe sought to perfect Washington's original policy, a rejection of it was well under way by the last days of his presidency. Frontier officials frequently reported that Indians were suffering from close contact with settlers, who brought violence, disease, and worst of all, whiskey. They recommended removal of the eastern tribes across the Mississippi River to save them from certain destruction. Native leaders like the Prophet, who was living on a Shawnee reserve in northwest Ohio, also worked to send the eastern Indians across the Mississippi. Many Americans, but not all of them, demanded that the last tribal holdings in their states be opened for sale and settlement. Georgia especially pressed the issue, claiming that the federal government had promised to remove the Cherokee when the state surrendered its western land claims to the United States.

By early 1825, pressure on Monroe to remove the Indians became so great that he reversed his own policy and recommended that the eastern tribes be sent across the Mississippi River. His successor, John Quincy Adams, agreed and would have started the removal process if his Secretary of War James Barbour had not intervened and offered a more humane Indian policy. If the Indians wanted to stay in the East, the government would provide whatever help they needed to enter the economic mainstream. But if they wanted to go west, the government would also support them by establishing Indian Territories near the headwaters of the Mississippi and along the Arkansas River. Here the tribes could live in peace, set up governments of their own, and hopefully bring the territories into the Union as states one day.[12]

Barbour's plans could not withstand the increasing calls for the removal of the tribes, which grew even louder as Andrew Jackson made his way to the White House in 1828. Jackson explained his plans for the eastern tribes in his first inaugural address and went on to discuss Indians in every State of the Union speech during the next eight years.[13] He implemented his plans with the passage of the Indian Removal Act in 1830. Tribes living east of the Mississippi would exchange their land for new reserves in what later became the states of Kansas and Oklahoma. What would happen to these Indians if someday Americans wanted to settle on these reserves was not a matter that troubled Jackson. Nor was the fact that even more tribes, many of whom lived as buffalo hunters on the Great Plains, would have to be pushed west to make way for the Indians being removed from back east. He shared the common assumption held by government officials and the public that somehow there was enough room on the vast prairies and plains of the Far West for all the tribes to live forever on "one big reservation."[14]

Jackson's decision to remove the Indians had a profound impact on future policymaking. From George Washington through John Quincy Adams, the presidents considered treaty making with the Indians the first step in the settlement of the West. They negotiated land sales with the tribes and set up annuity payments for them ahead of the flood of settlers coming their way. The system was not perfect, as Fallen Timbers, Tecumseh's confederation, and the War of 1812 proved. But at least it functioned regularly, with the nation's chief executive as the focal point of decision-making regarding the tribes. However, after Jackson initiated the removal process, responsibility for the tribes fell increasingly to the Office of Indian Affairs, established in the War Department in 1824, along with territorial governors, Indian agents, army officers, local militia leaders, and various senators and congressmen who took charge of the Indians west of the Mississippi.

The result can be summarized in one word: chaos. Americans soon overran the "one big reservation" west of the Mississippi River. Even before Jackson signed the Indian Removal Act, his countrymen were already on their way to Texas and the vast southwestern country, eventually acquired through the Mexican War and the Treaty of Guadalupe Hidalgo. They went even farther, to the Pacific Northwest, then down to California and back east through the Rocky Mountains. No government officials went regularly ahead of the traders, miners, stagecoach drivers, missionaries, and farmers to negotiate treaties with the Indians asking them to surrender their land in exchange for annuities. Conflicts with the Indians were handled on a case-by-case basis, with the ultimate decision-making power handed over to the commissioner of Indian affairs, a post officially established in 1832 to oversee the Office of Indian Affairs, which became part of the Department of the Interior after the department's founding in 1849.[15]

By the early 1850s, violence between settlers and tribes in the Far West was serious enough for Luke Lea, commissioner of Indian affairs under Presidents Zachary Taylor and Millard Fillmore, to propose a more coherent national Indian policy. On the recommendation of Thomas Fitzpatrick, the Indian agent at Fort Laramie in the Wyoming Territory, Lea proposed concentrating the tribes on the northern and southern plains, where they would be out of the way of Americans trekking west. In the summer of 1851, he directed Fitzpatrick to negotiate a treaty with the Sioux, Cheyenne, Arapaho, Crow, Assiniboine, Mandan, Gros Ventre, and Arikaree at Fort Laramie. In the final treaty, the United States promised to protect the tribes if they remained in these designated areas, stopped attacking Americans, and no longer fought among themselves. While forts and roads could still be built throughout their country, no Americans could settle there permanently. The Indians would also receive annual cash payments for the next fifty years, along with farm equipment, blacksmith shops, and manual labor schools for their children.[16]

Even though Congress reduced the payment schedule to ten years, the Treaty of Fort Laramie was relatively successful in bringing peace to the northern plains for the next decade. Two years after it was signed, Lea ordered Fitzpatrick to negotiate a similar treaty with the Kiowa, Comanche, and Apache at Fort Atkinson in Nebraska. The tribes agreed to move out of the way of the many wagon trains heading southwest along the Santa Fe Trail. In exchange, the government would pay them annuities, educate their children, and protect them from harm.[17]

But the desirability of almost every part of the West for the American people quickly brought an end to Lea's "concentration" policy. By the mid-1850s, politicians, especially Senator Stephen Douglas of Illinois, were determined to open the Great Plains for settlement. After the passage of the Kansas-Nebraska Act in 1854, Northern free farmers and Southern slaveholders raced into the Kansas Territory. Tribes that had been removed there from the eastern states a generation before faced increasing pressure to give up their land to farmers and railroad companies. Even more troubles came to the far western tribes as gold and silver were discovered throughout the Rockies. Now the Cheyenne in the central Rockies, the Navajo in the desert Southwest, and the Sioux on the northern plains were in the way of fabulous riches, not to mention the transcontinental railroads that must be built between the Mississippi Valley and the Pacific Ocean.

By the time General Lee surrendered to Ulysses Grant at Appomattox in April 1865, Congress was searching for an Indian policy that would bring a lasting peace to the West. Many people, both in and out of the government, now believed that the bloodshed would end only if the United States officially abandoned the concentration policy in favor of placing the tribes on much smaller reservations. The Office of Indian Affairs had already established dozens of these by treaties negotiated from the mid-1850s to the end of the Civil War. But this practice raised even more troubling questions. If the tribes were placed on small reservations, should there be a renewed focus on "civilizing" the Indians, making them live like modern Americans, a concern that had largely disappeared after Jackson's removal of the eastern tribes across the Mississippi? If so, how should this be accomplished? And once accomplished, should the Indians then be welcomed into the wider society and their reservations completely dissolved? As politicians debated these issues, some Americans, especially those who had seen their friends and families massacred on the western frontier, argued that the best approach to the Indians was simply to exterminate them, right down to the last man, woman, and child.[18]

Early in 1867, when news arrived in Washington that Sioux warriors had massacred Captain William Fetterman and his eighty soldiers in Montana, the Senate established the Indian Peace Commission to investigate this latest tragedy in the West. The members of the Peace Commission, as the group came to be known, were also charged with developing a comprehensive Indian policy that would end the wars across the Mississippi forever. The commissioners concluded that peace could be achieved only if the tribes, primarily for their own survival, were kept in separate districts on the northern and southern plains, where they could learn to live like the settlers who surrounded them and prepare for assimilation into American society. They delivered their final report to Congress as the race for the White House began in 1868.

Ulysses Grant, the Republican candidate for president, promised to follow the commission's recommendations if elected. His attitude was in keeping with the mood of many Americans who had endured enough bloodshed in their own Civil War. If Union soldiers and Confederate veterans, masters and their former slaves, and the many immigrants who were arriving daily from the farthest corners of the world could all live together in peace, then surely the American nation and the Indian tribes of the Far West could do the same. However, Grant did not reveal an important fact about his own plans to win peace. Even before the

Prelude

Peace Commission was appointed, he had already developed an Indian policy of his own, mainly with the help of Ely Parker. It would be overseen by the White House; directed by the Office of Indian Affairs, operating once again out of the War Department; and implemented by army officers, who would run the many superintendencies, agencies, and reservations across the Mississippi River. Grant was certain that his new approach would end the bloodshed in the Far West, protect the Indians from extinction, and ultimately bring them into full American citizenship.[19]

It was a tall order to fill, but sometime between the misery of Shiloh and the glory of Appomattox, General Ulysses Grant had ascended into the pantheon of American heroes who seemed capable of achieving the impossible. He now held out the promise of a peace that had eluded the likes of Washington and Jackson. Somehow, he would find a way, where so many others had failed, to persuade the soldiers, militiamen, miners, railroad workers, ranchers, laborers, farmers, and recent immigrants to live in peace with the Indians and welcome them into the nation as their fellow citizens. Perhaps he was confident he could do this because he had defeated the Confederates when no one else could. But maybe he should have heeded the warning that the nymph Calypso gave to his namesake, the hero Ulysses, who had also ended a terrible war long before:

> But if you only knew, down deep, what pains
> are fated to fill your cup before you reach that shore,
> you'd stay right here, preside in our house with me
> and be immortal.[20]

1. One Man's Journey

The simple words that President Grant spoke about the Indians in his first inaugural address touched on a truth that haunts Americans to this day. All who live in the United States, and for that matter the rest of the Americas, live on land where native peoples once lived, whether they recognize this fact or not. The cities and towns where they work and make their homes, the schools where their children learn, and the roads and highways on which they travel every day all were built on ground formerly occupied by indigenous tribes, some whose names are remembered and many more whose names will never be known. Even the reservations carved out for Indians through the late nineteenth century rest on land inhabited by other natives long forgotten. Trace the story of any living American back to his or her first ancestors in this country and another story runs alongside it filled with the lives of the many tribes that had to be defeated—on the battlefield, at the negotiating table, or by epidemics and other natural disasters—to make this one life possible.

The parallel stories can be seen in the life of Ulysses Grant, a man who could trace his family's ancestry far better than most Americans. As he proudly stated in the opening line of his *Personal Memoirs*, "My family is American and has been for generations, in all its branches, direct and collateral." Further on, he explained, "I am the eighth generation from Matthew Grant."[1] On May 30, 1630, twenty-nine-year-old Matthew Grant and his wife, Priscilla, along with their four-year-old daughter, also named Priscilla, arrived in Massachusetts from England after a two-month voyage. They had come across the Atlantic as part of the original flotilla of Puritans brought to the New World by John Winthrop. Sailing on the *Mary and John*, they landed on a small peninsula jutting out into the Atlantic called Nantasket, or the "low tide place," some ten days before their leader arrived in the *Arbella*. The Grants and their fellow passengers headed farther inland to a place called Mattapan. Here they established the town of Dorchester, later part of South Boston, where they lived for the next five years.[2]

Like the Pilgrims who had founded Plymouth ten years before, the Puritans who came to Dorchester in the Massachusetts Bay Colony considered it providential to find few Indians in their new home. An epidemic, probably smallpox, had decimated the local population. Entire villages, including Patuxet where the Pilgrims built Plymouth, and even whole tribes were wiped out. The Massachusett, or Blue Hill People, who lived on the land that would soon become Boston, had seen their numbers go from ten thousand to one thousand almost overnight. The Wampanoag, who lived farther south, helped the Pilgrims through their first year at Plymouth, in part to win their support in dominating the surviving tribes and to acquire manufactured goods, especially guns and ammunition. Under the leadership of their sachem Massasoit, members of the tribe taught the Pilgrims how to fish, plant corn, and trade with the local Indians. They led the Pilgrims to Nantasket on the Massachusetts coast, where they established a fur trading post, later known as the town of Hull. It was here that Matthew Grant's family and the rest of the Puritans on the *Mary and John* had landed in the spring of 1630.[3]

Life for the settlers of Dorchester was difficult in the beginning, just as it had been for the Pilgrims of Plymouth. But they endured, and five years after landing in Massachusetts, half of Dorchester's citizens, including Matthew Grant and his family, moved a hundred miles southwest into the Connecticut River Valley. Here they founded a new town, first called Dorchester and later renamed Windsor, on the west side of the river near a trading post set up by the Plymouth colony two years earlier. Matthew Grant made a name for himself as Windsor's first surveyor, a position he held for thirty-six years. He also served as the town clerk. In both posts, he dealt frequently with local Indians, a collection of Algonquin-speaking peoples known as the River Tribes. As settlers filled up Windsor, Matthew Grant measured out their town lots and farms, all purchased from local sachems. Grant's name appeared frequently in court records, testifying that his fellow townsmen paid the promised amounts of clothing, wampum, and corn to the chiefs for their land.[4]

But the peace between Windsor's citizens and the local Indians did not last long, especially after settlers in Massachusetts Bay launched a war against the Pequot, the most powerful tribe in southern New England, in the fall of 1636. The bloodiest fight in the Pequot War came in May 1637, when the English attacked the tribe's main town of Siccanemo on the Mystic River, some sixty miles southeast of Windsor. As the conflict spread, Matthew Grant played a key role in his town's defense by laying out a palisade at its center and clearing six acres within the fort himself. While fighting never reached Windsor, the war continued until September 1638 when the Pequot were finally defeated.

The two hundred surviving Pequot were divided among the English and their allies, the Narragansett, Mohegan, and Eastern Niantic, or sold into slavery in the West Indies.[5]

Four months after the Pequot War ended, the freemen of Windsor, Hartford, and Wethersfield, meaning the adult male property owners of the three towns, adopted a set of rules to govern their communities. Known as the Fundamental Orders, the rules called for the election of magistrates to a general court that met twice yearly to pass laws for Connecticut. Even greater stability came to Connecticut in 1662, when the English king Charles II granted a new charter to the colony. Its citizens were granted the "liberties and immunities" of Englishmen, and its western border was extended to the "South Sea on the West." The entire continent, all the way to the Pacific, now belonged to Connecticut and the other English colonies with sea-to-sea clauses in their charters.[6]

With a stable government firmly established, Connecticut prospered. Its farms now produced flour and livestock for export to the Atlantic market, while shipbuilding, lumber, fishing, and the fur trade would soon become profitable enterprises in the colony. By the standards of the day, Matthew Grant was one of his colony's well-to-do citizens, having a house with an orchard, three acres of pastureland, a five-acre meadow, and twenty-three acres of woods. His achievement was part of the wider success story of New England. By the late seventeenth century, more than fifty thousand English colonists lived in over a hundred towns from the coast of Maine in the north to Long Island Sound in the south and westward to the foothills of the Appalachians.[7]

But again, running alongside this bright success story of the colonists came the shadow story of the Indians. Their numbers, along with the territory they once commanded, continued to dwindle. Most could make a living only by working as servants for the English. Their customs, considered by most colonists as akin to the ways of Satan, were discouraged and in some cases outlawed. They could not practice their own medicine for fear of being accused of witchcraft. Their marriages had to be sanctified in the local churches. They faced a hangman's noose if they dared to question the Protestant faith. Life was especially difficult for tribal leaders, who found themselves under the constant scrutiny of colonial officials. King Philip, or Metacomet, who had become the sachem of the Wampanoag after the death of his father, Massasoit, and his older brother Alexander, or Wamsutta, came often to Plymouth to answer the many charges brought against his people. The descendants of the Pilgrims, who had survived only through the help of Massasoit, now humiliated his son, demanding that he acknowledge the sovereignty of the English king and pay them a fine of one hundred pounds each year.[8]

One Man's Journey

To save his people from ultimate destruction, King Philip united his Wampanoag with tribes throughout New England and launched a war against Massachusetts Bay. His warriors, who usually attacked in the dead of night, burned thirteen towns to the ground, including Springfield, just twenty miles north of Windsor. Settlers in Connecticut worried that the Indians, who haunted the woods about their towns "like the lightning on the edge of clouds," would strike their settlements next. While Windsor was spared a direct attack, Simsbury, only fourteen miles to the west, was destroyed. Matthew Grant and his three sons, Samuel, Tahan, and John, contributed money to help the people of Simsbury rebuild their settlement. Windsor also raised a militia company of three hundred men under the command of Captain Samuel Marshall to fight the Indians. Eighty of them, including Captain Marshall, never returned home.[9]

By the spring of 1676, the English colonists had defeated King Philip's confederation. Their victory made it possible for the people of Connecticut, including the Grant family, to live in peace with the Indians for the next three generations. However, they could not escape the growing tension between England, their mother country, and France for control of North America. This tension led to three wars between 1690 and 1745, which were fought primarily along New England's Atlantic Coast: King William's War, Queen Anne's War, and King George's War. No members of the Grant family served in these conflicts, but they could not avoid participating in the French and Indian War, which broke out in 1754 over control of the vast country west of the Appalachians. The French considered this land part of their fur trading empire, which they had built with their many Indian allies. The English colonists claimed this country by right of the sea-to-sea clauses in their charters. The conflict, which started when the Virginians challenged the French for control of the Ohio River and the land that lay beyond it, became a worldwide contest when Great Britain entered the war on the side of its colonists.[10]

In this bloody contest, Noah Grant Jr., the great-grandson of Matthew Grant's son Samuel, became the first member of the family in America to win fame on the battlefield. Along with his younger brother Solomon and his uncle Ebenezer Grant, he joined the campaign to take the French post of Fort Frédéric at Crown Point in northern New York in 1755. He fought side by side with the Haudenosaunee, a confederation of the Mohawk, Oneida, Cayuse, Onondaga, and Seneca tribes, better known as the Iroquois, who were staunch allies of the English. Noah, a master mason, helped construct Forts Edward and William Henry on Lake George in upstate New York. Every time Noah's three-month enlistment was up, he signed on again, serving well into 1756 when he joined Rogers' Rangers, the daring scouts commanded by the charismatic

Robert Rogers of New Hampshire. He became so well known in Connecticut for his "extraordinary services and good conduct in ranging and scouting" that the colony's assembly awarded him thirty Spanish dollars.[11]

But in September 1756, Noah Grant was killed while on a forty-day scouting mission with British soldiers and Mohawk warriors in upstate New York. His brother Solomon was also killed during a raid near Williamstown, Massachusetts. The war hit a low point for the English the following year, when the French took Fort William Henry and their Indian allies massacred the men and women retreating from the post after the surrender.[12] But just one year later, the tide turned in favor of the English. They captured Fort Duquesne at the headwaters of the Ohio; Fort Frédéric, which the French had burned to the ground and abandoned; and finally Québec, after a battle below the city on the Plains of Abraham. By the Treaty of Paris in 1763, which ended the conflict known in Europe as the Seven Years' War, France surrendered Canada and the Ohio Country, which stretched north and west from the Ohio River to the Great Lakes, to Great Britain.[13]

The war may have ended for Connecticut and the other colonies, but not for tribes living west of the Appalachians. Even before the Treaty of Paris was signed, the Ottawa chief Pontiac and his warriors had attacked more than a dozen British forts throughout the Ohio Country. They were angry at the British for treating them less generously than the French once did at these same forts. Although the British ultimately defeated Pontiac's confederation, the near loss of the vast country they had just won in the Seven Years' War led them to change their policy toward the many Indians who lived there. In the Proclamation of 1763, Parliament designated the land west of the Appalachians as a tribal reserve. The Indians would now be welcomed into the British forts, where they would be treated as valuable trading partners. The colonists, living from the province of Maine in the north to Georgia in the south, could settle to the crest of the Appalachians, but no farther. If they had crossed over this boundary, then they must leave at once.[14]

For the colonists, however, no imaginary line drawn down the Appalachians could cancel the sea-to-sea clauses in their charters. From the poorest scrub farmers to the wealthiest fur traders and land speculators, they were certain the western country belonged to them and they had the right to take it away from the Indians. They added the Proclamation of 1763 to their long list of complaints against Great Britain, including unfair taxes levied without their consent, restrictions on their trade and industry, and the abolition of legal rights belonging to them as Englishmen. In April 1775, when the American Revolution began on the village green in Lexington, Massachusetts, and then spread to the nearby town of Concord, one of the issues buried in the many grievances that had brought about the grand fight for America's future was what was to become of the country west of the Appalachians.[15]

Throughout his entire adult life, right up until his death in 1819, Noah Grant III, the fifth generation of his family born in America, claimed he had joined the Continental army as soon as news came to his home town of Coventry, Connecticut, that British soldiers had fired on his fellow New Englanders. His father had died fighting with the British when Noah was just eight years old, and now, with a hundred other men from Coventry, he marched to Cambridge, Massachusetts, to fight against them. According to stories he told his family, Captain Grant served in every major battle of the American Revolution, including Bunker Hill, the disastrous Long Island Campaign, and Saratoga.

Like many veterans, Noah found life difficult after the war ended. Back in Coventry, he had a harder time making a living than had any previous generation of his family in America. His wife, Anne, died just as the war ended, and he now struggled to support his two young sons, Solomon and Peter. His children later claimed that he simply did not know how to handle money, but many of his troubles were the troubles of the age. Most Continental army soldiers had received little or no pay. When they returned home, they had no money to start new farms or businesses. Prices for land were high everywhere, with property taxes steadily rising to pay off the war debts of the states. In most places, taxes had to be paid with hard money, a near impossibility in a nation without a currency or banking system. Farmers living just upriver from Coventry in towns throughout western Massachusetts followed Daniel Shays in his rebellion against high property taxes payable only in gold.[16]

With the nation's economy in ruins, many people made their way west toward the Ohio Country, which had been renamed the Northwest Territory after Great Britain surrendered the region to the United States in the Treaty of Paris, which ended the war in 1783. Two years later, Congress passed a land ordinance mandating that the Northwest Territory be plotted out like the New England towns, in six-mile-by-six-mile-square blocks. Each township was in turn subdivided into thirty-six one-mile-by-one-mile-square sections, which were opened for sale and settlement. In 1786, in exchange for Connecticut giving up its old colonial claims to the west, Congress set aside over three million acres at the southern end of Lake Erie for the people of the state. This swath of land, running 120 miles due west from the Pennsylvania border, was known as the Connecticut Western Reserve.[17]

In 1790, Captain Noah Grant joined the many immigrants from Connecticut heading across Pennsylvania toward the Western Reserve. He left his oldest boy, Solomon, behind with his in-laws and traveled west with his younger son, Peter. He made it as far as Greensburg, a small town twenty miles southeast of Pittsburgh. Although he may have wanted to continue, he settled in western Pennsylvania, probably for fear of the Indians who were at war with the United States across the river. Most of the tribes living there, including the Miami, Shawnee, Delaware, Ottawa, Seneca, and Wyandot, had joined the British in the Revolution, and when the war ended, they refused to recognize the surrender of the Ohio Country to the United States. Instead, they fought the many American settlers and soldiers who came into their country until General Anthony Wayne finally defeated them at the Battle of Fallen Timbers in August 1794. A year later, Wayne negotiated the Treaty of Greenville, which drew a line across the future state of Ohio. The Indians could live north of the line, while Americans could settle south of it.[18]

Thousands of people now headed into Ohio, with many moving to the Connecticut Western Reserve. In 1799, Captain Noah Grant joined the immigrant train west along with his son Peter; his second wife, Rachel; and the four children she had borne him, including a five-year-old boy named Jesse. Along with a horse, two cows, and a few household goods, they boarded a flatboat, traveled down the Monongahela to the Ohio, and disembarked at the small town of East Liverpool in Columbiana County. The Grants moved north into Portage County, where they settled in the village of Deerfield, which had been named after the Massachusetts town in the Connecticut River Valley attacked by Indians during Queen Anne's War. Once again, for this latest generation of Grants in America, they were starting over on Indian land. While warriors, who still hunted south of the Greenville Treaty line, sometimes menaced settlers in the Western Reserve, the greatest threat to life, for both people and livestock, came from the wolves and panthers lurking in the woods about their towns and surrounding farms.[19]

Life was not easy for the Grants in Ohio, not because of Indians, but because, as Jesse Grant later recalled, his father was no better a provider here than back east. His favorite occupation was reminiscing about his service in the American Revolution. Captain Grant cared little about money, letting an inheritance in Connecticut from his uncle Solomon, who was killed in the French and Indian War, slip through his fingers. In 1805, when Rachel died and he was left with eight children to support, he scattered his offspring among relatives and friends. Eleven-year-old Jesse, who had a drive to succeed that was lacking in his father, was sent to live in Youngstown with George Tod, an Ohio Supreme Court justice. The judge's wife taught Jesse to read, giving him a lifelong love of books and learning.[20]

Despite their struggles, the Grants were among the sixty thousand people who made it possible for Ohio to enter the Union as the seventeenth state in 1803. As American settlements grew south of the Greenville Treaty line, tribes living north of it came under increasing pressure to give up their land. Whereas older chiefs viewed the loss of their country as inevitable, younger leaders like Tecumseh and the Prophet refused to accept it. These two Shawnee brothers organized an Indian confederation to win a permanent homeland for the tribes in the old Ohio Country. They laid plans to launch a surprise attack on settlers in the West and drive them back across the Appalachians. However, their plans were disrupted when Governor William Henry Harrison of the Indiana Territory defeated Tecumseh's followers, then under the command of the Prophet, at the Battle of Tippecanoe on November 7, 1811. Angry congressmen known as War Hawks subsequently demanded a war against the British for supporting Tecumseh's confederation as well as for their impressment of American sailors and attacks on American shipping.

In June 1812, the United States declared war on Great Britain. Tecumseh now joined the British, who promised to win his people a homeland north of the Ohio River. Together, in the opening months of the War of 1812, they won victories at Detroit, Michilimackinac, and Chicago. But by the spring of 1813, the tide had turned in favor of the Americans. An army under the command of General Harrison turned back Tecumseh at Fort Meigs in northwest Ohio, while Oliver Hazard Perry and his sailors defeated a British fleet on Lake Erie. In October 1813, Tecumseh died fighting his nemesis Harrison at the Battle of the Thames in Canada. By January 1815, when General Andrew Jackson won his great victory over the British at New Orleans, the war was already over. A peace treaty had been signed in Ghent, Belgium, the previous Christmas Eve, thus ending the struggle for control of the country west of the Appalachians that had gone on since the French and Indian War. According to the treaty, this land belonged to neither the British nor the Indians, but the Americans.[21]

Settlers now poured across the Ohio River in even greater numbers. People long remembered the year 1815 as the start of the Great Migration into their state. By 1820, close to six hundred thousand people lived in Ohio, and its largest town, Cincinnati, was well on its way to becoming the "Queen City" of the West. Jesse Grant, now twenty-six years old, settled upriver from Cincinnati in Point Pleasant. He had taken no part in the War of 1812, preferring instead to learn the tanning trade from his brother Peter in Maysville, Kentucky. He had later moved back to Ohio, living first in Deerfield and later Ravenna, before opening his own tannery in Point Pleasant. By 1821, he was successful enough to take Hannah Simpson, a young woman known for her common sense and quiet ways, as his wife. On April 27, 1822, Hannah gave birth to a boy named Hiram, whom everyone called by his middle name, Ulysses.[22]

When Ulysses was a year old, Jesse moved his family to Georgetown in nearby Brown County. He built a two-story brick home that grew larger every year as his tanning business prospered. By the time Ulysses was eight, he was old enough to chop wood and cart it to the tannery. Soon he was plowing his family's farm and planting potatoes. A kind and thoughtful boy, he enjoyed playing with the other children in Georgetown, but if they went hunting in the nearby woods, he never raised a gun or pointed an arrow at an animal. He loved horses and was so good at handling them that people brought their most difficult mounts to the Grant tannery so Ulysses could train them. Jesse made sure his favorite child got a good education, sending him to a one-room schoolhouse in Georgetown, then for a year each to schools in Maysville, Kentucky, and Ripley, Ohio. When Ulysses told his father that he had no interest in learning the tanning business but wanted to go to college instead, Jesse secured his appointment to the nation's military academy at West Point.[23]

One of the most remarkable things about Ulysses Grant's early life was the fact that unlike every previous generation of his family, he grew up with no direct experience with Indians. During his childhood, he heard the most about them during the presidential election of 1828, when candidate Andrew Jackson, the hero of New Orleans, promised to remove all the tribes living in the eastern United States if elected. The Indians would be sent onto the plains west of Missouri and Arkansas, known as the Great American Desert, which for the moment no American wanted. Removal of the tribes across the Mississippi would open up millions of acres in the Middle West and Deep South for settlement by the people who Jackson hoped would elect him.[24]

Most of Ohio's citizens knew little about the Indians who lived in their state on reserves granted to them after the War of 1812. In a treaty signed at the Foot of the Rapids on the Maumee River in 1817, chiefs of Ohio's major tribes had given up most of their land in exchange for small reserves laid out within their surrendered territory. The Ottawa, who had lived on three small reserves along the Maumee since signing a treaty with the government in 1805, were given another tract east of the river plus the use of more land upriver. The Shawnee received three reserves at Wapakoneta, Hog Creek, and Lewistown, while the Seneca received a forty-thousand-acre tract east of the Sandusky River. Four townships known as the Grand Reserve, drawn around their main town of Upper Sandusky, went to the Wyandot, while the Delaware received a tiny plot of ground around the village of the aged chief Captain Pipe. Here the American government told the Indians that they had to "civilize" themselves, transforming overnight into successful farmers and businessmen, and so prepare to assimilate with the many settlers coming their way.[25]

Most of the Indians did everything the government asked of them. Missionaries came among them to help in the transition, with Quakers heading to the Shawnee reserve at Wapakoneta, Presbyterians to the Maumee River Valley to serve the Ottawa, and Methodists to the Wyandot's Grand Reserve. The Seneca, faithful to their own traditions, especially the Gaiwiio, or Good Word of Handsome Lake, built prosperous farms on their reserve that amazed visitors who traveled through their country. The Ottawa refused to change their ways, preferring to hunt and trade with local settlers. The Shawnee established farms with the help of the Quakers. They cultivated hundreds of acres of corn and wheat, planted apple and peach orchards, and raised large herds of cattle and horses. But no one succeeded like the Wyandot. After the tribe subdivided the Grand Reserve among individual landowners, the Wyandot quickly found themselves among the wealthiest farmers in the state. A Methodist mission school in Upper Sandusky trained young men in farming and young women in homemaking. Several scholars, as the students were called, went on to careers in law and the ministry.[26]

However, none of this mattered when President Jackson launched his fight for Indian removal in the spring of 1830. All the Indians, not just Georgia's Cherokee, who received national attention for their opposition to Jackson, had to go west, and their land had to be sold to American farmers. Ulysses Grant's parents supported Andrew Jackson, as did most people in the counties near Cincinnati. Both representatives of Ohio's First and Second Congressional Districts in southeastern Ohio voted for removal. But elsewhere in the state, including every district with an Indian reserve, congressmen voted against removal, even if they were Jackson's supporters. The state's two senators, Benjamin Ruggles and Jacob Burnet, who loathed the president as a madman, voted against removal. People throughout Ohio, including citizens of Brown County, where the Grants lived, and young women from the town of Steubenville, petitioned Congress not to do this terrible thing. But nothing could convince Jackson that he should change his mind. The story of the Indians, running parallel to the wider story of the United States, was over. If they refused to give up their tribal identity, then they had to move west of the Mississippi, out of sight and out of mind of the American nation.[27]

Ulysses Grant, as a boy growing up in Georgetown, was probably unaware of what the Indians passed through during their removal from Ohio. In 1831, the Seneca, who had frequently petitioned both Presidents John Quincy Adams and Andrew Jackson to send them west in order to escape the troubles that white men brought into their country, signed a treaty with the government exchanging their land on the Sandusky River for a new reserve along the Neosho River in the Indian Territory. They followed the first eastern tribe to head across the Mississippi, the Choctaw. The Delaware from Captain Pipe's village, who had sold their land to the American government in 1829, joined the Seneca. All three tribes suffered terribly on the journey across the Mississippi, with many people dying or becoming gravely ill along the way.

To avoid similar disasters, President Jackson's new secretary of war, Lewis Cass, developed a more orderly plan for removing the tribes. The government would hire conductors and assistants to organize the "emigration," Jackson's preferred term for removal. These officials would stay with their charges until they were safely beyond the Mississippi. With the new regulations in place, the remaining tribes in Ohio came under increasing pressure to give up their land and head west. The Shawnee of Wapakoneta and Hog Creek, the Mixed Band of Shawnee and Seneca from Lewistown, and the Ottawa living in the Auglaize River Valley surrendered their land in 1831 and traveled overland to Kansas and Oklahoma in 1832. The Ottawa of the Maumee River Valley signed away their reserves in 1833 but refused to move west until 1837, when half of the tribe was placed on lake steamers, canal boats, and finally paddlewheels for the long trip to Kansas.[28]

By the time the rest of the Ottawa left Ohio in the late summer of 1839, Ulysses Grant was starting his freshman year at West Point. If he had seen any Indians as they departed down the Ohio and Erie Canal or left by steamboat from Cincinnati, he never recorded the experience. Nor were Indians ever mentioned in his studies at West Point. The only Indians that Cadet Grant encountered were the ones he read about in the works of James Fennimore Cooper in the college library. If by chance he came across Cooper's *The Wept of Wish-Ton-Wish*, he might have learned what his ancestors had passed through in Windsor during King Philip's War. Similarly, *The Last of the Mohicans* told the story of the siege of Fort William Henry, which his grandfather Noah Grant helped build during the French and Indian War, and the attack on the English as they fled from the fort under a flag of truce. The only clue about what young Ulysses thought of Indians in his college years can be found in a painting that survives from his art classes at the academy. The work shows two Indians, a man with a dog and a woman with a child, bartering goods with a trader. Grant portrays them as peaceful individuals, not warlike savages.[29]

In the late spring of 1843, when Lieutenant Ulysses Grant returned home after graduating from West Point, the last Indians in Ohio, the Wyandot, were preparing to leave the state. They had held out longer than any other tribe,

One Man's Journey

Painting by Cadet Grant. Grant painted this watercolor of Indians trading as part of his art class at West Point in 1840. The painting measures 10½ by 14½ inches. COURTESY OF THE WEST POINT MUSEUM COLLECTION, UNITED STATES MILITARY ACADEMY.

resisting three official attempts to remove them before finally selling the Grand Reserve to the government. Unlike the other Ohio tribes, they organized their own journey west in July 1843 by steamboat from Cincinnati with no help from Washington. Grant, who left Ohio to join the Fourth Infantry near St. Louis that summer, traveled along the same route taken by the Wyandot. But their paths never crossed on his way west or at any other time during his stay in Missouri. During the year he was stationed at the Jefferson Barracks, Lieutenant Grant's main concern was neither Indians nor the army, but Julia Dent, the sister of Frederick Dent, his roommate at West Point. They became engaged in 1844 shortly before Grant's regiment was ordered to Natchitoches, Louisiana, in anticipation of a war with Mexico once the United States annexed Texas. Only when he finally marched to Corpus Christi in September 1845 and later headed for San Antonio and Austin did he have any chance of encountering Indians. Grant promised his fiancée that he would give her a full account of the Comanche he met in battle, but he never saw any. However, he did witness their destruction firsthand in the deserted towns and farms he passed along the way.[30]

When he finally met Indians, they were not the wild horsemen of the southern plains but the downtrodden poor of Mexico. Grant would always remember them, purebloods and half-breeds as best he could tell, sitting idly in the many villages he passed through during the Mexican War. These humble people were mercilessly abused by the proud elites who ruled their society. Grant found it awful to see Indians treated so badly in a country whose landscape he found so beautiful. It was almost as awful as the fact that the United States had fomented a war against this innocent nation and sent newly trained officers from West Point to prosecute it. Lieutenant Grant had no illusions that he and his fellow soldiers were fighting for anything but more land for Southern slaveholders, the elites of his own country. In his opinion, President James K. Polk had sent them into Mexico to win Texas and the entire Southwest all the way to California so more slave states could enter the Union.[31]

After the Mexican War ended, Grant did not meet Indians again until 1852, when he was assigned to the Columbia Barracks in the Oregon Territory. He had married Julia Dent right after coming home from the Mexican War, and they now had a two-year-old son and another child on the way. Fearing his family would not survive the long journey west, which would take them across the Isthmus of Panama in the midst of a cholera epidemic, he traveled alone. Grant was certain his regiment was heading to Oregon to "tramp over the country looking after Indians," but when he stopped in San Francisco, he met only a handful. He was stunned to see that the Indians were as badly treated here as in Mexico. Miners and soldiers had hunted the "Diggers," as the local tribes were derisively called for eating plant roots, and killed them like wild animals. Those who survived did whatever menial work they could find in the goldfields. Grant wrote to Julia describing how the poor Indians, desperate to find even the smallest speck of gold, brought all the dust they could carry into the trading posts. Later, when he was assigned to a fort in the Columbia River Valley, he hired local Indians to transport goods on their backs through the Cascades for railroad surveying parties. After his wife warned him to beware of Indians, especially when he was out riding alone, Grant answered that the "whole race would be harmless if they were not put upon by the whites." He openly mocked the claim that the abuse heaped on the Indians was done for their own benefit. In his opinion, tribes like the Clickitat and Dalles were wasting away before the two great "blessings" of civilization: whiskey and smallpox.[32]

The world that had crushed the Indians finally broke the spirit of Ulysses Grant. Tired of military life and missing his wife and children, he asked to return home but was instead sent to Fort Humboldt in California. There he drank to excess and fell into near despair. In April 1854, on the same day he received his captain's commission, he resigned from army, and by late summer he was back in Missouri. He moved from farm to farm, trying to make a living for his family. By 1858, he and his wife had four children: the oldest, Fred; Ulysses Jr.; their only daughter, Nellie; and the baby, Jesse. After years of struggling to make ends meet, his wife suggested that he ask his father for a job. In May 1860, Grant went to work as a clerk in his father's leather store in Galena, Illinois. Here he expected to live out his days far from the strife and misery he had seen since leaving West Point. All his efforts would be turned to bringing up the next generation of Grants in America, for his own ambitions for himself were over.[33]

However, at least one person in Galena recognized more than failure in Ulysses Grant. He was Ely Parker, a government engineer supervising the construction of a customhouse and marine hospital in the town. Parker noticed that "selling goods from behind a counter did not seem to be his forte." Whenever people came through the front door, Grant beat a hasty retreat to the back room, where he stayed until another clerk waited on them. While such behavior upset many customers, Parker, who was a Seneca Indian from New York, was intrigued by this quiet man. "I saw him quite frequently," he remembered, "becoming friendly by degrees as we became better acquainted." Parker was impressed that Grant, so reticent and composed, behaved more like the Indians he knew than a white man. It took a long time to get to know him, but once the "ice was broken," all his best qualities were revealed, especially his compassion for others. Little did he realize how deeply this man, who would become his close friend, sympathized with the Indians. Nor could he have ever suspected how his own life, rooted in the Wolf Clan of the Seneca, and Grant's life, bound eight generations back to the founding of New England, would come together to try to save the Indians of the Far West from what many believed was certain destruction.[34]

2. Parallel Lives

To tell the story of how Ulysses Grant, a clerk in a leather store in Galena, and Ely Parker, a civil engineer working in the same town, came together to try to rescue the tribes of the Far West is to tell the story of settlers spreading across a continent and the parallel story of Indians trying to survive against the press of them. By the time the two men met in Illinois in 1860, the story had grown more complex. The settlers who had united for nearly 250 years against tribes blocking their way west to the Mississippi now competed against each other for every last acre of their diminishing continent. Even as they raced from the Mississippi to the Pacific, with wagons and stagecoaches heading down the Oregon and Santa Fe Trails, waves of miners searching for every last ounce of gold and silver, and railroad men dreaming of crisscrossing the prairies with their transcontinental lines, a debate broke out between free farmers in the North and slaveholders in the South over who should settle the vast plains in between. The fight would shatter the nation, but one constant remained. Most Americans in the North and South still agreed that the Indians who lived beyond the Mississippi, at least three hundred thousand divided among some two hundred tribes by the latest count of the Office of Indian Affairs, must be pushed into the shadows of history to make way for them.[1]

When Grant and Parker lived in Illinois, at the eastern edge of the plains that stretched to the Rockies, the state became the center of the national debate over the future of the West. Senator Stephen Douglas, a Democrat from Illinois, had won passage of the Kansas-Nebraska Act in 1854, which opened the Great Plains to settlement according to the principle of popular sovereignty. Let the people who settle there, he argued, decide for themselves whether their states should be free or slave. He was certain that cash crops like cotton, rice, sugar, and tobacco would never grow on the Great Plains, so slavery would never take root there. Settling the "Great West," as Douglas named the central section of the country, would be the "hope of this nation—the resting place of the power that is not only to control, but to save, the Union." But the mere thought that

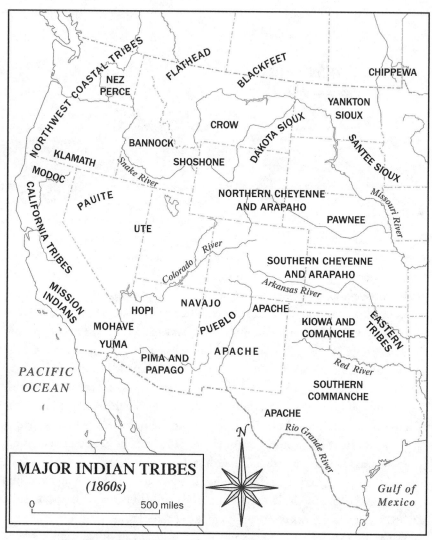

Major Indian Tribes (1860s). The map shows the location of the major Indian tribes at the start of Grant's presidency. COPYRIGHT © ROBERTA STOCKWELL, 2018.

slaveholders might gain a foothold in the last bit of territory opened for settlement was enough to give rise to a new political party, the Republicans, who anchored their ambitions on the principle that the West belonged to free white labor. Abraham Lincoln, an eloquent lawyer from Springfield, took the debate to a more profound level when he ran against Douglas as the Republican candidate for Senator from Illinois in 1858. "A house divided against itself cannot stand," Lincoln declared when nominated, "I believe this government cannot endure, permanently half slave and half free." Slavery must be banned from the Great West and eventually die out in the rest of the nation so the United States could at last live up to its founding principle that all men are created equal.[2]

When Douglas and Lincoln ran for president in 1860, Grant and Parker agreed that if they could vote, they would choose Douglas. Grant came from a Democratic family that had long supported Andrew Jackson. While his father later joined the Whigs, his mother remained a lifelong Democrat even when her son ran for the White House as a Republican. Grant's in-laws, the Dents, who migrated from Maryland to Missouri, were loyal to the Democratic Party as the defender of their rights as slaveholders. Parker supported Douglas even more strongly than did his friend Ulysses Grant, since he shared the Illinois senator's vision of the Great West as a place where democracy must triumph. He was certain Douglas would follow in the footsteps of James K. Polk, the president whom Parker most admired. He approved of Polk's annexation of the Oregon Territory and the vast country stretching from Texas to California so, in Parker's words, the "Genius of Democracy can travel in his great boots." As Parker saw it, "Republicanism should extend its sway over the whole American continent."[3]

However, in 1860, neither man could vote. Grant had just moved to Illinois and did not meet the residency requirements, while Parker, a Seneca Indian, was not an American citizen and therefore could not cast a ballot. After Lincoln was elected, and the Southern states seceded from the Union, both men were determined to join the fight to defeat the Confederacy. Shortly after the attack on Fort Sumter, Grant wrote to his father-in-law Frederick Dent, a slaveholder, predicting the downfall of the Confederates and the institution they had launched this war to protect. "I can but see the doom of Slavery," he asserted. Parker, too, saw the conflict as a "terrible contest" between the "slaveholding and non-slaveholding sections" of the country that the South had recklessly started. It was even more shocking to Parker than to Grant that Americans would attempt to destroy the United States, a nation he considered "his country" even if that same nation refused to consider him a citizen.[4]

After President Lincoln issued his first call for volunteers in April 1865 [1861], Grant struggled to win a commission in the Union army. Finally, the following June, Governor Richard Yates appointed him colonel of the 21st Illinois Infantry. Commanding men in a war whose outcome mattered to him, unlike the Mexican War, awoke a drive in Grant he had never known from the time he entered West Point until he resigned from the army fifteen years later. His newfound determination could be seen from the moment he got word a Confederate army planned to capture Paducah, Kentucky, at the strategic point where the Tennessee River met the Ohio. Clearly seeing that if the Tennessee could be secured, the Confederacy would be cut in two, Grant beat the rebels to the city and then proceeded along the river toward the major railroad crossing of Corinth, Mississippi. As he hurried south, he was promoted from a brigadier to a major general and won a reputation in Northern newspapers as "Unconditional Surrender" Grant for his refusal to give terms to the enemy.[5]

But both the press and the public turned against him when the Confederates finally stopped his push up the Tennessee at Pittsburg Landing, just twenty-five miles north of Corinth. Having failed to reconnoiter the countryside around the place, he stumbled into a bloody two-day battle near the Shiloh Church. Stories now filled the Northern papers that he had been drunk during much of the fighting. Few gave him credit for learning a valuable lesson from the mistakes he made at the Battle of Shiloh. He had discovered sooner than any other general, North or South, that this would be a long and terrible war of endurance. His newfound understanding helped him plan and persevere in the nine-month-long campaign to take Vicksburg, the Confederacy's last stronghold on the Mississippi.[6]

As his friend fought his way south from Paducah to Shiloh and finally to Vicksburg, try as he might, Ely Parker could not secure a place for himself in the Union army. Rejected by recruiters in his home state of New York, even as they signed up other Indians, he traveled to Washington to ask Senator William Seward, just appointed Lincoln's secretary of state, for help. He was stunned when Seward told him, "This fight must be made and settled by the white man alone." Seward sent Parker back to New York with one last piece of advice: "Go home, cultivate your farm, and we will settle our troubles without Indian aid." Years later, when Parker was a much older man looking back on the accomplishments of his long life, he could still recite the stinging rebuke of Lincoln's secretary of state word for word.[7]

Seward seemed unaware that he had turned away a man far more accomplished than most Union officers, including General Grant. Born in 1828 on the Seneca's Tonawanda reserve in western New York, Parker could count leaders like Red Jacket, Cornplanter, and Handsome Lake among his ancestors. Great things had been expected of him even before his birth. When his mother, Elizabeth Parker, was pregnant with him, she dreamed of a rainbow that stretched from Tonawanda to the farm of the tribe's Indian agent. A Seneca dream interpreter explained that her child would be a renowned "peacemaker" between the "pale faces" and his own people. When her son was born, she named him Hasanoanda, meaning "Leading Name" in the Seneca language. He was also given the English name of Ely Samuel after a well-respected Baptist minister who worked among the tribe.[8]

Unlike Grant, who showed little enthusiasm for formal schooling, Parker was driven to educate himself from an early age. He studied at a Baptist mission school at Tonawanda and later attended academies in western New York, where he mastered English in both speech and writing. He developed a love of reading, and as an adult, he was known for the breadth of his knowledge, especially in history and literature. By the time he was eighteen, he was ready to enter Williams College, but the Seneca had other plans for him. They chose him as their official spokesman to help them in their fight to stay in Tonawanda.[9]

Much like the Indians in Grant's Ohio, the Seneca had already lost millions of acres in their former territory. In 1797, they surrendered much of western New York and Pennsylvania to Robert Morris, the nation's top financier, while retaining reserves at Buffalo Creek, Cattaraugus, Allegheny, and Tonawanda. White settlers quickly surrounded these reserves, bringing violence, disease, and whiskey with them. The Seneca regularly petitioned the American government to find them a new home west of the Mississippi, and in 1831, Jackson's administration purchased 250,000 acres in the Wisconsin Territory from the Menominee for the Seneca, but the tribe refused to move there. In 1838, after selling their remaining reserves to Thomas Ogden, a New York City businessman, and Joseph Fellows, his partner from nearby Batavia, the tribe promised to move to Wisconsin within five years. But as the time drew near, the Seneca were reluctant to move there. Instead, they signed another treaty with the American government in 1842 confirming the sale of their land to Ogden and Fellows and promising to move to a new reserve in Kansas, not Wisconsin, within the year.[10]

But in 1843, the Seneca once again refused to leave Tonawanda. They claimed their leaders had not been present at the previous negotiations and therefore the treaties were invalid. Since assessment of improvements on their land had to precede removal, they refused to allow assessors onto their reserves, believing that if their property was never assessed, they could never be removed. Violence broke out in 1846, when Joseph Fellows and his employee Robert Kendle entered the lumberyard owned by John Blacksmith, the chief of the Wolf clan, striking him at gunpoint before forcibly removing him. Blacksmith hired local attorney John H. Martindale to represent him. Martindale sued Fellows and Kendle for assault, battery, and trespassing and won a jury trial against them in Genesee County.

Fellows eventually took his case to the New York Court of Appeals, where he argued that only the Seneca nation and not an individual Indian could sue him for trespassing. He claimed that he and Ogden were the true owners of Blacksmith's land, having won it in two treaties with the Seneca. Therefore, they had every right to evict the chief from their property. The court, however, ruled in Blacksmith's favor on the grounds that an individual Indian could sue for trespassing and, just as important, that Fellows and Ogden did not own the land because the Seneca had not been paid for improvements on it. Since the validity of the 1838 and 1842 treaties had been called into question, the court sent the case on to the United States Supreme Court under a writ of error, as required by Article XXV of the 1789 Judiciary Act. It would take more than a decade for the highest court to hear the case.[11]

While the case made its way through the state courts, Ely Parker traveled regularly to Washington to fight against the removal of his people from Tonawanda. He impressed everyone he met, including President Polk, officials in the War Department, and important senators such as Henry Clay, Daniel Webster, and John C. Calhoun. The well-spoken Parker made a striking figure as he met with leading politicians in the nation's capital. He was tall for his time, standing five feet, eight inches. He was stocky, too, weighing two hundred pounds and with shoulders so broad that he had a hard time finding clothes that fit him. Parker became so well known that once when First Lady Sarah Polk rode past him walking down a street in Washington, she stopped her carriage and invited him to ride with her through the city.[12]

For his remarkable leadership, the Seneca named Parker their grand sachem when he was just twenty-three. He was given the honorary title of Donahogawa, or "Open Door." His skill in defending others led him to study law for three years in the office of William P. Angel, an Indian agent and district attorney of Ellicottville. He further developed his talent as a public speaker by joining local debating societies and the Masons. Parker was prepared to take the bar exam in the state of New York but was not allowed because he was an Indian. Blocked from a career in the law, he turned to engineering, taking a short course on the subject at Rensselaer Polytechnic Institute in Troy before securing positions on the Erie Canal in New York and the Chesapeake and Albemarle Ship Canal between Virginia and North Carolina.

But Parker had become so proficient in the law that in January 1857, when the Supreme Court finally heard the case of *Fellows v. Blacksmith*, he sat at the side of John Martindale, giving him advice throughout the two days of oral arguments. There seemed little hope that Chief Justice Roger B. Taney, a Jackson appointee, would rule in the Seneca's favor. But on March 5, 1857, Justice Samuel Nelson read the court's unanimous decision written by Taney himself. While the court upheld the validity of the disputed treaties, it ruled that only the federal government could remove the Seneca from their land and only after paying the tribe for improvements on it. The decision was a victory for the Seneca, who had found the key to resisting removal that had eluded other tribes. If the assessment of their property could be delayed, then their removal could be prevented. The significance of the decision was largely missed by reporters of the day, who were anxiously awaiting another decision to be handed down the following morning. Chief Justice Taney had stayed home on March 5 to put the finishing touches on the opinion he would read on March 6 in the Dred Scott case.[13]

When the *Fellows v. Blacksmith* decision was announced, Parker had just arrived in Detroit to take up his new position working for the Treasury Department as the superintendent of lighthouses on the Upper Great Lakes. He was soon reassigned as the superintendent in charge of constructing the new customhouse and marine hospital in Galena, Illinois. But just a few months after moving to Galena, he learned that James W. Denver, President James Buchanan's newly appointed commissioner of Indian affairs, had come to Tonawanda to pay for improvements and remove the Seneca. Parker quickly headed to Washington, where he proposed selling the Seneca's land in Kansas to the government and using the money to purchase the Tonawanda reserve. The Buchanan administration agreed, and in early November 1857, Parker returned to Tonawanda to negotiate a new treaty. The Seneca sold their land in Kansas to the government for $256,000, which was enough to purchase three-fifths of the Tonawanda reserve. Parker could be proud of the fact that his people were one of the few bands of Indians who successfully resisted the government's thirty-year struggle to remove the eastern tribes west of the Mississippi River.[14]

It was this highly accomplished man—a master of the English language, a spokesman for his people, a trained attorney who helped win a case in the Supreme Court, a well-respected engineer employed by the Treasury Department, and a successful treaty negotiator—whom Seward had turned away at the start of the Civil War. Parker not only was refused a place in the Union army but also was fired as a government engineer. Salmon P. Chase, Lincoln's new secretary of the treasury, removed Parker from his position in Galena because he was a Douglas Democrat. Returning to his farm in Tonawanda, Parker continued to petition state officials for a commission in the army, but his every request was denied. He finally asked Congress to make him an American citizen, believing he would then be allowed to enlist, but the House Committee on Indian Affairs turned him down, claiming that citizenship could be granted only to a tribe and not to an individual.

Parker turned for help to his friends from Galena, including John E. Smith, the town jeweler, who was now a brigadier general serving with their old friend Ulysses Grant at Vicksburg. Smith, who knew that he was an excellent writer with perfect penmanship, petitioned the War Department to name Parker his adjutant general. Grant also wrote on his behalf, explaining, "I am personally acquainted with Mr. Parker and I think [him] eminently qualified for the position." He added, "He is a full blooded Indian but highly educated and very accomplished." Even before Grant's letter arrived at the War Department, Parker was appointed as a captain on Smith's staff.

He arrived in Vicksburg in July 1863, just after the Confederates had surrendered to the Union army. When he made his way to Grant's headquarters, Parker found his quiet friend from Galena quite talkative and even overjoyed about defeating one of the best armies of the Confederacy. But amid his great victory, troubles swirled about Grant's staff. Charles Dana, the assistant secretary of war, had been appalled at the quality of the men serving with Grant when he visited the general during the siege of Vicksburg. He described them as "a curious mixture of good, bad, & indifferent" and was especially troubled by John Rawlins, Grant's lawyer friend from Galena and current assistant adjutant general, who took hours to compose letters and then struggled to copy them out in a clear hand. Dana complained that "illiterateness" seemed to be the main characteristic of Grant's entire staff, along with his generals and regimental commanders. Knowing well Parker's talents, the War Department soon moved him from Smith's headquarters to Grant's staff. Parker welcomed his appointment as Grant's assistant adjutant general and remained with him for the rest of the war. He could usually be seen walking beside General Grant or sitting near him with a stack of papers in a leather portfolio and a bottle of ink tied around a button on the front of his jacket.[15]

As they made their way from Vicksburg to Lookout Mountain and finally to Virginia, Grant and Parker paid little attention to the many Indian wars raging across the Mississippi. The first one had started in August 1862 along the Minnesota River when four Santee Sioux warriors, who had returned empty-handed from a hunt, taunted each other into murdering a family of settlers. Frustrations among the Santee, also known as the Dakota, had been building for some time. After signing two treaties with the American government in 1851, they moved to a tiny reserve only 20 miles wide and 150 miles long on the upper Minnesota. In exchange for giving up their former territory, the tribe received a onetime payment of $220,000 and a yearly annuity of $88,000. The government would invest another $1,160,000 on the Sioux's behalf and pay regular dividends to the tribe. But the money was slow in coming, especially once the Civil War started. Most of the funds that did arrive went straight into the hands of corrupt agents and traders licensed by the government. In the summer of 1862, the corn, which could hardly grow in the barren soil of the Santee Sioux reserve, burned up in the hot sun and sparse rain, while the once plentiful buffalo, antelope, and elk disappeared. With his people starving, Chief Little Crow, on learning that his

Ulysses Grant and Ely Parker. Artist Alfred R. Waud sketched Captain Ely Parker standing behind General Grant as he wrote a telegram announcing that the Union army had crossed the Rapidan River in May 1864. COURTESY OF THE LIBRARY OF CONGRESS.

warriors had killed settlers, decided the time was right for his people to fight for their former homeland.[16]

While some Americans were sympathetic to the plight of the Sioux, most were shocked at the brutality of their attacks. Warriors swept down on homesteads, frontier towns, and stagecoach stations, murdering the men and raping the women. Not even children were safe from the wrath of the Sioux. Many died with their heads bashed in, while others were cut from their mothers' wombs and nailed to trees. In the chaos, a desperate governor Alexander Ramsey, charged with handling Indian affairs in his state, begged President Lincoln for help. General John Pope, fresh from his failure at Second Bull Run, was finally dispatched to Minnesota to put down the rebellion along with local volunteer companies. By the time the Santee Sioux War ended, at least eight hundred settlers were dead, and more than three hundred were still held captive by the tribe. Hundreds of warriors were tried and sentenced to hang for their crimes, but President Lincoln, reading through their cases one by one, commuted the death penalty for all but thirty-eight of them. Only those he could identify as having attacked white people for their own gain or pure pleasure met death at the gallows.[17]

A Union officer named James Carleton started the second major Indian war in the West about the same time that Grant launched his campaign to take Vicksburg. As the colonel of the 1st California Regiment, Carleton had been assigned the task of ferreting out Confederates in Texas, New Mexico, and Arizona. Finding none, he turned his attention to rounding up the Mescalero band of the Apache, who lived in the canyons of the Pecos and Rio Grande Valleys. He ordered this fiercest band of the tribe, derisively known as "lizard eaters" by soldiers and settlers alike, to a reservation in eastern New Mexico called Bosque Redondo. The place was hot and dry in the summer and bitterly cold in the winter. There were no trees from which to build shelters or make fires. Nor was there any wildlife to hunt. The water of the nearby Pecos River, which was high in alkaline, was bitter if not undrinkable.

After Carleton imprisoned the Apache there in early 1863, he set his sights on the Navajo, a people who lived higher up in New Mexico's canyons and called themselves the Diné. The tribe lived by farming and raising livestock. With no authority from Congress, the White House, or the Office of Indian Affairs, Carleton ordered the Navajo to join the Apache, their traditional enemies, at Bosque Redondo. He set July 20, 1863, as the date when the Navajo were to assemble and march toward the reservation. When they failed to arrive that day, he hired the Indian scout Kit Carson to take a militia company into the hills and hunt them down like wild animals. Carson set fire to the fields and ranches of the Navajo. He poisoned their wells and murdered their livestock. He killed men, women, and children, and by the wintertime, he had trapped the survivors in a place called Canyon de Chelly.[18]

Unable to escape from Carson's soldiers, the Navajo finally surrendered and started the "Long Walk," traveling three hundred miles on foot toward Bosque Redondo. The army guessed between eight thousand and nine thousand Navajo headed for the reservation, with perhaps two hundred dying along the road. Many who could not keep up with the rest, including pregnant women about to give birth, were gunned down by the soldiers who escorted them. At Bosque Redondo, the Navajo found life little better than hell on earth. They planted corn, but after cutworms destroyed the crop, they faced starvation along with the Apache. No shelter had been provided for them, so they burrowed into the ground for protection from the sun. They came out only to beg the soldiers in nearby Fort Sumner for food and water.[19]

By the time Grant took command of the Army of the Potomac, trouble in the West now centered on the Colorado Territory. In 1851, at the treaty negotiations at Fort Laramie, the government had promised the country around the central Rockies to the Cheyenne and Arapaho as part of the new policy of concentration. But when gold was discovered near Pikes Peak, tens of thousands of miners came west seeking their fortunes and completely ignoring the Treaty of Fort Laramie. Ten years after the signing of the treaty, government negotiators were back at Fort Wise in the Colorado Territory, demanding that the Cheyenne and Arapaho surrender the land just guaranteed to them. Six chiefs of the Cheyenne, including Black Kettle, and four Arapaho leaders signed a new treaty in which they gave up nearly ninety percent of the land promised to them at Fort Laramie and moved to a small reservation in eastern Colorado.[20]

But the new treaty brought no peace to the territory. Many young warriors, especially the elite Cheyenne fighters known as the Dog Soldiers, were furious

Ely Parker at Grant's headquarters. Parker, shown here seated on the right side of the doorway, waits with other members of General Grant's staff, including John Rawlins, who sits on the left side of the doorway, outside army headquarters at City Point, Virginia, in 1865. COURTESY OF THE LIBRARY OF CONGRESS.

Parallel Lives

at their chiefs for signing away their land at Fort Wise. They vowed to avenge the death of the many men gunned down as they hunted buffalo and the women and children slaughtered in their villages. Militia companies burned with a similar rage to avenge the death of farm families, railroad workers, and travelers on the stagecoach lines, all struck down without mercy. Both sides attacked without warning, murdering everyone they came across, with no regard for guilt or innocence. Even in the midst of the bloody Civil War, Colorado became known as one of the most violent places in the nation as warriors and settlers battled for control of the central Rockies.[21]

John Evans, governor of the Colorado Territory, moved in two opposite directions to contain the violence. He called together a volunteer company, under the direction of Colonel John Chivington, a Methodist minister who had once worked on behalf of the Ohio Indians, with every man determined to kill as many Indians as possible. However, he also invited Cheyenne and Arapaho chiefs who wished to live in peace to assemble at Fort Lyon. Black Kettle of the Cheyenne and White Antelope of the Arapaho accepted the offer and settled with their people forty miles northwest of the fort at Sand Creek under the American army's protection. Chivington and his volunteers paid no attention to this guarantee. On November 29, 1864, they swept into the Indian camp at Sand Creek, killing and wounding hundreds of men, women, and children. Nothing could stop the slaughter of the Sand Creek Massacre—not the American flag or the white flag of surrender flying over Black Kettle's tepee and not White Antelope's arms outstretched as a sign of peace. The soldiers hacked the dead to pieces and took body parts as souvenirs back in triumph to Denver. Here they displayed their trophies for the cheering crowds who had paid for the privilege of seeing them.[22]

Many Americans, even those who had grown numb to bloodshed during their long Civil War, were horrified at the Sand Creek Massacre. No recent battle, including Cold Harbor and the Crater, with casualties in the thousands, seemed quite as horrible as the brutal slaying of nearly 175 Cheyenne and Arapaho, all supposedly under the protection of American soldiers. A rumor circulated that General Grant himself, sitting in his tent in the mud of Petersburg, condemned the massacre as nothing less than the cold-blooded murder of Indians who thought they were under the protection of the federal army. Several official investigations of what had happened at Sand Creek were soon under way, including a military commission, a study by the Joint Congressional Committee on the Conduct of the War, and the Doolittle Commission, under the leadership of Wisconsin's Senator James Doolittle.[23]

Both the military commission and members of the joint congressional committee reached their conclusions quickly.. The Sand Creek Massacre had been caused by the "fiendish malignity of officers" in the Colorado Militia, who committed barbarous acts of the "most revolting character, such as never before disgraced the acts of men claiming to be civilized."[24] But finding a solution to the never-ending violence in the West would take much longer. During both the Lincoln and Johnson administrations, top officials in the Department of the Interior and the Office of Indian Affairs, including Caleb Smith, John Usher, James Harlan, and Orville Browning, each serving as secretary of the interior, and William Dole, Dennis Cooley, Lewis Bogy, and Nathaniel Green Taylor, all commissioners of Indian affairs, had struggled with this problem in their annual reports.

For all their differences, the officials described the situation in the Far West as the last chapter in the violent encounter between two races, one savage and one civilized, one red and one white, that had been at each other's throats for centuries. Citing John Marshall's opinion in *Worcester v. Georgia*, a case decided in 1832 regarding the Cherokee, these same officials blamed the Indians in part for the conflict. When the two races met, unlike other times in recorded history when inferior and superior peoples encountered one another, the Indians refused to join their conquerors in building a new society. Instead, they tried to maintain their independence and struck back viciously against settlers who encroached on their land. They fought, too, against injustices done to their people that any civilized man would oppose.[25]

But the officials also blamed their own government for the continuing troubles on the western frontier. In their opinion, presidents from Washington to Lincoln treated the tribes, which migrated frequently and had no stable governments, as nation-states. They wrote treaties with them as if they were dealing with France, Great Britain, or Spain. They regularly bought territory from chiefs who had no concept of national boundaries or private ownership of land and who often did not understand the treaties they signed. Unlike the rulers of actual nations, the headmen of the tribes were incapable of implementing these agreements. While treaties brought peace to the frontier, it was only for a moment. They were quickly broken as Americans settled on land promised to the Indians, which in turn set off a new round of wars and still more treaties.

Both sets of officials lamented that if only something else could have been done, right from the nation's founding, the situation in the Far West would not be so dire now. Looking back, they believed that the most intelligent policy would have been to establish an Indian reserve in the North, perhaps in the Wisconsin Territory, and another in the South, near the Arkansas Territory. Here all the tribes could have lived together, making sure that traditional enemies did not settle side by side. Once in their new homeland, the Indians would have slowly realized that their traditional way of life was disappearing. With the help of the American government and the aid of Christian missionaries, who seemed to have lost interest in helping the tribes after Andrew Jackson implemented his removal policy, the Indians would have learned the ways of the modern world. They could have been taught to read, write, and keep records like educated Americans. They would have taken up farming and the mechanical trades. They might have governed themselves well enough for their territories to enter the Union as new states.

But now, it seemed that the only solution to ending the violent cycle was to confine Indians on small reservations throughout the West. Many of these places would be within the boundaries of the Indian Territory, but others would be inside states or territories on the road to statehood. At first the tribes assigned to these reservations would find life difficult. White people, who hated them, would still surround them and bring every manner of misfortune into their lives. Likewise, the game on which the Indians depended would disappear, and thus they would be forced to find new ways of supporting themselves. As difficult as the transition might be, it must be done, for Indians were capable of a "high degree of civilization." With time, patience, and training, they would eventually adopt modern values, including the appreciation of private property. Once they had achieved this understanding, the reservations could be subdivided into individual holdings, thus allowing the Indians to join the quest for an ever better life that marked American society. If this transformation did not take place, then the tribes would be defeated in one terrible war after another until every Indian was exterminated.[26]

While General Grant had condemned the Sand Creek Massacre, he had no immediate suggestions for reforming the nation's Indian policy. For the moment, his only goal was to defeat General Robert E. Lee's Army of Northern Virginia. When the Confederates broke free from the trenches around Petersburg and raced west across Virginia toward the Danville Railroad Line, Grant finally caught up with them at Appomattox. On Palm Sunday, April 9, 1865, Lee made his way to the McLean House in Appomattox to agree on the terms of the surrender. He greeted Grant and his staff politely but was taken aback when Ely Parker reached out to shake his hand. His face flushed at the supposed insult of meeting a black man on Grant's staff. But then Lee looked more carefully into Parker's face and realized that he was an Indian. He regained his composure, took Parker's hand, and said, "I am glad to see one real American," to which Parker replied, "We are all Americans."

After the terms of the surrender were discussed, Colonel Joe Bowers, the first secretary to try to write down the terms, became flustered at the momentous task and threw down his pen, saying, "Parker, you will have to do this, I can't do it!" Parker calmly wrote out the terms, handing the paper back to Grant and Lee to sign. The next day, he met with both men as they sat on horseback under a grove of trees working out the details of the surrender. Parker placed his portfolio of papers on a tree stump as a desk and recorded every word said and every agreement made, regretting all the while that no artist was present to capture this even more momentous scene than had occurred the day before.[27]

In the summer of 1865, Ulysses Grant was appointed the general of the army, a title no man, not even Washington, had held before him. He was now responsible for overseeing the federal army in the South as well as the many soldiers stationed in the Far West. The war to save the Union seemed almost simple in retrospect compared with the twin tasks before him. He had defeated the Confederates at Vicksburg, Chattanooga, and finally Appomattox, but at least he could find them. Yet now in the South and the West, there were no armies, only bands of fighters who appeared and disappeared at will. They came out of the night in the South, wrapped in robes with their faces covered, wreaking vengeance on freedmen who tried to better themselves and anyone who tried to help them. In the West, they came out of the endless wind and beating sun, covered in paint and beaded clothing, leaving smoldering farms and ruined ranches in their wake. What was a general with so grand a title to do in either place?

Grant had at least seen the troubles of the South for himself. He knew the masked men, many of them ex-Confederate soldiers, who came in the dark to terrorize black people. But he had to admit that he had no experience with hostile Indians. He remembered the pitiful ones he had seen in Mexico and California and along the Columbia River. But the kind of warriors who could be collected by the thousands in the West he had never met in battle or even seen in person. As he explained to his friend General William Tecumseh Sherman, now commanding the army's Department of Missouri, which included most of the Great Plains, "I have never had any experience among hostile Indians myself and have never been in their country." He needed someone to be his eyes and ears in the West who would go beyond the simplistic views of General Sheridan, who commanded the army on the Southern Plains. Believing Indians to be locked in the Stone Age, with savagery deeply ingrained in them, Sheridan saw no need to defend the tactics he used to fight them, especially after warriors had committed heinous acts against frontier settlers. "I have to select that season when I can catch the fiends," he explained to Sherman; "and if a village is attacked and women and children killed, the responsibility is not with the soldiers but with the people whose crimes necessitated the attack."²⁸

While Grant respected Sheridan, the man who had fought with him bravely at Chattanooga and Cold Harbor and who had finally defeated the Confederates in the Shenandoah Valley, he refused to countenance such brutal methods. He did not believe that every Indian should be exterminated or, as many government officials did, that they were on the certain road to destruction. Instead, he pressed Sherman to come up with a real strategy that would preserve every life, Indian and American, west of the Mississippi River. Sherman finally concluded that the two peoples must be kept apart. The West should be divided into separate districts, one for the tribes and one for the settlers. The Sioux should live in a district in the northern plains—more specifically, west of the Missouri, north of the Platte, and east of the road to Montana. The Cheyenne and Arapaho should live farther south near the Indian Territory. This would leave the central district open for the construction of the Transcontinental Railroad. Sherman was convinced that once the railroad was completed, things would settle down. Americans would cross back and forth from Kansas to California, and the Indians, staying on either side of the great line, would be free to hunt buffalo and antelope and continue their traditional way of life with no interference.²⁹

Grant also learned a great deal from General John Pope, who, after his disastrous loss to the Confederates at Second Bull Run, was transferred to Minnesota with orders to defeat the Santee Sioux. He had prosecuted the war to a successful conclusion, and after the Santee were exiled from Minnesota, he kept up the fight against other Sioux bands through the summer of 1865. Even as he battled the Indians, he had little sympathy for "emigrants," the standard name for recent settlers in the West. He frequently complained about them to General Grant. In his view, they caused most of the trouble with the Indians. They seemed incapable of living in peace with the tribes. Whether they were miners, farmers, or railroad men, emigrants as a rule ignored treaties, trampled through reserves, and disrupted what remained of the Indian hunting grounds. Their actions set off attacks by warriors, which in turn led to retaliation and more bloodshed.³⁰

By the time Grant became the general of the army, Pope had come up with a solution, at least in Minnesota and the Dakota Territory. As he explained to Grant in letters and telegrams written throughout the spring and summer of 1865, it is "impossible for Indians and white men to live in contact on the frontier." Therefore, he further argued, "it is my purpose to keep the two races separated by a line of soldiers and by broad extents of country." He built a string of forts starting at Fort Abercrombie, heading west toward Spirit Lake, and finally ending at Pierre in the Dakota Territory. He directed the Sioux to settle near the forts, where they could raise their crops and hunt in the vast prairies in between. Pope likewise banned all white people, except for "military officers and teachers of religion," from settling near the Indians. The banishment even included Indian agents appointed by the government. Traders could sell their wares only within forts under the watchful eye of the army.[31]

Pope was adamant that soldiers alone could keep the peace on the frontier. They would do this not by attacking Indians, but by providing safe havens that protected them from settlers. He believed his approach should become the nation's new Indian policy and traveled to Washington in the summer of 1865 to present his ideas directly to Grant.[32] For his part, Grant was in complete agreement with Pope's suggestions right from the start. He regularly passed Pope's recommendations, along with his official endorsement, to Edwin Stanton, the secretary of war, and James Harlan, the secretary of the interior. As Grant explained to Pope, "It may be that Indians require as much protection from [t]he whites as the whites do from the Indians. [M]y own experience has been that but little trouble would have ever been from them but for the encroachment and influence of bad whites."[33]

There was one more person to whom Grant turned for advice. That man was Ely Parker. Like Grant, Parker had no experience with hostile Indians. He had seen warriors, who were now but a memory to the Seneca, for the first time when he met a group of them, including many Comanche, at the White House. They had come from Texas and Mexico to visit President Polk. At first they refused to believe that Parker was an Indian because he wore no paint and instead had the scrubbed face of a white man. They were fierce looking in their native costumes, wearing "very little clothing," as Parker explained to his family, "covered with paint, and ornamented from head to foot with all kinds of brass rings & beads & shells." He told his friends back in Tonawanda if only he had men like this at his side he would easily save his people from destruction: "If I had such Indians at the north, I could whip the Ogden Company & all their accomplices in less time than you could say 'Jack Roberson.'"[34]

But while Parker had no experience with hostile tribes, he understood what it was like to be pressed all around by a people who demanded everything and gave little in return. If Grant had a natural sympathy for the Indians just from witnessing their mistreatment when serving in the army in the West, Parker, who had spent much of his youth defending the Tonawanda Seneca, had still more. In September 1865, Grant assigned him to help resolve the conflicts that had developed during the Civil War among the tribes in the Indian Territory. Parker hurried west to attend a grand council of twelve tribes at Fort Smith, Arkansas.

These included the Cherokee, Choctaw, Chickasaw, Creek, and Seminole, whom President Jackson had removed from the South. The Seneca from the Sandusky River were also there, along with Shawnee and Seneca from Lewistown, Ohio. These Indians had lived on reserves in Grant's home state before being removed to the West. The Osage and Quapaw, who were among the first western tribes pushed across the plains to make room for the eastern Indians, were also present. The Comanche and Wichita rounded out the group.

When the Civil War started, Confederate troops had invaded the Indian Territory. They raided farms and ranches for food and supplies, and then demanded that the tribes join the fight against the Union. They promised annuities that matched the ones paid by Washington. Southern tribes that owned slaves enlisted willingly, while those from the North generally remained loyal to the Union. The Cherokee had been the most deeply divided over which side to take in the war. Chiefs of the Western Cherokee, who had moved across the Mississippi in the late eighteenth century, headed to Washington, asking for Union troops to defend them, while members of the Eastern Cherokee, who had been pushed out of Georgia by Andrew Jackson, fought for the Confederacy. Still another seven thousand Indians, whose ancestors had mainly been removed from the Northern states, fled to their kinsmen living in Kansas.[35]

The Indians who had gathered together in Arkansas were amazed to see one of their own among the commissioners. Shortly after Parker arrived, Grant ordered him to attend another council in the Colorado Territory, but the tribes at Fort Smith refused to let him go. As they explained, Parker had "inspired them with confidence," and they would not negotiate without him. He remained with the other commissioners, including President Johnson's recently appointed commissioner of Indian affairs, Dennis Cooley; Brigadier General William S. Harney, an Indian fighter; Elijah Sells, the superintendent of the Southern tribes; and Thomas Wister, a leading Quaker known for his calls to treat Indians fairly. Tensions ran high between Indians who fought the Confederacy and those who supported the Union, but Parker and the commissioners laid the groundwork for new treaties reconfirming the ties between all the tribes and the United States.[36]

Parker's work at the Fort Smith council led to even more assignments working with Indians. Commissioner Cooley asked for his help in negotiating treaties with the many delegations arriving in Washington from the Indian Territory. Parker also helped the Tonawanda Seneca pay off their debts and obtain government money for a new council house and a bell for their church. Grant likewise welcomed his help not just in the West but also in the South. Parker was sent on an inspection tour of forts in Kentucky, Tennessee, and Mississippi. He determined which installations should be closed, how many troops should be mustered out, and what supplies should be sold. Parker also noticed how much the condition of the former slaves resembled that of the Indians. They were surrounded by white people who despised them and, in his opinion, could survive only as wards of the government. He therefore recommended that the Union army stay in the South to protect the freedmen.[37]

Grant forwarded Parker's recommendations on forts in the South to the Johnson administration and came to rely on his judgment in matters related to the Indians. In the fall of 1866, when there was trouble with the Comanche in Texas, he asked Parker to investigate. The governor of Texas had demanded that federal troops be deployed to stop the tribe's depredations in the state's interior. Grant worried that this was a ruse to move soldiers away from the eastern part of the state, where they were protecting black people. After studying the situation, Parker explained what was happening in Texas and what to do about it. Before the Civil War, the government of Texas had ignored treaties between the United States and the Comanche, pushing the tribe out of the reserves promised to them by the American government. Once the war began, state officials demanded that the Comanche join the fight against the Union. The Comanche refused, saying they wanted no part in the white man's war, and fled to Mexico. When the Civil War ended, they returned to Texas, expecting to live on the land originally promised to them. To end the conflict between Texas and the Comanche, Parker suggested that a council be called. The tribe should be brought into the meeting with a full military escort meant to protect the Comanche from harm. At the council, the American government must offer the tribe a new reserve west of Arkansas. Here they would be supported by the Interior Department and guarded by the American army. Once again, Grant endorsed Parker's suggestions and forwarded them to the War and Interior Departments.[38]

Early in 1867, Grant asked Parker to help him develop an overall policy for dealing with the Indians in the West. This policy, as Parker explained, would establish a "permanent and perpetual peace" between the Indians and the United States. In his four-point plan, Parker first and foremost proposed that the Office of Indian Affairs be moved from the Department of the Interior back to the War Department. General Sherman had also suggested this move to Grant. The transfer of the office to the Interior Department may have seemed like a good idea following the Treaty of Guadalupe Hidalgo when the prospect of wars for the continent against the English, French, Spanish, and Mexicans had finally come to an end. But the Interior Department had been unable to resolve the growing conflicts between settlers who raced into the newly acquired territory and dozens of tribes that already lived there. Its agents were political appointees who were usually uninterested in protecting the Indians. Many were corrupt, taking goods promised to the tribes, selling them for a profit, and leaving the Indians starving and desperate. In contrast, Parker believed that army officers would protect the Indians, if so ordered. They would carry out their responsibilities more faithfully and thus make better Indian agents. Once the army was in place overseeing Indian affairs, the system of licensed traders, who thought only of making money rather than protecting the tribes, could be abolished.

Second, after so much fighting and so many treaties, the Indians must finally be guaranteed land of their own. Once permanent territories had been carved out for the tribes, the proper government for these territories must be determined. In this second point, Parker echoed government officials from Secretary James Barbour, who had served under President Adams, to the commissioners of Indian affairs under Lincoln and Johnson, and even General Sherman, who all argued that two territories, one in the North and one in the South, should be set aside for the Indians. Parker recommended that the best government for the territories would be the three-part process outlined in the Northwest Ordinance of 1787. The territories would eventually enter the Union, and the Indians would become citizens of the United States. While Parker restated the proposals of many who had gone before him, he did so with greater urgency because he believed the tribes were truly in danger of extinction. He knew many Americans wanted to wipe out the Indians, but he believed a Christian nation like the United States would not allow "such an appalling calamity befalling a portion of the human race."

Third, before the Office of Indian Affairs was officially transferred back to the War Department, an "inspection board" must be set up to oversee all the Indian agencies. The members of the board would inspect the books of every agency to make sure the money promised to the tribes, down to the last penny, was paid out to the Indians. This would end the corruption in the Indian service and provide a signal to the tribes that the government meant what it said. The Indians would be protected as they made the transition to modern ways of living. Since the transformation could not be made overnight, government officials must be patient. They must take the time to help the Indians, with the goal of welcoming them into the nation as citizens.

Finally, another permanent commission must be established, consisting of both white people and educated Indians, to meet regularly with the tribes. Its members would tell the Indians quite honestly that their days of freedom were over. Just as Parker's own people, the Seneca, had adapted to the white man's ways, so now all the tribes who still roamed the West must do the same. They were about to be overrun by settlers, many of whom wanted them hunted down and killed like wild animals, and only swift actions on their part and the part of the government could save them. The Sioux, Blackfeet, Cheyenne, Arapaho, Kiowa, Comanche, Apache, and all the other tribes must give up their traditional livelihoods and take on the hardworking habits of the settlers who surrounded them. Parker admitted that all this would be difficult for the tribes, but the transformation must take place to save the Indians from destruction and to preserve the honor of the United States.[39]

Grant took everything Parker had written to heart, forwarding his suggestions to Secretary Staunton with both a personal endorsement and a request that they be sent on to Congress. He also added one more idea of his own. The system of treaty making with the tribes that had gone on since the days of President Washington and even before, during the Confederation Congress, must be abolished. Grant disliked treaties not because settlers always overran the boundaries set in them, starting new wars, which in turn led to new treaties, but because the government often promised in them to give guns and ammunition to the Indians, who invariably used these weapons against the Americans. As Grant saw it, negotiators armed the tribes while soldiers fought them, often dying at the hands of the guns provided to the Indians. He also believed the Indians were no fools. Knowing the goods promised during treaty negotiations, they often stirred up trouble just to win these rewards.

If Grant had any say in the future of the West, he would end the treaty system and put the army completely in charge of Indian affairs. Once the army was in control, local commanders would decide which tribes received guns and which did not. They would likewise take over the distribution of annuities and other goods to the tribes in place of agents who were usually political appointees with no real concern for their charges. Private traders would also be banished from the Indian Country. Grant could only hope that his plans would be implemented, especially now that the United States was at war against the Sioux and by all accounts the Sioux were winning. But no matter what, long before he gave any thought to becoming president of the United States, Ulysses Grant already had the major outlines of his Indian policy in place.[40]

3. A Better World Ahead

*T*he mighty Sioux, who could field thousands of warriors against Grant's Civil War veterans, were not one people but many. The Santee Sioux, also known as the Dakota, lived farthest to the east in the great tribal confederation. They had hunted, farmed, and gathered wild rice on Minnesota's lakes until they were banished from their homeland after rising up in a desperate bid to win back their country from the Americans. They were sent to live with the Yankton Sioux, who hunted and sometimes farmed along the streams in the tall prairie grass at the eastern end of modern-day North and South Dakota. Beyond them to the west, fanning out on the northern plains toward the Rockies, lived the seven bands of the Teton Sioux, or Lakota: the Oglala, Brulé, Hunkpapa, Miniconjou, Sans Arc, Ooinunpa, and Blackfeet. Buffalo hunters who followed the herds year-round as far west as Montana and Wyoming and as far south as Nebraska and Kansas, they were fierce warriors who often joined the Cheyenne, Arapaho, Kiowa, Comanche, and Apache in raids defending their vast territory against the encroachments of settlers.

Like so many tribes that made the Great Plains their home, the Sioux originally came from the woodlands east of the Mississippi River. The Santee remained there until they were sent west following their revolt in 1862. But the Yankton and Lakota moved out onto the plains when the American colonies launched their war of independence against Great Britain. By the time the United States adopted the Constitution, the Sioux knew how to ride horses, the descendants of the first mounts brought to the Americas by Spanish conquistadors. The young men of the Lakota were some of the best horsemen on the Great Plains. They wandered with their people from the foothills of the Rockies in the north to the flat, arid grasslands in the south, not living in permanent villages but gathering every summer with the rest of the Sioux for tribal councils on the northern prairies. One of their favorite meeting places was in the Black Hills of the Dakota Territory, a sacred spot for the tribe where, between the cool forests of the highest mountains and the starry skies above, the Sioux could trace a path from this world to the next.[1]

A Better World Ahead

When the Santee Sioux uprising broke out in Minnesota in 1862, the Yankton and Lakota living farther west continued to live in relative peace with the United States. Roaming beyond the farthest reaches of territorial government, they had few encounters with settlers. Even when they met Americans more regularly, especially after the Oregon Trail opened between Kansas and the Pacific Northwest in the early 1840s, peace was maintained through the treaty negotiated at Fort Laramie in 1851. Based on the new national Indian policy of "concentration," the treaty carefully delineated the country belonging to the Sioux, bordered at the north by the Heart River, at the east by the Missouri, and at the south and west by the White, Platte, and Powder Rivers. Here the Sioux could maintain their traditional way of life without interference. They, in turn, agreed not to harm the many people traveling through their country along the Oregon Trail and its branches that turned south through the Rockies.[2]

The peace promised in the treaty was maintained for close to a dozen years. The large annuity that the government paid the tribes helped keep the peace. Likewise, so did the Sioux's promise to allow the construction of roads and forts on their land and make restitutions to Americans harmed while passing through their country. There were periodic skirmishes between Sioux, Cheyenne, and Arapaho warriors and travelers heading through the reserve, but no large-scale military operations were launched against the tribes in retaliation. However, the situation changed dramatically after gold was discovered in Montana in the early 1860s. Miners now regularly traveled through the country of the Sioux down the Bozeman Trail between Fort Laramie and Bozeman, Montana.

In late August 1865, to protect miners and other settlers from Indian attacks along the trail, President Johnson, with the full support of Ulysses Grant, the newly appointed general of the army, sent an expedition against the Lakota and their allies living along the Powder River Valley. After fighting several skirmishes and burning one Arapaho village to the ground, the army retreated back east.[3] The administration, however, remained determined to secure the Bozeman Trail. To accomplish this, three new posts, Fort Reno, Fort Phil Kearny, and Fort C. F. Smith, would be built along the trail in Wyoming and Montana the following summer. Still hoping to avoid an all-out war with the Sioux, the government called a grand council of the Indians at Fort Laramie in June 1866, hoping that Oglala chief Red Cloud, the most respected leader among the Lakota, Cheyenne, and Arapaho, would attend.

As the council got under way, Red Cloud rode into Fort Laramie with his fellow chiefs. At first, it seemed likely that he would sign a treaty with the United States, especially if this meant increased annuities for his people. But when Colonel Henry Carrington and thirteen hundred soldiers and their families came into the fort, along with support personnel hauling supplies to build posts along the Bozeman Trail, Red Cloud stormed out of the meeting with his followers after declaring:

> The Great Father sends us presents and wants a new road. But the white chief already goes with soldiers to steal the road before the Indian says yes or no. I will talk with you no more now. I will go now, and I will fight you. As long as I live I will fight you for the last hunting grounds.[4]

Government officials continued the council with the few remaining chiefs who had no authority to speak for their tribes. As a result, the treaties they negotiated were not worth the paper they were written on. Red Cloud, with usually no more than five hundred Lakota, Cheyenne, and Arapaho warriors at his disposal, now directed attacks on wagon trains and against woodcutters and haymakers sent out from forts in the Powder River Valley. As winter approached in late 1866, travel along the Bozeman Trail came to a halt. Colonel Carrington and his small company of soldiers became virtual prisoners in the newly built Fort Phil Kearny.

In December, Captain William Fetterman, a Civil War veteran, arrived at the post with a heavily armed supply train. According to legend, he boasted that with just eighty men he could ride safely through the Sioux country. He got his chance on December 21, when Carrington told him to take eighty soldiers and rescue the woodcutters under attack a few miles from the fort. The colonel warned him not to pursue any Indians on his way to relieve the woodcutters. But Fetterman met a small party of mounted Indians, including the noted Oglala warrior Crazy Horse, who taunted his men from high atop a ridge. He ordered his soldiers after them, chasing them over the hill and down into a valley, where three thousand warriors stood ready to ambush them. Cheyenne and Arapaho attacked from the west, while the Lakota closed the trap from the east. Fetterman and his soldiers were all killed, some by gunshots but many more by arrows and knives. Remembering the Sand Creek Massacre, the warriors hacked the soldiers' bodies to pieces, beheading and castrating many of them. Only one young man, a bugler who bravely fought off his attackers, was left untouched with a buffalo robe carefully placed over his dead body.[5]

News of the Fetterman Massacre arrived in Washington, DC, at the same moment that Senator James Doolittle finally delivered his commission's report on the Sand Creek Massacre to the Senate. After collecting more than five hundred pages of testimony, the commission concluded that the Indians, the "inferior race," were trapped in an impossible situation. They were being overrun by white people, the "superior" race, who were coming west in a "steady and relentless emigration." Bringing whiskey and disease with them, the white people incited violence against the Indians, who retaliated but to no avail. The tribes could not hold back the tide of white people, nor could they be saved from certain destruction. Their final ruin began when miners came west hunting for gold and silver and would end once the Transcontinental Railroad was completed. The buffalo, on which the Indians depended, would quickly disappear, and then "all the powerful tribes of the plains would disappear with them."[6]

Congress paid little attention to the findings of the Doolittle Commission, preferring instead to focus on the Fetterman Massacre. The Senate passed a resolution demanding to see every report coming into the War Department about the tragic event. Grant, the nation's top general, provided the information to Congress but recommended that a military court of inquiry at Fort Phil Kearny should investigate the incident. Still sympathetic to the Indians, he was certain a review of the facts would show that Fetterman and Carrington were incompetent. A more public investigation by Congress would only succeed in further embarrassing the army. President Johnson disagreed and instead appointed a new commission charged with discovering the cause of the army's humiliating loss. General Grant was one of the few people in Washington who thought this was a bad idea. When his concerns were dismissed, he made sure that his most trusted advisor, Ely Parker, was appointed to serve in the commission's military escort.[7]

By now, Grant had developed a more coherent picture of the troubles in the West and what a successful Indian policy should look like. He was receiving almost daily reports from military commanders on the state of Indian affairs across the Mississippi. He quickly concluded that a much larger force was needed to protect both the settlers and the tribes. This was another reason why the Office of Indian Affairs should be moved from the Interior Department to the War Department. Grant also more clearly understood that managing Indian affairs in the West was a balancing act. The concerns of settlers, Indians, and the army must be weighed against one another before any decision was made. However, several steps could be taken to make these decisions easier. Settlers should head west through the vast central section of the country on designated routes where they would never meet Indians. White men bent on corrupting the tribes, including agents and traders, should be kept away from the Indians unless they could be fully under military control. The army should deal swiftly with hostile Indians and refuse to reward them with gifts, especially guns and ammunition, once they had sued for peace. Even if soldiers made mistakes, destroying friendly Indian villages or failing to move swiftly enough to protect

A Better World Ahead

settlers from attacks, their commanders should give them the benefit of the doubt because, as Grant was fond of saying, there were "always two sides to a question."[8]

When Parker and the commissioners returned to Washington, they reported, as General Grant had suspected, that Fetterman and Carrington were responsible for the massacre. Fetterman had expressly ignored the instructions of his commanding officer, while Carrington had waited three hours to relieve the troops under attack. But beyond finding fault with these two men, the commissioners reported that they had made a great deal of progress with the Sioux and other tribes. Parker had been especially helpful in their negotiations with the Indians. He had assured the chiefs that President Johnson, their Great Father, was doing his best to protect their people. He likewise listened to their many complaints about the government's broken promises, the corrupt officials who stole goods from them, and the much-hated Bozeman Trail, which they said had to be shut down. The commissioners were certain that they had prevented many warriors from joining Red Cloud, but few in the nation's capital paid any attention to this achievement, since Congress had authorized yet another commission to review the nation's Indian policy and propose specific actions to end the wars in the West.[9]

Known as the Peace Commission, its members, all appointed by President Johnson, included Nathaniel Taylor, the commissioner of Indian affairs; Lieutenant General William Tecumseh Sherman; Brevet Major Generals Alfred Terry, William Harney, Christopher C. Augur, and John B. Sanborn, who were experienced Indian fighters; Senator John B. Henderson of Missouri, who served on the Senate's Committee on Indian Affairs; and Colonel Samuel Forster Tappan, a well-known defender of Indian rights who had investigated the Sand Creek Massacre. Their work had been clearly outlined in the legislation that created the commission. They had to "establish peace" by first determining and then removing the causes of the Indian Wars; secure the safety of frontier settlements and protect the many railroads under construction; and devise a plan to civilize the Indians.[10]

In August 1867, as the commissioners made their way to St. Louis and then to Fort Laramie, they sent runners ahead to call the Indians to two great councils. The first would be held with tribes living in the Dakota and Montana Territories, including the Lakota and Northern Cheyenne, at Fort Laramie on September 13, 1867. The second would take place with tribes living below the Arkansas River, including the Southern Cheyenne, along with the Arapaho, Kiowa, Comanche, and Apache, at Fort Larned in Nebraska on or about October 13, 1867. Everywhere they went, the commissioners met bands of desperately poor Indians begging for food and complaining about the government agents who ignored their every need.[11]

By the time the commissioners opened the council at Fort Laramie, they had come to the same conclusions about the Indians that Ulysses Grant had arrived at long before. If Indians acted badly, it was because they were treated badly. Any further theorizing about their actions served no purpose. Say what one might about how uncivilized they were, there was no denying the fact that Indians were human beings who responded to "magnanimity and kindness." The Golden Rule of "doing good unto others" must be applied to all the tribes, whether or not they were currently at war with the United States. The only way, in fact, to bring peace with the Indians in the West was to "conquer by kindness."[12]

But coming up with specific ways to help the Indians was far more difficult. This was especially true in the matter of guns. Grant believed the government should stop delivering guns to the tribes as a regular part of treaty negotiations. Instead, local military authorities should determine which bands received guns and which did not. He had even defended his position in heated exchanges in several cabinet meetings with Orville Browning, Johnson's secretary of the interior. Grant told Browning that the army could play a greater role in keeping the peace if given total control over distributing goods to the Indians. All supplies purchased for the Indians should be sent directly to military posts on the frontier. Local commanders, not agents or traders, should decide which bands received items and which did not based on their behavior. These officers should also decide when and where the distribution took place. Only in this way could guns be kept out of the hands of hostile bands who promised peace only to use the weapons against soldiers and settlers alike.[13]

However, the Brulé chief Swift Bear, the first chief to speak at Fort Laramie, did not agree. He explained that the buffalo and antelope were fast disappearing, and the bows and arrows used to hunt them could not bring in enough food. His men must have guns to hunt more efficiently or their families would starve to death. Contrary to what Grant believed, Swift Bear complained that the government never delivered the guns and other gifts promised during negotiations with the tribes. It was no wonder that the Indians did not trust the white man. "Whatever our people may choose to say of the insincerity or duplicity of the Indian," the commissioners would note in their final report, "would fail to express the estimate entertained by many Indians of the white man's character in this respect."[14]

From Fort Laramie, the commissioners planned to head to the Powder River Valley and meet with the Oglala, but with Red Cloud's War raging, it was too dangerous to proceed farther north. They went back down the Platte to the

Kansas, and then traveled to a place eighty miles south of the Arkansas River called Medicine Lodge Creek. Here the Kiowa, Comanche, and Apache were waiting for them. But there was no sign of the Southern Cheyenne or the Arapaho, who had camped some forty miles away. Their warriors had been attacking settlers since the previous April. They were now on the run from General Winfield Scott Hancock and his soldiers, who hunted them down like wild animals, often killing any Indian they came across, whether hostile or peaceful. Hancock's methods were so vicious that General Grant often demanded an explanation from him about his tactics. Unaware of this, the tribes could not believe that the United States, after launching Hancock's War, might be considering a more humane policy toward them. They kept their distance but sent a few warriors to Medicine Lodge to report back on the proceedings and, even more important, gauge the true intentions of the officials gathered there.[15]

On October 21, 1867, after a week of negotiations, the commissioners concluded treaties with the Kiowa and Comanche, along with the Apache, who agreed to be incorporated within the other two tribes. Just one week later, the Cheyenne and Arapaho finally met with the commissioners and signed an identical treaty. From the American perspective, the most important articles included promises by the Indians to stop attacking settlers, wagon trains, and stagecoach lines. They also agreed that railroads could be built across their country. For the Indians, the most important articles designated the country between the Washita and Red Rivers as their reserve. They could leave this place temporarily to hunt buffalo along the Arkansas River, but they could not settle there permanently. No white person, besides army officers, Indian agents, or other government officials, would be allowed onto their land. In return, the government would construct an agency with a warehouse and a home for their agent on the reservation, along with a church, schoolhouse, sawmill, and gristmill. Likewise, a doctor, carpenter, farmer, blacksmith, miller, and engineer would be sent west to help them.[16]

After they delivered annuities to the southern tribes, which had been put on hold during the Civil War, the commissioners headed back to Omaha and then up the North Platte to Fort Laramie, where they again hoped to meet with Red Cloud. A delegation from the Crow nation was present, waiting to give the commissioners a long list of complaints, but Red Cloud and his warriors were nowhere in sight. Deeply disappointed in their failure to end the war that had "spread terror throughout this entire region," they started back on the long trip to Washington. By the time they delivered their report to Congress on January 7, 1868, they were happy to learn that Red Cloud had promised to come to a council in the upcoming spring or summer.[17]

The final report of the Peace Commission formally laid the blame for the violence in the West, including Red Cloud's War, squarely at the feet of the Americans, not the Indians. Instead of honoring the claims of the Sioux, Cheyenne, Arapaho, Kiowa, Comanche, and Apache to their traditional homelands, Americans had raced west to Oregon, California, and Montana, hungry for land and even hungrier for gold and silver. The government had done nothing to stop its citizens from tramping over the country of the Indians. Chiefs were expected to protect their people in the ensuing chaos with no help from the American government. What else could they do, the commissioners asked, but send their warriors in one raid after another against the white people to save their kind?[18]

If any politician, journalist, or average citizen thought that the only solution to peace in the West was the extermination of the Indians, the commissioners did their best to set them straight. From a practical point of view, killing more than three hundred thousand people spread over a vast territory was impossible. There were simply not enough soldiers or tax dollars available to accomplish this brutal task. Just as important, from the perspective of common decency and the values of the supposedly Christian American nation, the demand to exterminate all the tribes was reprehensible, especially given the fact that the Indians were, in the commissioners' opinion, truly noble. The Indian, as the commissioners explained, was the "very embodiment of courage." He may have been driven from the home he loves, tortured, and killed, but "it never could make him a slave."[19]

The only solution to the misery that Americans, both settlers and their government, had brought to the Indians was to establish "districts" with territorial governments where the tribes could reside permanently. The Indians must be persuaded to come to these places, away from the violence that white people brought to the West, and there learn to give up hunting and become farmers. As the commissioners concluded, "Aside from extermination, this is the only alternative now left us. We must take the savage as we find him, or rather as we have made him. We have spent two hundred years in creating the present state of things. If we can civilize in twenty-five years, it will be a vast improvement on the operations of the past."[20]

Beyond these general recommendations, the commissioners ended their report with specific steps that must be taken to implement their vision. Following the suggestions that Sherman had made to Grant on a new national Indian policy, reservations should be concentrated in two separate districts, one near the country of the Lakota on the northern plains and the other near the reserve established for tribes on the southern plains in the Medicine Lodge Treaty. Next, the overall structure for handling Indian affairs had to be reconfigured. Matters dealing with the Indians had to be taken away from local authorities and handed back to the federal government. The Office of Indian Affairs had to be maintained, but Congress would have to decide whether it remained in the Interior Department, moved back to the War Department, or became a separate cabinet department.

But no matter what Congress finally decided, no governor or legislature of any state or territory should ever again be allowed to carry on a war against the Indians. The United States Army instead would be given full authority to protect the tribes on their reservations and punish any white person who trespassed there or on any other unceded Indian land. Congress had to pass new laws that banished greedy traders from the reservations and ensured that high-quality goods were delivered to the tribes. Finally, the United States had to negotiate a new treaty with the Navajo, who had suffered so mightily at Bosque Redondo. Likewise, a new national commission had to be appointed to meet with the Sioux in the upcoming year, and since the Union Pacific Railroad would soon reach the country of the Snake, Bannock, and other tribes, treaties should be negotiated to move them to one of the new districts.[21]

No one in the nation's capital was more accepting of the commission's findings than Ulysses Grant. Through all the proceedings, he had stayed in constant communication with General Sherman. He was impressed that his friend had greatly tempered his original approach to the Indians and could thus better analyze the situation beyond the Mississippi in all its complexity. Sherman had advised Grant that the problems faced by the army out west were far worse than either of them had imagined. He even said that they were more difficult than anything he had faced during his march through Georgia in the last year of the Civil War. He characterized the West as a vast, empty place where tribes were constantly on the move. An army could march for hundreds of miles and not see one Indian. It was no wonder, he confessed to Grant, that soldiers had such a difficult time determining which tribes were friendly and which were hostile.[22]

Despite his friend's growing despair, Grant still believed that Sherman was the best man to negotiate a treaty with Red Cloud's Sioux. He would support his efforts by standing ready to order the permanent evacuation of the three forts on the Bozeman Trail, even if this meant barring miners and other settlers from the Powder River country of the Lakota. He was not as well versed with the problems of the Navajo because their Long Walk had occurred during some of his most trying days in the Civil War, but he hoped that Sherman would also negotiate a treaty with them and thus find a way to rectify the damage done to them and restore this persecuted people to their traditional homeland.[23]

Grant had a greater stake in the outcome of the negotiations with the Sioux and the Navajo than did Sherman or the other commissioners because he knew the Republican Party would probably nominate him at its convention in the spring of 1868. In all likelihood, he would be elected president of the United States next November. The task of implementing the recommendations of the Peace Commission and the specific details in the treaties signed at Medicine Lodge would fall on his shoulders. He would be responsible for continuing the great shift already under way in the nation's Indian policy. The government had once again taken on the responsibility of civilizing the tribes. This had been part of the nation's original Indian policy established by President Washington. However, since the days when Andrew Jackson sent the eastern tribes across the Mississippi, any concern about teaching modern ways to the Indians so they could join the nation's mainstream had fallen by the wayside. But now Ulysses Grant, who had so long sympathized with the Indians, would be required to clothe the tribes, build houses for them on their reservations, teach them the value of privately owning land, educate their young in modern ways and the English language, and train everyone, both adults and children, to become self-supporting farmers. No president to date had been handed so specific a list of responsibilities toward the Indians even before he assumed office.[24]

If elected, Grant would also be required to implement the treaties signed with the Sioux and Navajo in the spring of 1868. In April, General Sherman and several negotiators, including Nathanael Taylor, Johnson's commissioner of Indian affairs, had met with Red Cloud and his fellow chiefs at Fort Laramie. The opening lines of the treaty they wrote pointed to a new era in the relations between the United States and the Sioux, which Grant, if he became president, would have to oversee: "From this day forward all war between the parties to this agreement shall forever cease. The Government of the United States desires peace, and its honor is hereby pledged to keep it. The Indians desire peace, and they now pledge their honor to maintain it."[25]

Implementing the treaty would be difficult because, while the Indians and Americans had both signed the document, they believed far different things about what the agreement meant for the future. For the Sioux, the document laid out the permanent boundaries of their country. Its eastern border followed the course of the Missouri, cutting the modern state of South Dakota in two and giving the western half to the Sioux. The sacred site of the Black Hills was clearly delineated as belonging to the tribe. An agency would be established on the Missouri River at the center of the reservation. The tribe could still hunt in Nebraska, but no white person could settle in the Powder River country, which was now designated as "unceded territory." Most important, the government promised to abandon the three military posts there and close the Bozeman Trail.

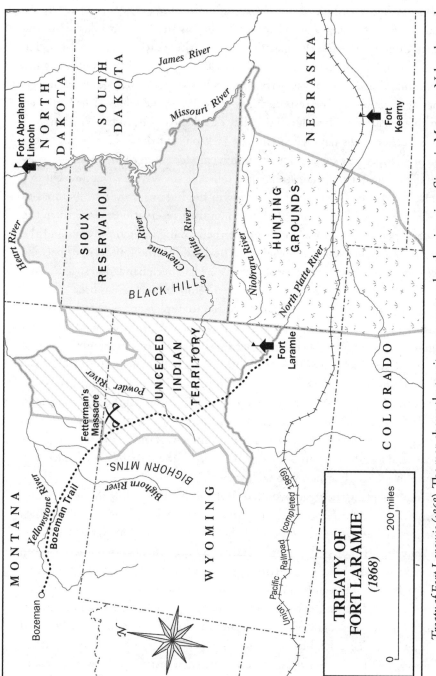

Treaty of Fort Laramie (1868). The map shows the territory guaranteed to the victorious Sioux in Montana, Nebraska, and the Dakota Territory at the conclusion of Red Cloud's War. COPYRIGHT © ROBERTA STOCKWELL, 2018.

In the treaty, the Sioux appeared to have won a complete victory. However, important concessions had been wrested from the tribe. The Sioux must stop attacking white people passing through their country and allow railroads to be built across it. They must also begin the slow process of looking and acting like Americans, already required of the Southern Cheyenne, as well as the Arapaho, Kiowa, Comanche, and Apache. They would receive the same clothing as the tribes who signed the treaties at Medicine Lodge Creek. Government surveyors would make sure there was enough arable land on their reservation for all adults to own land. The government would establish an agency on the Missouri, but a schoolhouse would also be built. The latter was important because the treaty contained all the same provisions for teaching modern skills to the children, including learning the English language, as the previous treaties signed on the southern plains.[26]

As president, Grant would also have to implement the conflicting aims of the treaty that General Sherman concluded with the Navajo on June 1, 1868, at Fort Sumner in the New Mexico Territory. From the Navajo perspective, the treaty allowed them to return to their traditional homeland in eastern New Mexico from which Carleton and Carson had driven them. Their new one-hundred-square-mile reservation included Canyon de Chelly. The government also promised to deliver fifteen thousand sheep and goats and five hundred head of cattle to the tribe, along with one million pounds of corn. However, from the American perspective, the treaty pointed to a new cultural life for the Navajo. The tribe promised never to attack Americans and to allow the construction of railroads through their country. Likewise, the Navajo had to change the way they dressed, owned land, and educated their children. It might take a generation or two, but by the end of the century the Navajo would look and act exactly like most Americans.[27]

When Sherman and his fellow negotiators were meeting with the Navajo, Grant was chosen as the Republican candidate for president. In the telegram he sent accepting the nomination, he promised to bring peace to a nation that had suffered from so many wars. He could make this pledge with utter sincerity when looking toward the Indians in the West. He was in complete agreement with the treaty just signed with the Sioux at Fort Laramie and the one about to be signed with the Navajo. For the moment, he saw no contradiction in either. In his opinion, the Indians had promised to live on reservations where the American government would protect them. Just as important, they had agreed to stop interfering with the march of American civilization, represented so perfectly by the Transcontinental Railroad, and someday to blend in with that same civilization.

Grant had been behind the scenes throughout the treaty negotiations, urging Sherman to make peace with the tribes, especially the Sioux, even if it meant closing the Powder River Country to Americans. Instead of sending armies against the tribe's warriors, many of whom had murdered his fellow citizens, he had consistently advocated signing a treaty with the Sioux that prohibited settlement in their territory. He was more than ready to abandon Forts Reno, Phil Kearny, and C. F. Smith on the Bozeman Trail, which ran directly through the tribe's hunting grounds. Emigrants foolish enough to travel along it on their way to the imagined riches of goldfields in Montana would need more soldiers to protect them than the three forts could provide. Grant also saw no purpose in maintaining Fort Fetterman, farther to the south in the North Platte River Valley. In March 1868, he had recommended to the War Department that all four posts be closed. Although Fort Fetterman would remain open, Grant's recommendation to abandon the forts on the Bozeman Trail was incorporated into the Treaty of Fort Laramie, signed one month later. In August, after the War Department withdrew the last soldiers from forts along the trail, Lakota warriors burned the hated posts to the ground.[28]

Whereas Grant was concerned with establishing peace with the Indians, neither the Republicans nor the Democrats were troubled for the moment about violence in the West. The platforms of both parties agreed that the nation's debts must be settled and immigrants welcomed. The greatest disagreements came in the parties' differing attitudes toward the defeated Southern states and the rights of black people. The Republicans stood by their repudiation of the Confederate debt, their condemnation of Andrew Johnson, and their support for black suffrage. In contrast, the Democrats called for removing the army from the former Confederate states and dismantling the Freedmen's Bureau, an agency for "negro supremacy." Their platform also demanded greater support for working people, including the many farmers who were steadily heading west. Without ever mentioning the many Indians who lived across the Mississippi River, the Democrats stood for the principle that "public lands should be distributed as widely as possible among the people." This should be done through preemption or homestead laws. Land should also be sold in reasonable amounts and at reasonable rates, with the minimum price set by the American government. The words of the platform echoed the spirit of the Democratic Party from Jefferson to Jackson that the West belonged to the people, not the Indians, and must be opened for settlement.[29]

While the problem of Indians in the West was not a major matter in the campaign, it remained an important issue for candidate Ulysses Grant. In fact, he had already shaped his Indian policy more completely than any other policy

A Better World Ahead

he would implement if elected president. His primary goal was a simple one. As he explained to General Sherman, "Any expense, or course, that will preserve the peace with the Indians is to be commended."[30] Like Sherman and the other members of the Peace Commission, Grant was determined to end the debates over who had caused the unending violence in the West. He was certain most Americans now understood that the settlers who overran the Indian country were to blame for the continuing unrest in the region. Nor did he plan to set up any more commissions to determine appropriate actions to take with regard to the western tribes. There was simply no more time for this. Grant instead would intervene on behalf of the Indians to save them. Once elected, he would do this by fully implementing the provisions of the treaties signed at Medicine Lodge Creek, Fort Laramie, and Fort Sumner. The tribes would be granted reservations where settlers would not be allowed to enter. The army would play a key role in protecting the Indians. They would prevent settlers from coming onto Indian land, except for specific personnel sent west to help them. The army would also help the Indians by inspecting goods delivered to the reservations and making sure they were of high quality.[31]

Even when news of another massacre in the West made it to Washington, DC, barely three weeks after Grant was elected, the new president did not waver in the course he had already set for himself, his nation, and the army. On November 21, 1868, Lieutenant Colonel George Armstrong Custer and five hundred soldiers attacked the camp of the Cheyenne chief Black Kettle on the Washita River in the Indian Territory. Black Kettle and his people had moved to the valley, which had been granted to the Cheyenne, along with the Arapaho, Kiowa, Comanche, and Apache, as part of the reservation designated in the Medicine Lodge Creek treaties. While older leaders generally accepted the provisions of the treaties, many younger warriors did not. They were especially frustrated that they were being kept away from the hunting grounds farther to the north and west. Humiliated and hungry, bands of warriors headed into Kansas throughout the summer and fall of 1868, chasing buffalo and attacking American settlements.[32]

Black Kettle traveled to nearby Fort Cobb to tell the soldiers that his people had no part in these attacks and wished instead to move farther south away from the Washita. They were in desperate need of food, since the weather had already turned bitterly cold by the late fall. Colonel William Hazen, the fort's commander, informed him that General Sherman had ordered General Sheridan to punish the warriors causing depredations, even allowing him to enter the new reservation just set up in the Indian Territory. Hazen added that Sheridan's army had been told to leave all peaceful Indians alone. However, the colonel was unaware that General Sheridan had envisioned his orders in terms of a total war waged in the South during the final days of the Civil War. Sheridan directed his soldiers, including Custer's 7th Cavalry, "to destroy their villages and ponies, to kill or hang all warriors, and bring back all women and children."[33]

Returning with his people to the Washita River, Black Kettle ignored rumors that soldiers were on their way through the deep snow to attack the many Indian camps in the valley. On the morning of November 28, 1868, General Custer's 7th Cavalry stormed into Black Kettle's camp from four directions. While Custer lost only one man directly under his command in the fighting, losses to the Indians were high. Over one hundred men lay dead, including Black Kettle with a bullet in his back, and at least that many women and children. After the battle, Custer ordered all goods that could not be carried away destroyed and also had at least 675 Indian horses and ponies killed. He later defended himself against charges that he had led a massacre into a camp of friendly Indians on the grounds that his cavalry had followed a trail of warriors directly into Black Kettle's village.[34]

As Congress and the press debated whether the attack on the Washita was a massacre or a battle, as Custer believed, President-elect Ulysses Grant steadily maintained the path he had set for dealing with the Indians. In this frightening time for the tribes, so clearly seen in the troubles along the Washita, he agreed with Ely Parker that the Indians must be considered "wards of the state." The government must support them until they were brought into full American citizenship. The first step in accomplishing this must be to bring the tribes onto reservations. Here the army would protect them from any further harm by Americans, both "bad men" who fomented violence and "good men" who wanted their land. Superintendents and agents currently working in the West would be dismissed and replaced by army officers who would carry out orders sent directly from the Office of Indian Affairs, which would be moved back to the War Department.

Custer's actions did not alter Grant's plans to send army officers west to manage the reservations. His faith in the integrity of the soldiers who had fought so bravely with him during the Civil War was unshakable. He considered them far more trustworthy than the average civilian. They would faithfully deliver annuities to the tribes, making sure they were of high quality and provided in the exact amounts prescribed by treaties. They would never sell these goods, pocketing most of the profits for themselves and spending only a few dollars on poor-quality items for the Indians, as so many agents and traders did under the current system. The army officers would also oversee the work of the many people sent to the reservations, including teachers, doctors, farmers, millers, and engineers, to help the Indians make the transition to a modern way of life. If an officer disobeyed orders with regard to the tribes, he could easily be dismissed through a court-martial.

It might take time, but slowly, under the watchful tutelage of the army, the Indians would learn to give up their old ways and prepare to become individual landowners and citizens of the United States. This belief was packed into the simple yet startling phrase that Grant spoke in his inaugural address. Ely Parker was one of the few people who understood the careful reasoning behind the president's pledge to uphold the "proper treatment of the original occupants of this land—the Indians."[35] For his part, Grant had only one concern about his policy. Would he be able to appoint Ely Parker as the next commissioner of Indian affairs to help him implement it? In the weeks leading up to his inauguration, he came under increasing pressure from Protestant ministers to retain Nathaniel Taylor, "an accomplished Christian gentleman," or to name General John B. Sanborn, who, in the opinion of Sherman and the other peace commissioners, had the "integrity and ability" to run the Indian service. Ignoring these opinions, Grant considered Parker his first and only choice. However, he worried that the Senate might block the nomination because Parker, a Seneca Indian, had never been formally declared a citizen of the United States.[36]

Many Indians had been granted American citizenship under treaties signed with the United States. Most recently, members of tribes removed from the Northern states to Kansas, such as the Wyandot, had received individual tracts of land and American citizenship when the government purchased their tribal reserve to make way for settlers and railroads in the 1850s. The Civil Rights Acts of 1866 had granted citizenship to "all persons born in the United States and not subject to any foreign power, excluding Indians not taxed." The final clause distinguished between Indians who lived on tribal reserves and therefore paid no taxes, property or otherwise, and Indians like Parker, who lived in the wider American society and paid a variety of taxes including ones on property.

The Fourteenth Amendment to the Constitution, just ratified in July 1868, defined American citizenship by this simple phrase: "All persons born or naturalized in the United States, and subject to the jurisdiction thereof, are citizens of the United States and of the State wherein they reside." The amendment made a passing reference to Indians by stating that "representatives shall be apportioned among the several states according to their respective numbers, counting the whole number of persons in each state, excluding Indians not taxed." Grant reasoned that Parker had paid taxes when he worked as a government engineer, military secretary, and treaty negotiator and therefore was an American citizen. His new attorney general, Ebenezer Hoar, agreed, ruling that Parker was eligible to serve. Republican Senator John Thayer of Nebraska, who had fought with Grant from Fort Donelson to Vicksburg, also encouraged Grant to nominate Parker. As Thayer saw it, who else "could exercise so favorable an influence upon the Indians?" The Committee on Indian Affairs agreed, approving his nomination on April 15, 1869, with the full Senate confirming him four days later by a vote of thirty-six to twelve. Parker immediately resigned his army commission and assumed his new post.[37]

No one of Parker's caliber had ever taken on the position of commissioner of Indian affairs to date. Most who served in the position had been political appointees only. They were faithful party workers, including several newspapermen, who had been given the post for supporting the candidate who won the presidency. Parker, by contrast, had trained as a lawyer and engineer, negotiated on behalf of his people, helped argue a case on Indian rights before the Supreme Court, and served in the Treasury and War Departments. For the last four years, he had worked for commissions investigating Indian unrest on the frontier and had even helped negotiate treaties with the southern tribes. But most important, he was the living embodiment of the nation's original Indian policy that had guided the country from Washington up until Jackson. His people had given up most of their tribal land in the East and settled on individual farms. Parker was himself an excellent farmer. Like many of his family members, he had studied at mission schools on the Tonawanda Reserve and local academies attended primarily by white people. He was a master of the English language and had blended into the wider American society. In 1869, he had married a white woman, Minnie Sackett, which had been the final hope of Washington's original Indian policy. At some point in the future, the two peoples, white and red, would become one through intermarriage.

The two friends Ulysses Grant and Ely Parker had made plans for the Indians of the Far West that would require not just hard work on their part but also a great deal of money. The usual budget for the Office of Indian Affairs was $5 million to $6 million annually. The office had thirty-eight clerks working in the Washington office, fifteen superintendents, and nearly seventy agents in the field. Along with the many other people employed by the Indian service, including the personnel described in the latest treaties, such as blacksmiths, farmers, millers, teachers, and doctors, the total climbed to six hundred people. The office's responsibilities were enormous and included day-to-day dealings with the Indians, distributing annuities to the tribes, and managing everyone who worked on the reservations. Since many changes were coming in Indian affairs, one of Grant's first requests to Congress was to increase the annual budget of the Office of Indian Affairs by $2 million. Parker also made a further change related to money: any matter dealing with Indian claims must come directly to him. He was determined that no agent would ever again cheat the Indians. He also decided to inspect personally the yearly purchase of annuity goods for the western tribes.[38]

With Grant's approval, Parker's first major action as the new commissioner of Indian affairs was to remove most of the superintendents and agents currently in the Indian service. While a handful of agents kept their positions, and five superintendencies—Oregon, Wyoming, Nevada, Colorado, and the Dakota Territory—were granted to Republican politicians, Parker replaced most of the remaining officials with army officers (see Appendix A). He asked the War Department to help him assign soldiers who had some knowledge of Indians. They must be men of "rank, experience, and sobriety." Parker gave the new agents detailed instructions on how to treat the Indians. They must do everything in their power to bring the tribes onto the reservations. This would not be easy. The agents must at all times be honest, explaining that the traditional Indian way of life, especially the year-round hunt of the buffalo, was over. The tribes must be encouraged to come to the same conclusion. They must accept the fact that they would survive only if they moved to designated reserves where they would be out of the way of American settlers and learned to farm.

While Parker kept a few former agents, mainly in the Pacific Northwest, he followed Grant's directions on appointing agents in the Northern and Central Superintendencies. A delegation of Quakers from Iowa had met with the president-elect in Washington on January 25, 1869, and urged him to take a "more liberal and attentive consideration of the welfare of the Indians" than previous presidents. The next day, another delegation of Quakers from Philadelphia met with Grant and recommended a similar approach. He welcomed the suggestions of both delegations, since they agreed with many ideas of his new policy. On February 15, Grant directed Parker to write letters to both the Orthodox and Hicksite branches of the Quaker faith, asking each group to recommend several of their own members to serve as Indian agents. Parker ultimately appointed eighteen Quaker agents. He likewise placed the Northern Superintendency in Nebraska under the control of the Orthodox Quakers and the Central Superintendency in Kansas and Oklahoma under the care of the Hicksites. They joined the ranks of many more agents whom Parker had chosen from the ranks of the army.[39]

As he implemented the new Indian policy in the opening months of the Grant administration, Parker admitted that the Indians might have a hard time trusting army officers at first. But he believed that with time and patience, they would see the peaceful intentions of the government and be won over by the kind treatment they received. The newly appointed agents would oversee the delivery of high-quality food, clothing, and shelter to the Indians, while slowly getting them used to a more settled life. Their toughest assignment would be convincing the tribes that they should stop attacking Americans, especially when retaliation seemed justified, and to view them instead as their fellow citizens. A difficult task, no doubt, but in Parker's opinion, not impossible. If they could not bring every Indian onto a reservation and still encountered "roving bands," they must let their fellow officers posted in nearby forts decide whether these wandering Indians were friendly or hostile and deal with them accordingly. After so much effort and money had been spent on Indians in the past without bearing much fruit, Parker believed the tribes would now come out of the darkness into the light. Indians of the Far West, like his own people, the Seneca, long before them, were at last on the road to joining the civilization of modern America. As he looked forward to the success of Grant's Indian policy, Parker never guessed that a revolt was already under way against it.[40]

4. The Dawn of a Revolt

During his first months in office, President Grant never doubted his Indian policy was working. Anyone who honestly studied the matter, which hopefully included members of Congress and the press, could appreciate how similar his new policy was to the nation's original Indian policy. From the founding of the nation, starting with the Confederation Congress and George Washington's administration, the United States had always hoped "to ameliorate and civilize the tribes." Grant had followed suit by envisioning Indian reservations as places where the tribes would slowly take on the habits of modern Americans. He had been able to obtain an extra $2 million from Congress to fund civilization programs on the reservations. Looking ahead to the coming years, more reservations would be established in Montana, Nevada, Arizona, and New Mexico. Here army officers appointed by his administration would manage day-to-day operations and help the Indians along the road to civilization. Here, too, the tribes would be treated honestly for all goods purchased for the tribes would be delivered by the Office of the Commissary of the Army, not private traders.[1]

But whether Grant admitted it, there were increasing problems implementing his policy across the Mississippi. Not every Indian living in the West was happy with the changes coming from Washington. Many did not want to move onto reservations where they were expected to live like white men. They saw no reason why they must give up their traditional way of life, which for them was a civilization far superior to that of the Americans. While the Sioux were generally content for the moment with their latest treaty, the tribes of the central plains, especially the Cheyenne, Arapaho, and Kiowa, were on the brink of uniting to avenge the many deaths along the Washita River at the hands of Custer and his 7th Cavalry. Farther south, the Comanche living in northern Texas and the Apache in Arizona were determined to maintain their territory with no interference from President Grant and his strange ideas about how they must live their lives. If they had to kill every settler and soldier who came their way to maintain their independence, then they would do so.

The Dawn of a Revolt

Many Americans who lived in places as far flung as Montana, Arizona, and Texas were just as certain that President Grant had set their nation on the wrong path. The Indians might be civilized at some future date, but for now they were violent and not to be trusted. The chiefs who signed peace treaties with the United States could not control the bands of young warriors who attacked frontier outposts, killing and maiming without mercy. Nor was every military man certain that protecting Indians and teaching them the finer points of civilization should be among his primary duties. As soldiers in the Arizona Territory were fond of saying about themselves, they did not go into the army to be Indian agents. The army came west to keep the peace, but only if this meant rounding up the tribes and making them live like prisoners on reservations. A soldier's main job was to protect American settlers from Indian attacks, whether or not those same settlers had played a part in instigating these attacks. Many were willing to carry out this task with great brutality.[2]

The ideals of Grant's Indian policy and the realities of life in the Far West were bound to collide and finally did so in the Marias or Piegan Massacre, which occurred in the Montana Territory on January 23, 1870, less than a year after Grant took office. The origins of this terrible event, which left upward of two hundred Piegan Indians dead at the hands of the American army along the Marias River, could be traced to a tangled story of violence and revenge that not even the most humane Indian policy could have prevented. The Piegan, who along with the Blackfeet and Blood Indians formed the Blackfeet Confederation, had frequently attacked settlers in the Montana Territory. Commissioner Parker believed that part of the tribe's unrest stemmed from the government's failure to designate a reservation for the confederation where the three tribes could live in peace. However, he had been unable to accomplish this since assuming office. But even if he had secured a reservation, the tribes might have continued retaliating against settlers for the latest wrongs done to them. The desire for vengeance, working its way out over many years, helped lead to the Marias Massacre.

Sometime in 1867, according to Piegan oral tradition, a white trader and rancher named Malcolm Clarke had raped the wife of a Piegan warrior named Owl Child. The woman later gave birth to a mixed-race infant, who by some accounts was stillborn but by others was murdered by the elders of the tribe. Owl Child avenged the shame of his wife by stealing horses from Clarke's ranch. Clarke retaliated by beating Owl Child in the presence of Piegan warriors and thus humiliating him. The cycle of violence reached its climax on the night of August 17, 1869, when Owl Child, feigning forgiveness, came to dinner with the Clarke family. After the meal, he murdered Malcolm and wounded his fifteen-year-old son, Horace. Clarke's Indian wife, Cothecocona, a cousin of Owl Child's wife, along with another son and two daughters, hid in the house and thus escaped from harm.[3]

Caring little about the long-standing feud between Malcolm Clarke and Owl Child, General Philip Sheridan, now commander of the army's Department of the Missouri, ordered Major Eugene Baker and the 2nd Cavalry to hunt down Owl Child and Mountain Chief, an important leader among the hostile Piegan who lived along the Marias River. While Baker was to distinguish between friendly and hostile bands, Sheridan, on the direct orders of Sherman, encouraged him to "strike them hard." Baker and his two hundred soldiers, now including mounted men from the 13th Infantry, headed for the Marias River Valley in late January 1870, traveling at night through the bitter cold. Passing by several camps of friendly Indians, Baker came upon another settlement, which his scout Joseph Cobell deliberately misidentified as Mountain Chief's village. Cobell was married to Mountain Chief's sister and wanted to keep Baker from attacking the camp of his brother-in-law, which was actually ten miles farther up the Marias River.

Shortly after sunrise on January 23, Baker ordered his men to open fire on the sleeping camp. Hearing the guns, a Piegan man holding a piece of paper in his hand raced from his lodge toward the soldiers. He was Heavy Runner, the leader of the camp, who was a well-known friend of the Americans. The paper he carried was a promise of protection from the Office of Indian Affairs. Cobell, knowing full well who the chief was, shot him dead. The attack on Heavy Runner's camp continued, with the soldiers using their new Springfield rifles to rapidly fire hundreds of bullets at the Piegan. The soldiers shot any Indian who tried to escape. They gunned down the poles that held up the buffalo hides of the lodges. Many of the hides caught fire as they collapsed, trapping the sleeping Indians beneath them. By the time the attack was over, anywhere from 170 to 200 Piegan lay dead, almost all of them women, children, and old men. Another 140 women and children had escaped to the Marias River, where they tried to hide in the icy waters.

After the fighting was over, Baker finally realized that he had attacked a friendly Piegan camp. Many of the people who died had been sick with smallpox. Few warriors were present, since most were off hunting. Baker and his men threw the bodies of the dead into the fire to consume the smallpox, rounded up the shivering Piegan still standing in the Marias, and then hurried along the river toward Mountain Chief's camp. They found the place deserted. As soon as Mountain Chief learned about the attack on Heavy Runner's camp, he had fled with his people to Canada. Baker now returned to his command post at

Fort Shaw. He released the women and children he had captured but gave them no food, clothing, or tents. They walked ninety miles in the freezing cold to Fort Benson, many of them dying along the way. Baker, a known alcoholic who would eventually die from cirrhosis of the liver, refused to write a report about the attack for several weeks. When he finally alerted General Sherman, who had been promoted to general of the army when Grant was elected president, about the tragic events at Heavy Runner's village, he assured him that he had attacked the village of Bear Chief and Big Horn, two well-known hostile chiefs. His soldiers had killed 125 Piegan and Blood warriors and 53 women and children, and captured three hundred horses. They had taken many more women and children prisoners but had set them all free.[4]

As the story of the massacre spread through the nation's newspapers, the decency of the American army, the very linchpin of Grant's Indian policy, was called into question. Debates over Baker's actions raged across the country, with western papers generally supporting Baker and eastern ones condemning him. However, the worst fighting took place within the highest ranks of the army. The men whom Grant and Parker had appointed to oversee Indian affairs in the Montana Territory condemned the drunken Baker and his misguided soldiers. General Alfred Sully, who headed the Montana Superintendency, attacked the many lies in Baker's official report. Sully rightly pointed out that the camp of the friendly chief Heavy Runner had been attacked and that hundreds of women, children, and old men had been gunned down and burned alive without mercy. Lieutenant William B. Pease, the Blackfeet Indian agent, joined Sully in condemning Baker. A week after the massacre, Pease met with a delegation of Piegan, who told him only fifteen of the dead were men of fighting age. He forwarded a report to Sully, who endorsed it and sent it on to the Grant administration.[5]

Sherman and Sheridan, the army's two highest-ranking officers, soon entered the fray on the side of Major Baker. Sherman issued a statement to the press saying he preferred to believe the report that most of the dead were Mountain Chief's warriors. He added that the army had stopped shooting at the very moment the Indians no longer resisted the attack on them. The soldiers accepted the surrender of all who asked and let at least a hundred women and children go free. While Baker could be faulted for not immediately reporting the exact number of Piegan killed, Sherman stated point-blank that he had total faith in his leadership. Both he and Sheridan urged Congress, as well as President Grant and Commissioner Parker, to ignore Sully's request for a full investigation.[6]

At a critical time in the implementation of his Indian policy, President Grant decided to accept Major Baker's version of events. He would order no official investigation of the incident beyond asking the Board of Indian Commissioners to study the matter. He had decided when he became the general of the army to trust the judgment of military commanders in the field, and he would not change his position now. For his part, Parker believed that even if wrongdoing had occurred along the Marias River, the Blackfeet had brought it on themselves by their frequent attacks on settlers. Looking for something positive in this terrible event, he concluded that the army's assault on the Piegan camp along the Marias River, which had sadly killed many innocent women and children, had at least ended the Blackfeet's resistance to Grant's Indian policy. The smallpox epidemic that swept through their country had a similar effect.

Parker promised that the Office of Indian Affairs would do everything in its power to halt the further spread of smallpox by vaccinating the far western tribes. But there would be no turning back from the president's demand that the Blackfeet stop their depredations against Americans, settle down on a reservation designated for them by the government, and begin the slow process of adapting to modern ways, which would be accomplished under the watchful eye of army officers. Congress accepted Grant's decision, but because of the trouble with the Piegan, his request to move the Office of Indian Affairs back to the War Department, a key feature of his new Indian policy, was voted down.[7]

Another feature of Grant's policy met with growing resistance not from Congress, but from the tribes themselves. Many were simply not interested in moving onto reservations where they were expected to transform their lives. The Utes, for example, who had been assigned a reservation in Colorado in an 1868 treaty with the government, refused to move there. Many of the Cheyenne, Arapaho, Kiowa, Comanche, and Apache, who had settled in the Indian Territory in accordance with the Medicine Lodge Creek treaties signed in 1868, had no intention of taking up farming. Instead, warriors from these tribes raided the homesteads of eastern Indians who had been living in Oklahoma since their removal during Jackson's administration. They also headed to northern Texas, where they killed settlers, captured women and children, and stole horses and cattle. The Apache in New Mexico and Arizona made similar raids on settlers throughout the Southwest.

To counter their resistance, Parker initiated a policy within the Office of Indian Affairs to deliver annuities only on reservations. He hoped this practice would entice the Utes and every other tribe reluctant to move onto their designated reservations to do so. He also refused to listen to any complaint from Indian warriors that they were attacking Americans in retaliation for mistreatment. "In my judgment they know better" was his frequent response. He recommended constructing a string of forts from the southern border of the

The Dawn of a Revolt

Chickasaw reservation in Oklahoma across northern Texas to deter Indian raids. Knowing that the Apaches spared only priests when they attacked settlements, he urged the Department of the Interior to recruit Catholic clergy to persuade the Apaches to make peace with the United States, settle down on land provided for them by the government, and start the process of joining the white man's world.[8]

Never once did the president or his commissioner of Indian affairs consider the possibility that the Indians might reject the future offered to them. If some tribes refused to settle on reservations, they were simply misguided. If they did not want to conform to the values imposed on them, learning to own land and be educated in schools, all so that someday they could become citizens of the United States, they were lost in dreams of a past that was fast disappearing. If they preferred to follow the buffalo herds, believing the life they currently lived in the West would never change, they were doomed to destruction. Miners pursuing every last ounce of gold and silver in the Rockies, the mighty Transcontinental Railroad connecting east and west, and settlers by the hundreds of thousands filling up the plains from Texas to the Dakota Territory would roll over the painted warriors on horseback, destroying them and their people and wiping out every memory of the tribes that once roamed the Far West.

To help the Indians understand what lay ahead of them if they refused to accept his Indian policy, Grant asked tribal leaders to meet with him in person in Washington, DC. After the Marias Massacre, an invitation went out to the chiefs of the Lakota, including Spotted Tail and Swift Bear of the Brulé and the far more influential Red Cloud of the Oglala. Hoping for a positive response from the tribes, the president was unaware of the degree to which his views on the future of the Indians differed from those of the Sioux. However, once officials in his administration and tribal leaders finally met in Washington in June 1870, the differing viewpoints, which included a fundamental disagreement about the meaning of the treaties signed at Fort Laramie, could no longer be ignored.

Jacob Cox, Grant's secretary of the interior, opened the first meeting with Red Cloud and his fellow chiefs shortly after they arrived in the nation's capital. A former Union general from Ohio who had fought with McClellan at Antietam and Sherman in Georgia and North Carolina, Cox generally supported the Indian policy that Grant and Parker had developed. However, he brought a more urgent sense that corruption in the Indian Department must be eliminated through civil service reform. Cox had seen the troubles of the Far West firsthand after the Civil War when he rode the Union Pacific from Chicago to its terminus on the Great Plains. While he was not convinced that the Indians would ever give up war, especially after witnessing their harassment of railroad

Red Cloud's first visit to the White House. With the words "Let us have peace," President Grant and his secretary of war, William Belknap, greet Red Cloud, who is drawn as a heroic figure, along with his fellow chiefs, on the cover of *Harper's Weekly*, June 18, 1870. COURTESY OF THE LIBRARY OF CONGRESS.

workers along the transcontinental line, he assured Red Cloud and his followers that the American government wanted peace. He could only hope they felt the same way.[9]

After their opening meeting with Secretary Cox, Commissioner Parker took the Indians on a tour of the city, showing them the wonders of American civilization, which he and the president wanted the Sioux to join, from the top of the Capitol dome, then back down to the Senate Chamber, and finally out to the Armory and the Naval Yard. He also explained the provisions of the 1868 Treaty of Fort Laramie and urged the Lakota to live up to them. President Grant welcomed the Sioux to a candlelit dinner in the East Room of the White House. Sitting alongside members of the diplomatic corps, officials from the Interior Department, and many congressmen, the Indians ate a sumptuous meal capped off with a dessert of ice cream and strawberries. But nothing they heard or saw convinced them that embracing this world would lead to a better future for their people. When an official whispered to Red Cloud that he could have food like this if the Sioux learned to farm, he responded sarcastically that he would gladly farm "if you always treat me like this and let me live in as big a house."[10]

The opposing views of both sides were especially clear on June 8, when the council between the government and the Indians officially began. Secretary Cox opened the meeting by telling the chiefs that their visit should prove President Grant wished only good for the tribes. He then proceeded to explain Grant's Indian policy, point by point, in the clearest terms possible. First, the president was determined to find places where the Indians could live in peace and be totally undisturbed by his own people, who were racing west across the plains. Second, he had sent General Sherman west in 1868 to negotiate a treaty at Fort Laramie, which guaranteed a homeland for the Sioux. Third, the president would not allow settlers to overrun the Indian country but would instead protect the tribes. He, in fact, would give the Sioux everything they needed to survive except powder and ammunition, which he would grant only if they stopped attacking their white neighbors and fellow Indians. Finally, the president asked the Sioux "to try to learn the ways of the white man and to persuade others to do so."

Red Cloud listened politely to Cox's words as they were translated for him. Then he rose and walked across the room toward Cox. He sat down on the ground directly in front of him, facing west, the place where he was born and the direction from which he had just come. He explained that he had not traveled to Washington to argue the finer points of Grant's Indian policy. He had instead journeyed over two thousand miles to tell the president about the troubles that his people, the Americans, were causing for the Sioux. Despite what Secretary Cox said about Grant's intentions, Red Cloud argued, the white people did not want peace. Instead, they were taking over the country that the government had promised to the Lakota. "The white children have surrounded me and have left me nothing but an island," he explained. "We are melting like snow on the hillside while you are growing like spring grass."

As Red Cloud explained, there were ways that President Grant could help the Sioux, not in the abstract world of policy-making, but in the real world where the tribe's warriors and their families actually lived. First, the Americans must stop building roads on Sioux land, especially through the Black Hills and the Bighorn Mountains. Second, posts already built nearby, such as Fort Fetterman in the Wyoming Territory, must be abandoned. Third, an agency must be established for the Lakota near the heart of their country, not far away down the Missouri River. Red Cloud repeated his requests to the president the following day, asking for food and clothing for his people and emphasizing again that Fort Fetterman must be abandoned. Grant said he could not close any more forts in the West because, in accordance with his new policy, he had stationed soldiers in these posts to protect both Indians and his own people.

On June 10, during his final meeting with Commissioner Parker and Secretary Cox, Red Cloud questioned President Grant's belief that army officers had a pivotal role to play in bringing harmony among the many people of the Far West. The chief dismissed the soldiers appointed to run the superintendencies, reservations, and agencies with a bitter phrase: they are all whiskey drinkers. Before he left for his home in the Powder River Country, Red Cloud threw a last parting shot at Grant and his Indian policy. He now denied he had ever agreed to any treaty at Fort Laramie promising to settle his people on a reservation. He could only remember signing a document at Fort Laramie that promised peace alone.[11]

Ely Parker, who had been warmly greeted by all the chiefs as their red brother, was the most stunned of all the officials in Grant's administration at what Red Cloud had said. He and the president had worked together to lay out an Indian policy that placed the tribes on reservations where they would be fed and clothed under the watchful eye of army officers. Here they would slowly learn to support their families through farming and become citizens of the Unites States. But now he was horrified to learn that the Sioux, who should have been the exemplars of the new policy, were suffering as white people overran their country and American soldiers fell drunk all around them. Though many promises had been made in the latest Treaty of Fort Laramie, none seemed to have been kept.

With many other tribes on their way to Washington, including delegations from the Cheyenne, Pawnee, and Osage, Parker was determined to prove that the government lived up to its promises, at least if his friend Ulysses Grant was president. This became even more imperative after officials in the army's commissary office notified him that they would stop delivering food to the Indians after July 1. Agents along the Missouri River informed him that this change meant they would soon run out of food. Parker surmised that he must immediately purchase food and other supplies and ship them west to the waiting agents. He had to do this to maintain the peace and keep the tribes moving down the path toward civilization. In Parker's opinion, treating the tribes with great generosity at the agencies was the first step in the process of civilizing the Indians, which would take several generations to accomplish. Even after the difficult meetings with Red Cloud, he and Grant still believed their plans must be achieved or the many tribes still wandering the West would simply disappear.[12]

Maybe if Ely Parker had been solely responsible for implementing the president's new policy, he could have succeeded in winning the Indians to his cause. However, there was another line of authority in Indian affairs, which he himself had helped establish but which frequently worked against him. Even before Grant was elected, Parker had proposed appointing commissioners who would advise the Office of Indian Affairs on all matters related to the tribes. Just one month after Grant was inaugurated, Congress, on the president's recommendation, established the Board of Indian Commissioners as Parker had envisioned the new organization, with one exception. There would be no Indians, educated or not, on the board. Instead, as described in Section 4 of the act appropriating money to the Indian Department, the president would select up to ten men "eminent for their intelligence and philanthropy." They would serve on the board for unspecified terms and without pay. They would "exercise joint control," along with the secretary of the interior, over all appropriations related to the Indians. Up to $25,000 would be set aside to pay for the board's transportation, expenses, and staff of one clerk.[13]

Beyond the bare outlines described in the 1869 appropriations act, Parker expected the commissioners to act primarily as advisors to himself, the secretary of the interior, and ultimately the president. He prepared a list of questions for the commissioners, hoping that their answers would help the administration perfect its Indian policy. First, what should the legal status of the Indians be? More specifically, what rights did Indians currently have under the law, including treaties? Second, should the treaty system continue? If yes, why should the system continue? If no, what should become of the promises made in previous treaties? Third, was the president's plan to place Indians on reservations a good one? If yes, would the Indians ever be allowed to leave these places? If no, what was to become of the tribes still roaming the West? Fourth, how should the government handle conflicts between the tribes and local settlers? Were there times when the army should take control of a region away from civil authorities? Finally, and most important, what should be done about corruption in the Indian service? The government might purchase the best food and other goods for the tribes, only to have agents sell them, keep most of the profits, and spend a pittance on poorer-quality items for the Indians. Was there a better way to deliver supplies, as well as annuities, to the tribes?[14]

In contrast to Parker, Grant saw the Board of Indian Commissioners as auditors of the Indian service rather than advisors to his administration. He thus gave them full authority to inspect the records of the Office of Indian Affairs. He likewise encouraged the commissioners to travel to superintendencies and agencies throughout the West. Here they were to review records and interview local officials and Indians alike. They could also be present at the purchase of goods for the tribes and monitor the distribution of annuities on reservations. If they saw problems in any area, including bad behavior on the part of officials, they were to notify the commissioner of Indian affairs, who would pass the information up the chain of command to the secretary of the interior, the White House, and finally Congress. The board was also to work diligently on developing specific plans for civilizing the Indians. All this must be done within the constraints of the budget appropriated by Congress. Likewise, the board must keep perfect records of its activities and be willing to share its findings with any new congressional commissions.[15]

However, the wealthy, accomplished men whom Grant appointed to serve on the Board of Indian Commissioners considered themselves neither auditors nor advisors, but supervisors of the Indian service. They were likewise determined to actualize the vague calls made by both Grant and Parker to "civilize and Christianize" the Indians. William Welsh, a prominent Philadelphia merchant and philanthropist, was named the commission's first chairman. Felix R. Brunot, who was appointed the board's first secretary, owned steel mills and a railroad in Pittsburgh. John V. Farwell ran a profitable dry goods business in Chicago with his partner, Marshall Field. George H. Stuart was a wealthy merchant of imported goods from Philadelphia. Robert Campbell of St. Louis had made a fortune in mining and real estate. As a former fur trader, he was the only commissioner who had worked with the Indians. William E. Dodge of New York City, better known as the "Merchant Prince of Wall Street," had made millions in land sales in Georgia after the Civil War and in railroads that crisscrossed the Great Plains. Edward S. Tobey was a wealthy shipping magnate from Boston. Nathan Bishop of New York City was a lawyer and experienced educator, who had worked as the superintendent of the public schools in Providence and Boston and as a trustee of Vassar College. Henry S. Lane, the only professional politician in the group, had served most recently as a Republican senator from Indiana.

There was much more to the men appointed to the Board of Indian Commissioners than mere business acumen. Most were deeply involved in philanthropy with a distinctly Protestant bent. William Welsh, a devout Episcopalian, was a staunch supporter of the church's many missionary societies, both at home and abroad. Felix Brunot, another Episcopalian who participated in his church's annual conventions, had founded the Pittsburgh Sanitary Fair to raise money for Pennsylvania's soldiers and sailors during the Civil War. George Stuart served as the chairman of the Christian Commission, an organization formed to minister to Protestant soldiers in the Union army. William Dodge, a devout Presbyterian, was a longtime supporter of the temperance, antislavery, and Sunday school movements. He was also a prominent fund-raiser for the Christian Commission in New York. Nathan Bishop, a Baptist; John Farwell, a follower of the dynamic preacher Dwight L. Moody; and Edward Tobey, a Congregationalist, were deeply involved in the charitable activities of their respective churches. Each man also chaired the local branch of the Christian Commission in his hometown during the Civil War.[16]

The members of the board knew most about the troubles of the Indians through the writings of Reverend Henry Whipple, the first Episcopal bishop of Minnesota, who ministered to the Santee Sioux, Chippewa, and Winnebago. When Whipple headed west in 1859, he had no personal knowledge of Indians. A native of New York, he studied at Oberlin College in Ohio and then, after his ordination to the Episcopal priesthood, served in parishes in the eastern United States. But from the moment he moved to the small town of Faribault, some fifty miles south of Minneapolis, he became a staunch defender of Indian rights. He argued that his fellow Americans, and not the Indians, had caused most of the troubles on the frontier, including the Santee Sioux War. As he later explained in *Lights and Shadows of a Long Episcopate*, his 1899 memoir of his life in Minnesota, the Indians in the West lived "without protection, subject to every evil influence." They were the "prey of covetous, dishonest white men" who brought violence, disease, and most terrible of all, "firewater," which flowed in "rivers of death."[17]

Whipple wrote frequently to the nation's politicians, including James Buchanan, Abraham Lincoln, and future president Ulysses Grant, describing how the American government had contributed to the suffering of the tribes. He condemned the practice of negotiating treaties with them, not because they were always broken, but because these agreements assumed wandering bands of Indians were actual nation-states. Whipple argued that the tribes had no true political structure to enforce the responsibilities assigned to them in treaties. Nor did the chiefs have any power to stem the tide of misery coming from the settlers who surrounded their people. If violence was perpetrated against the Indians, no hand of justice was ever raised in their defense. But if any Indian was suspected of harming an American, he was swiftly punished, usually without due process or a trial of any kind. If annuities failed to arrive, or if the goods delivered to the Indians were poor in quality or insufficient in quantity, the chiefs had no way to rectify the situation. Corruption in the Indian service was rampant, and sadly, not a single soul, from the lowest agent to the president, had lifted a finger to stop it.

For Whipple, an even more profound tragedy lay at the heart of his nation's mistreatment of the tribes. Americans wrongly believed that Indians were bloodthirsty savages past all reforming. His experience in Minnesota had taught him that nothing could be further from the truth. Whipple had instead discovered that Indians were innately spiritual. They recognized the presence of God in all creation. They were likewise deeply moral and treated each other with greater respect than he had ever seen among white people. They were especially fond of their children and cherished them in a way no other people did. While some clung to their traditions, many were more than willing to learn commercial farming and modern business practices. They welcomed schools on their reservations where their children could learn to join the wider American society. To help the Indians undergo this transformation, Whipple urged the government to recognize them as wards of the state and provide them with all possible aid. No greater help could be given than sending missionaries among them to convert the tribes to Christianity, which, in Whipple's view, was the heart of American civilization.[18]

While the men placed on the Board of Indian Commissioners agreed with Whipple's main arguments, they went much further than he did in analyzing how badly the American government had treated the Indians. From Washington to Grant, top officials in the government had always claimed that they were trying to save the tribes and not destroy them. The commissioners admitted that many people, even including some in the military, had tried their best to help the Indians. But none had stemmed the tide of "broken treaties and unfulfilled promises" that characterized the implementation of the nation's Indian policy. Nor had they controlled the "border white man," the worst specimen of humanity, who arrived first on the American frontier. Violent and aggressive, this type of individual persecuted the tribes and drove them to retaliate in brutal ways.

Sadly, tales of Indian attacks on frontier outposts, which just a generation before took months to travel across the country, now raced instantly over the telegraph lines to every hamlet in the nation. Americans were outraged when they read newspaper accounts of men, women, and even children murdered in horrible ways. But few paid any attention to the injustices that drove the Indians to these dastardly acts. The long list included agents who stole from the tribes to enrich themselves, drunken soldiers who infected women with venereal disease, and traders who plied the Indians with whiskey. Just as terrible, many people hired by the government to help the Indians, including interpreters, wagon masters, and day laborers, worked instead to keep the tribes in their current state of barbarity. Only in this way could they retain their jobs in the Indian service.

To right these wrongs, Chairman Welsh believed the commissioners must play a more active role in Indian affairs than either Parker or Grant envisioned. His goal was to take total control of spending in the Office of Indian Affairs. He likewise demanded the right of board members to inspect all government purchases for the tribes, including items set for delivery to agencies in the spring of 1869. When Ely Parker refused Commissioner George Stuart's request to review these same purchases, arguing that the items had already been packaged for transfer out west, Welsh resigned his post. He did so in the hope that his fellow commissioners would follow suit and thus embarrass Grant into firing Parker. However, none of the others resigned. Instead, Felix Brunot assumed the chairmanship, while Vincent Colyer, an accomplished artist, antislavery activist, and founder of the Young Men's Christian Association, took his place as a board member and its secretary. For the moment, the remaining commissioners were not interested in taking immediate control of spending in the Indian service. However, they remained in constant communication with Welsh, who traveled frequently through the West and reported his findings back to them. With or without their support, he remained determined to win control over spending for the board, believing that the surest way to accomplish this was to topple Ely Parker from his post.

Chairman Brunot carried on the board's work with a zeal rarely seen in the Indian service. The commissioners had decided to organize into three groups that would investigate the northern, central, and southern plains. Traveling west in the summer of 1869 as a member of the Central Plains Committee, Brunot led his fellow commissioners William Dodge and Nathan Bishop, along with his wife and Mrs. Dodge, more like a mission family than a group of civil servants. Arriving first in Chicago, where they interviewed General Sheridan's staff, they headed next by train, carriage, and horseback over one "desolate prairie" after another toward the Indian Territory. As they traveled on, Brunot and his party learned that life on the Great Plains was mainly a battle to survive in the beating sun and endless wind. Even with all their modern conveniences, they spent many a day searching for food and water and many a night fending off wolves and snakes.

In this difficult world, Brunot and his companions came to the same conclusion about the Indians that Lieutenant Ulysses Grant had come to twenty years before: they were more to be pitied than feared. Their sufferings were almost beyond comprehension. The men struggled to feed their families and seemed just as desperate to find whiskey for themselves. Brunot was especially horrified when he watched a young warrior trade a pony worth thousands of dollars for a cup of whiskey. The Indian women appeared even more downtrodden. Accustomed to dressing animal skins to clothe their families, they were fascinated by the reams of bright calico offered to them by the commissioners' wives. Mrs. Brunot and Mrs. Dodge, who never complained about the strain of traveling through the West, were visibly shaken at the sight of the mothers and grandmothers grabbing the cloth from them. Their hands were little more than stumps, since they cut off their fingers as signs of mourning when their family members died.

Once they arrived in the Indian Territory, the commissioners met with chiefs of the Cheyenne, Arapaho, and Kiowa at Camp Supply. They quickly surmised that hunger was the worst problem facing the tribes. Not only were the buffalo fast disappearing from the Great Plains, but also most of the supplies promised in recent treaties with the government were slow in arriving. The commissioners concluded that corn, rice, coffee, and sugar must be delivered immediately, along with fodder for the horses, or the Indians would simply perish. They also recommended that reservations be moved closer to the remaining wildlife on the Great Plains. Agencies, in fact, should never be more than eight to ten miles from the people they served. The agency of the Cheyenne, Arapaho, and Kiowa, for example, should be located near Camp Supply on the North Fork of the Canadian River.

As they reflected on their first trip out west, Brunot and his fellow commissioners concluded that much of Grant's Indian policy should be overturned. They demanded that army officers be immediately removed from their posts as superintendents and agents. In their opinion, the president could only have appointed these men as a "temporary expedient." Certainly no one in his right mind could believe that military training "fit a man to civilize and Christianize the Indian race." The few remaining agents who had gotten their jobs under the old patronage system must also be removed. In place of these "irreligious men," Grant must choose devout Christians to oversee the reservations. The process used to appoint Quaker agents in the Northern and Central Superintendencies should be "writ large" throughout the West. The administration should ask the missionary boards of the various Protestant denominations for the names of agents, along with subordinates like teachers, farmers, doctors, millers, and blacksmiths. Once deeply religious civilians were appointed to run the agencies, then the many scourges that plagued the Indian service in the West, including disease, graft, and drunkenness, could be eliminated.

Furthermore, in the opinion of the commissioners, Grant and Parker seemed only slightly aware of the role that religion should play in civilizing the tribes. They might talk of Christianizing the Indians, but both men were really more interested in the Indians becoming self-supporting farmers. By contrast, the commissioners believed the key to civilizing the tribes lay in converting them to Christianity. The president and his commissioner of Indian affairs had failed to grasp this point, they felt, and were instead interested only in the day-to-day operations of the reservations. The commissioners blamed this on the fact that neither man was particularly religious. Only practical questions seemed to interest them, especially that of whether to move the Office of Indian Affairs back to the War Department, a proposal that the commissioners vowed to do everything in their power to prevent.

In even harsher terms, the board condemned the nation's treaty-making system and demanded that Grant abandon the process at once. The commissioners disliked treaties not because, as the president viewed the situation, they made guns available to the Indians. Agreeing with Bishop Whipple, they believed that treaties rested on the "fiction" that a few thousand "savages" had the "capacity, power, and right to negotiate like a civilized nation." Sounding more like Andrew Jackson than Ulysses Grant, they mocked the "preposterous idea" that the Indians were the actual owners of the "fabulous tracts of country over which their nomadic habits have led them or their ancestors to roam." Every treaty was nothing more than a "devil's bargain" in which both sides made promises they would never keep. Government officials who negotiated treaties were "particeps criminis," or partners in crime, for telling the Indians that the reservations described in them would belong to tribes forever. How could a nation like the United States, which was so committed to "civilization and the progressive movement of the age," ever promise such nonsense?

In the opinion of the commissioners, the treaty system was also wrong because it forced negotiators to deal with only a handful of chiefs, usually older men, who had no power to control their tribes. They might agree to peace, but if younger chiefs chose war, they had no power to stop them. The commissioners demanded a new system where officials met with an entire tribe in a general council and won the support of everyone. This was the only way that agreements with the Indians could ever be upheld. Having argued all this, the commissioners still believed that promises made in previous treaties, especially annuities payable to the tribes, must be continued into the indefinite future. These payments should be to purchase farm equipment for Indian families, thus allowing the reservations to be divided into individual allotments as soon as possible.

As the commissioners prepared to visit more reservations in the summer of 1870, they identified another serious flaw in the nation's Indian policy. Neither Grant nor Parker seemed interested in winning the support of the American people for the immense changes under way among the tribes. Instead, both men were satisfied with allowing the Indians to transform their lives with little fanfare and were likewise certain that this change would take place over several generations. In contrast, the commissioners were deeply committed to the belief that there was a "race to civilize, there were agents to humanize, and there was a great nation to educate in the principles of Christian love toward an oppressed and heathen race." They eventually came to see Ely Parker, more than Ulysses Grant, as the main obstacle in the way of achieving their noble ends. Agreeing with William Welsh, they planned to oust him from his post. Once Parker was gone, the Board of Indian Commissioners could take complete control of the Indian service, including all spending. With the support of the American people, they could transform the "wild Indians" of the western prairies into good Christians. Racing toward the future, they even came to believe that they, and not President Grant or the Seneca chief who served as his commissioner of Indian affairs, had crafted the nation's new Indian policy.[19]

5. Interrupted Odyssey

As he completed his first year of managing the Office of Indian Affairs, Ely Parker never suspected that the Board of Indian Commissioners, along with its former chairman William Welsh, was actively working to remove him from his post. Instead, his main concern was making sure the food he promised Red Cloud in June 1870 arrived in the Dakota Territory before the chief and his party returned home from Washington. If the most influential leader of the "great family of the Sioux," as Parker described the twenty-five thousand confederated Indians of the northern plains, had faith in the promises of Ulysses Grant, then a lasting peace could be secured between the Lakota living in the Powder River Valley and the United States. Hopefully, this would inspire other tribes throughout the West to follow the lead of the Sioux.[1]

Parker, like the president he served, could not bear the thought of another Indian war breaking out in the Far West. Grant had helped end Red Cloud's War by abandoning the forts along the Bozeman Trail. More recently, he had squelched the efforts of a mining company in the Wyoming Territory to send exploring parties into the Bighorn Mountains to search for gold. If settlers could be kept out of the Sioux Country, the chiefs and warriors of the great confederation might remain within the bounds of their reservation and come to depend on the agencies set up along an eight-hundred-mile stretch on the Upper Missouri River to serve them. In the last year, the Santee and Yankton had attached themselves to these agencies after hunters killed more than fifty thousand buffalo in the eastern Dakota Territory. With game disappearing farther west, Parker hoped the Lakota would follow their lead. But if he could not deliver the supplies promised to Red Cloud's Oglala, or to the many other Sioux bands living on the northern plains, another war with the tribe seemed inevitable. Officials in the army's Commissary Department told him that they would stop delivering food to the tribes after June 30, so Parker saw no way to prevent a renewed conflict.[2]

Just as worrisome, the appropriations bill to fund the Office of Indian Affairs had stalled in Congress. If the bill was not passed soon, money for the entire

Indian service would run out on July 1. The bill had been held up in the House when James A. Garfield, an Ohio Republican, questioned the traditional duties assigned in the Constitution regarding treaties. He argued that while the Senate was given the power to ratify treaties with the Indians, the House was expected to appropriate the funds promised in these same agreements, including onetime payments in cash, annuities of more cash and goods, and money for purchasing supplies like farm equipment. Garfield asked why the House, which according to the Constitution controlled the nation's purse strings, should continue rubber-stamping financial decisions made by the Senate. His question was enough to delay passage of the appropriations bill for the Office of Indian Affairs past the June 30 deadline.[3]

Since he felt sure that the bill would be stalled in Congress well into the summer, Parker decided that he had to act quickly. If he did not purchase food for the Sioux on the Upper Missouri immediately, another Indian war seemed inevitable. He would forgo the usual method in his department for buying beef, flour, and other foodstuffs for the tribes. This process took at least two months, with four weeks spent advertising for bids in the nation's newspapers, another two to three weeks reviewing the bids, and still more weeks for the winning bidder to fill the order. Convinced he could not wait this long in an emergency situation, Parker searched for a contractor willing to provide a three-month supply of beef, flour, bacon, sugar, coffee, tobacco, and soap for the Indians without the firm assurance of ever being paid. James W. Bosler, a trader from Carlisle, Pennsylvania, accepted the contract, promising to deliver the items to Indian agencies along the Upper Missouri on July 17, August 10, and September 10.[4]

Parker soon found that solving the problem of delivering food to the Sioux did not end the troubles in the Office of Indian Affairs. In fact, these problems grew worse once the House of Representatives finally passed the last round of appropriations on July 15, 1870. The bill funding the army for the next year added a prohibition against officers on the active list serving in any "civil office, whether by election or appointment." If any soldier accepted a civil post, he would automatically lose his commission. Many congressmen resented the president's use of soldiers as superintendents and Indian agents, since the practice prevented them from awarding these posts as political patronage. Some also claimed that they supported the prohibition because the Piegan Massacre proved soldiers were unfit for duty in the Indian service. But no matter why congressmen voted for the change, the prohibition attached to the appropriations bill meant that every officer recently appointed to serve in the Indian service had to be dismissed. Politicians in the nation's capital stood ready to dole out these same positions to constituents who helped them get elected.[5]

Interrupted Odyssey

Just as troubling, the House of Representatives added a clause to the appropriations bill for the Indian service clarifying the responsibilities of the Board of Indian Commissioners. Several current members of the board, its former chairman William Welsh, and well-respected churchmen like Bishop Whipple had urged Congress to state clearly that the commissioners were supervisors of the Indian service and not merely auditors or advisors as Grant and Parker believed. Therefore, all purchases made for the Indians had to be authorized and inspected by the board. After listing specific payments to the nation's many tribes in the minutest detail, Congress added these demands at the close of the appropriations bill:

> And it shall be the duty of said commissioners to supervise all expenditures of money appropriated for the benefit of Indians in the United States, and to inspect all goods purchased for said Indians in connection with the Commissioner of Indian Affairs, whose duty it shall be to consult said commission in making purchases of such goods.[6]

For Grant and Parker, the changes embedded in the spending bills came as a complete surprise. They had been cautiously optimistic that their approach, which brought the tribes onto reservations, appointed army officers as superintendents and agents, and restored control over Indian affairs to the executive branch, was working. Grant had described its success just months before in his first State of the Union message. The Indians, long abused by both the American government and settlers on the frontier, were now protected as "wards of the Nation." While Quakers managed a few agencies, he noted that the majority had been placed under the control of army officers.[7] Although more aware of the day-to-day problems in implementing the new policy, Parker also had only good things to say about the practice. As he planned to say in his next report to Congress, "military gentlemen . . . have faithfully, and with much credit to themselves, efficiently managed the trust devolved upon them." He would now have to add, "It is to be regretted that they cannot be continued in service."[8]

Dismissing these accomplishments, the members of Congress instead dismantled key features of Grant's Indian policy with no discussion or debate because they clearly understood that the president had shifted control of the Indian service to the executive branch. To win back their influence, they banned officers from serving as superintendents and agents. By so doing, they gambled that Grant would have to reopen the reservations to political appointees and thus restore control of the Indian service to Congress. The Board of Indian Commissioners, whom Grant and Parker had viewed as supporters of the executive branch, would likewise play a part in stripping the administration of its authority. While the president would still appoint the board's ten commissioners, he would have little control over them. Neither would the commissioner of Indian affairs, who by law was now required to work in conjunction with them and not as their superior.

Grant had to decide quickly how to respond. He refused to veto either spending bill, since both funded the military and the Indian service. However, he could not in good conscience go back to the spoils systems. He was truly frustrated since, in his opinion, he had good reasons for appointing army officers to run the reservations in the first place. Wherever Indian agents were sent, troops would also be sent. Thus there was a strong economic motive to place officers in control of superintendencies and agencies, along with the fact that an army officer served for life, unlike an agent, who only served as long as the president who appointed him was in office. A military man was therefore more interested in "establishing a permanent peace" with the Indians than an agent who moved on after four or eight years. As a permanent resident of the West, an officer wanted the Indian to join him within the bounds of "civilized society," in contrast to an agent who had "no such personal interest" and would soon move back east. Finally, and most critically, the president, as the commander in chief, could control soldiers better than he could ever control civilian agents.[9]

Parker was just as distraught that Congress had not given Grant's policy time to take effect. He was prepared to tell Congress in his annual report about the many excellent military superintendents serving in the West. Major Samuel Ross, who watched over more than sixteen thousand Indians in the Washington Territory, was a good example. As soon as he took up his post in Olympia, he had become a stalwart defender of the Indians. He dismissed the worthless agents who had pocketed annuities and let the reservations fall into shambles. He then ordered an inventory of all goods delivered to the tribes, distributed annuities directly to the tribes, and repaired the many ramshackle buildings on the territory's five reservations. He considered the white people who surrounded these same reservations little more than troublemakers who coveted land that did not belong to them. As Major Ross explained to Parker, "A mania prevails among a certain class of citizens in this direction. I verily believe that were the snow-covered summits of Mount Rainier set apart as an Indian reservation, white men would immediately start 'jumping' them." As a military man, Ross could stand up to settlers who demanded Indian land with an authority that a civilian agent never could. He did so for his own honor as a soldier and for the honor of the American government, which had "solemnly pledged" this land to the Indians.[10]

Besides such army officers, Grant had left a handful of political appointees in place. In Parker's opinion, at least one of them was doing an excellent job implementing the president's Indian policy and should not be removed. That man was Alfred Benjamin Meacham, the Oregon superintendent. He had a sympathy for the western tribes that far surpassed what even Grant or Parker felt for them. Growing up in Ohio, Meacham often wondered what had become of the Indians who once roamed the woods and fields near his family's farm. Later, after he moved with his parents to Iowa, he was hired as a wagon master to move the Sac and Fox west from their traditional homeland. He never forgot the sorrow of the tribe and the injustice of their forced removal. Later, when he was a young man heading west on the Oregon Trail, he believed none of the stories about the savage warriors attacking wagon trains. Even when he saw people dead along the way, their bodies riddled with arrows, he was certain the Indians had good reasons for attacking the endless stream of emigrants trampling through their country. He maintained this belief even after he became one of Oregon's leading citizens and a top Republican politician.[11]

As the territory's Indian superintendent, Meacham sometimes faulted Grant's Indian policy for moving in too many directions at once. The president appeared unable to decide whether to run the reservations as a branch of the military, a civil service, or a Christian mission. Still, Meacham championed Grant's plan to win citizenship for the Indians. He had, in fact, seen a transformation among Oregon's many tribes just knowing that the president wanted to make them part of the United States. That Grant considered them his wards or, from their point of view, his "children" was a great comfort to them. This convinced them that he would watch over them and protect them from harm. He would care for their every need not as "aliens," but as his fellow countrymen with all the rights and privileges of Americans. The promise of citizenship was especially important to the chiefs who could now look to the government with confidence, not suspicion. Meacham confessed to Commissioner Parker in almost poetic terms how the promise had inspired the local tribes. "I assert, fearless of contradiction," he explained, "that this very 'idea' has done more in one year to elevate the Indians in Oregon than all the cruel and inhuman regulations ever invented could accomplish in ten years. Few Indians are so low or so depraved that there is no soil on the heart where hope and ambition may not take root."[12]

But nothing Parker might have said in defense of Grant's Indian policy would have mattered now. Instead, the president had to find a way to keep the Indian service from slipping back into the clutches of political patronage with all its attendant corruption. Years later, General Sherman remembered this trying time for his friend Ulysses Grant. He recalled an angry meeting at the White House when congressmen arrived to inform the president that they had just passed a bill prohibiting the use of army officers in the Indian service. Grant responded with both disgust at their maneuver and a solution that would trump them. "Gentlemen," he said, "you have defeated my plan of Indian management; but you shall not succeed in your purposes." He added, "I will divide these appointments up among the religious churches, with which you dare not contend."[13]

Grant had decided that the practice he used for appointing officials in the Northern and Central Superintendencies should be employed across the nation. The Board of Indian Commissioners had, in fact, recently recommended this change to Cox. Grant directed his interior secretary to ask religious denominations that had "heretofore established Missionaries among the Indians" to submit possible candidates for appointment as superintendents and agents. Volunteers would likewise be sought from other denominations willing to set up missions among the Indians. Until enough people could be found to fill these openings, Grant would direct army officers to continue serving on reservations throughout the West. He also decided that the appointees would not be subjected to the civil service requirements he had recently outlined for his administration. They would instead win their positions through the recommendations of their respective mission societies.

As to the matter of the board overseeing all purchases for the Indians, Grant agreed with Parker that this was simply impractical. The ten wealthy commissioners, who lived and worked in various parts of the country, could never be gathered together at the same place and time to make every purchase. They could possibly check dry goods, like blankets or cloth, but inspecting herds of cattle on the open range would be impossible. Instead, Grant would continue the practice already established by Parker: board members who lived in Philadelphia and New York would be invited to join the commissioner of Indian affairs on his yearly trips to purchase annuity goods for the tribes in these two cities.[14]

Parker was willing to go along with Grant's plan to appoint missionaries in part because the Quakers had performed remarkably well in their first year in the Northern and Central Superintendencies. He was especially surprised that Orthodox Quakers had been able to deal with some of the most hostile tribes on the southern plains. Lawrie Tatum, a young farmer from Iowa, had been chosen by the Quakers to serve the Kiowa, Comanche, and Wichita. He knew nothing about Indians or how to run an agency and only did what the elders of his religion asked of him. He brought his wife and seven-year-old son with him to the Fort Sill Agency, but fearing for their lives as Indian raids grew more frequent, he soon sent them home.

Working at times completely on his own, Tatum prepared the Indian fields for planting and built fences around them. He found the women generally friendly and willing to live near the agency, but the men remained hostile and mocked President Grant's offers of peace. They told Tatum that they could get more goods from the government by attacking settlements and raiding agencies than by behaving themselves. After every war, they signed treaties with the government that made them richer. But no matter how much they tried to disrupt Tatum's agency, by stealing horses and kidnapping settlers, he refused to be intimidated. He watched over the herds of cattle delivered to the tribes, built flour and saw mills for them, and made plans for a school for their children. Coming always unarmed to councils, he slowly won the respect of the chiefs and warriors of the tribes he served.[15]

Despite the success of Lawrie Tatum, Parker still doubted whether Christian missionaries could do a better job than army officers as superintendents and agents. However, he hoped they might be more successful in teaching modern ways to the Indians than the many government officials who had worked with the tribes for nearly a century. Parker admitted that even under his tenure as commissioner of Indian affairs, there had been little progress "in educational, in agricultural, and general industrial pursuits" on the reservations. Despite his best efforts, along with those of the president, the Indians still seemed to learn only the vices, not the virtues, of the modern world when they encountered it. Perhaps missionaries could teach the tribes to cherish the highest values of the American people: intellectual development, moral growth, and the steady acquisition of wealth. Beyond calling for the "civilization and Christianization" of the Indians, neither Grant nor Parker had been able to develop specific plans to accomplish this.[16]

Still, Parker worried how men who were chosen for "possessing good Christian characters" could handle the many conflicts in the West. Although no official Indian war had broken out since the beginning of Grant's presidency, reports of trouble came in daily to the Office of Indian Affairs. Some of the worst violence occurred in the Southwest, where settlers clashed with Apache bands led by the daring Chiricahua leader Cochise. The number of people killed in gruesome ways, livestock stolen or left for dead, and ranches burnt to the ground could hardly be counted. Arizona's legislature compiled page after page of testimony from its citizens describing Indian attacks throughout the territory. No one was safe—not farmers and their hired hands, not stagecoach drivers and their passengers, not even soldiers and militiamen. Many worried that the new settlements springing up everywhere would soon go the way of the ruined Indian towns found all over Arizona. As territorial officials explained in their report to Congress, "The cause of their destruction was undoubtedly the ravages of the implacable Apache, and our people now begin to realize, that unless assistance is given them, that they only await a similar fate."[17]

Lieutenant Colonel George Andrews, Arizona's Indian superintendent, who would soon be replaced by a missionary, told the administration point-blank that all its best intentions would never subdue the Apache. While Americans might applaud President Grant's determination to treat the Indians humanely, Andrews argued, only the army could conquer the tribe. Officers in the field, in coordination with soldiers running Indian agencies, must work together to defeat the warriors, disarm them, and finally bring everyone onto reservations. Parker agreed that if missionaries had to be sent to Arizona, they would have to be Catholic priests, since it was a well-known fact that Apaches never killed them. Knowing how difficult managing Indian affairs would be for the many new superintendents and agents, he could do little more than hope that the "prayers of all good Christians go with them, that they may succeed in the great work for which they have been specifically chosen."[18]

Even with the changes passed by Congress, Parker remained confident that the administration would still be able to achieve the goal of citizenship for the Indians. He believed that many tribes living in the Indian Territory would be the first ones brought into the American body politic. This would be accomplished by supporting the Indians in their effort to write and ratify a constitution, which would in turn be the first step toward statehood for the territory. On the instructions of President Grant and Columbus Delano, a lawyer and Republican politician from Ohio who had become secretary of the interior after Jacob Cox had resigned in November 1870, Parker traveled one month later to Ocmulgee, the capital of the Creek Nation, in the Indian Territory to help write the constitution. The Creek had called the council because they were alarmed that Congress was debating plans to establish a territorial government there without consulting them. They also worried that railroad companies were on the brink of buying up as much Indian land as possible. If the tribes did not act quickly, control of the territory set up for them would slip away forever.

When Parker arrived at the council, the Indians were happy to see him. Enoch Hoag, their Quaker superintendent, as well as Commissioners Campbell, Farwell, and Lang, were already present. But the tribes were most impressed that the commissioner of Indian affairs was in attendance, since this meant that President Grant had not forgotten them. Four years previously, Parker had attended the council where tribes that had fought for the Confederacy signed new treaties with the United States. In these treaties, the Creek, along with the Cherokee, Choctaw, Chickasaw, and Seminole, promised that one day they would set up a government for themselves. That day had finally arrived. The Creek had called together the southern tribes along with the Shawnee, Ottawa, Wyandot, and Seneca, whose ancestors had been forced west from Ohio. Tribes removed from elsewhere in the Midwest, including the Peoria and the Sac and Fox, were also present, as were tribes that had long lived west of the Mississippi, the Big and Little Osage and the Quapaw. After less than a week of debating, the fifty-six representatives of the tribes sent to the Ocmulgee council were able to write and approve a constitution for the Indian Territory.[19]

The Ocmulgee Constitution stated that the Indians considered their government both a confederation, the type of joining together that had been traditional among the Indians for centuries, and a union like the one that had brought the thirteen original American states together in 1787. Beginning with a simple acknowledgment that Almighty God watched over them, the Indians proposed a government with three departments: a bicameral legislature called the General Assembly, an executive branch, and a court system. The legislature would consist of a House of Representatives and a Senate. The tribes would elect one representative for every thousand people and one senator for every two thousand. All spending bills and calls for impeachment would originate in the House. Any other bill could originate in either the Senate, which held the power to try impeachments, or the House. The governor, who would be elected directly by the people, would lead the executive department. He signed into law all bills passed jointly by the General Assembly and could veto any legislation he deemed inappropriate. There would be a court system, too, made up of a supreme court, whose three justices would be appointed by the governor, as well as three district courts and inferior courts set up by the General Assembly.

The constitution concluded with a Declaration of Rights, which included thirteen specific rights that paralleled the Bill of Rights of the United States. Freedom of religion and worship were guaranteed. So were freedom of speech and the press, as well as the right to assemble. Every right regarding due process embedded in Amendments Four through Eight of the Bill of Rights was also specifically addressed. But there were three important additions that went beyond the parallel American ones. First, the people, who were the source of all power, were guaranteed the right to change and even abolish the government and create a new one in its wake. Second, no person could be imprisoned for debt. Finally, any powers not specifically guaranteed to the people were reserved to the separate Indian nations in accordance with their treaties with the American government.[20]

Parker was certain that with a few changes, Congress would gladly accept the Ocmulgee Constitution as a framework for the government of the Indian

Territory. The most important change would allow Congress to review and revise, as necessary, any of the laws passed by the Indian Territory's General Assembly. Likewise, the president of the United States, not the governor of the Indian Territory, should be given the authority to name justices to the Supreme Court. If these changes were made, Commissioner Parker, along with President Grant, had no doubt the Indians would take a major step toward self-government. By so doing, they would take an even bigger step toward joining the Union as citizens of the United States. Both men were determined that all government positions in the territory, even judgeships appointed by the president, went to Indians.[21]

Having accomplished so much, Parker was stunned when he found himself embroiled in a scandal just days after the council adjourned. William Welsh, the former chairman of the Board of Indian Commissioners, had worked for more than a year to remove Parker from office. He finally got his way in the summer of 1870. While accompanying Episcopal missionaries to their new posts in Minnesota, Welsh noticed a flood of goods at Indian agencies along the Upper Missouri. Taking it upon himself to investigate the matter, he discovered that Ely Parker had negotiated a large contract with a trader named James Bosler to deliver cattle and other foodstuffs to agencies along a large stretch of the river. Welsh was furious that the Board of Indian Commissioners, with whom he had stayed in close contact, had neither authorized nor inspected these purchases. Even worse, since he considered the purchases unnecessary, he concluded that Parker and Bosler were working together to defraud the Indians and the government of hundreds of thousands of dollars.

When he returned to Philadelphia, Welsh was determined to alert Secretary Delano about the widespread corruption he had supposedly discovered in the Indian service. Delano, knowing that Welsh was accompanying Episcopal missionaries to Minnesota, had asked him to observe whether Indians might make good cavalry officers. Congress had authorized the army to recruit a thousand warriors into the army in 1866. On November 21, while visiting the Santee Sioux, Welsh had penned a short note to Delano stating that the Indians would make fine officers. But now, on December 7, he composed a much longer letter to the secretary of the interior detailing the "startling observations" he had made about secret and illegal activities in the Office of Indian Affairs, as he characterized it, the "one department" in the Grant administration that "needs the powerful grasp of a master hand." Welsh claimed that "adroit manipulators" had awarded a $250,000 contract to supply cattle, flour, and other foodstuffs to Indians along the Missouri River without advertising for bids in public newspapers. The Board of Indian Commissioners, which in his opinion should have authorized the contract and inspected the items purchased by it, had never been consulted. Since the goods could have been bought for less than two-thirds of the stated price, someone had pocketed the difference.

Although he never mentioned Ely Parker by name, the point of Welsh's accusation was clear. The person who negotiated and profited from the corrupt contract was none other than Grant's commissioner of Indian affairs. Welsh added that he knew for a fact that Indian agents along the Missouri River did not want the beef delivered to them. They were offered bribes to accept the cattle and not to question the fact that the animals weighed far less than the contract stated. Welsh added that he saw large herds of cattle on their way up the Missouri River from Texas in October when he was out west. If their cost, which Welsh estimated at $155,000, was calculated into the value of the secret contract, and allowances were made for labor and transportation fees required to move and care for the animals, the final cost to the government would be in excess of $1,000,000.

Welsh concluded his letter by thanking the president for his determination to civilize the Indians and his decision to appoint Christian missionaries as superintendents and agents. He was certain that if Grant had his way, the western tribes in just one more year would raise enough food on their own farms to sustain themselves without government handouts. He believed the one person standing in the way of the president civilizing the Indians was Ely Parker, the Seneca whom Grant had placed in charge of the Office of Indian Affairs. According to Welsh, Parker was more than willing to see the tribes remain in a state of dependence and savagery so he could make money supplying their every need.[22]

Worried that Secretary Delano might ignore his suspicions, especially since President Grant was so fond of Commissioner Parker, Welsh sent a copy of the letter to Washington and Philadelphia newspapers, which promptly published his charges. On December 12, 1870, just as Parker arrived at the Ocmulgee council in the Indian Territory, Aaron Sargent, a Republican congressman from California, introduced a resolution in the House of Representatives directing the Committee on Appropriations to "inquire and report back" whether key provisions of the July 15, 1870, appropriations bill, which authorized the Board of Indian Commissioners to supervise and inspect all purchases for the Indians, had been violated. Specifically, had the recent purchases of beef and other foodstuffs for agencies along the Upper Missouri River ignored this law? Had more goods been purchased for the Indians than necessary, and if so, was the contract to buy them "corruptly and improvidentially made?" The House passed the resolution, adding a further charge that Welsh had made after sending his accusatory letter to Secretary Delano the previous November. The committee

William Welsh. Welsh, the first chairman of the Board of Indian Commissioners, led a crusade to oust Ely Parker from the Office of Indian Affairs. FROM MORRIS, *MAKERS OF PHILADELPHIA*, 259.

was to investigate whether all or part of a $90,000 payment made recently to the Quapaw Indians had been illegally diverted to "other parties."[23]

Parker learned about these charges in late December 1870, when he was still in Ocmulgee. When he arrived back in Washington in January, he hoped the letter he submitted to Secretary Delano would be enough to answer the committee's questions. He explained that an emergency had existed on the northern plains the previous summer after Congress failed to pass a funding bill for the Indian service. As a result, money for the entire Indian service was set to run out on July 1, 1870. The Sioux, who had just been promised food and other supplies at a meeting with President Grant in Washington, would receive none. Other tribes that depended on food from agencies along the Missouri River would also be in trouble. To keep the hungry Indians from attacking American settlements, and thus igniting a series of frightening wars throughout the West, Parker had signed a contract with James Bosler, who was willing to provide food with no assurance that he would ever be repaid. Parker mentioned, too, that he had not violated the July 15, 1870, appropriations act since he negotiated the contract before the bill was passed. He also added that he did not understand why William Welsh was so interested in this matter when he had no official role in Grant's administration. He suspected that the accusations were part of Welsh's continuing efforts to remove the government completely from the Indian service and place it solely in the hands of Christian missionaries, specifically those of Welsh's own Episcopal faith.[24]

Parker's letter did nothing to halt the investigation. Instead, Congressman Sargent, who would chair the investigation, continued to prepare with his fellow committee members, William Lawrence, an Ohio Republican, and James Beck, a Democrat from Kentucky, for the public hearings that would start in late January. They were already so convinced of the validity of the charges that they invited Welsh to submit a list of witnesses and join the committee in questioning them. To help the House in its investigation, Welsh submitted a thirteen-point list that clarified his charges against the Office of Indian Affairs. Although he again did not mention Ely Parker by name, the implication was clear. The Seneca, whom President Grant trusted enough to run the nation's Indian service, was as rotten as the department he managed.[25]

In mid-January, Parker received a request from Sargent to respond to Welsh's charges in writing. He did so by denying every one of them. He did not violate the July 15, 1870, appropriations act, which required him to work under the supervision of the Board of Indian Commissioners, since he had purchased the beef and other goods the previous month. The Bosler contract had gone into effect before the bill became law. It likewise made no sense to criticize him after the fact for failing to check how much food the army commissary might be able to deliver to the Indians before June 30. Nor could he be faulted for paying higher-than-average prices for food and its transportation in an emergency situation. The records of the Indian Office would prove his dealings with traders, superintendents, and agents had all been above board. There was no collusion, graft, or bribery, as Welsh implied. Nor was there double-dealing with any "political friends." Parker demanded the right to cross-examine witnesses and review all evidence in advance of committee hearings, and then openly criticized Welsh's tactics:

> Your committee will observe, upon reading the charges numbered from one to thirteen, that, in some cases, they contain statements of facts which I can have no knowledge; that they abound in inferences of the person making them which do not necessarily follow from the facts themselves; that they cover a wide range of inquiry, not only the particular transactions, but the general policy of the Indian Office; that they are often vague and uncertain in allegations of facts, but of this I care

little. There are substantial averments that concern me personally and officially, and all such I stand ready to answer.[26]

Despite his brave comments, Parker was so distraught over the charges that he took to his bed, refusing to come to the hearings, which began on January 17, 1871. Welsh had compiled a long list of witnesses, many of whom he had already interviewed, along with dozens of letters and telegrams he had collected from the Office of Indian Affairs. It was clear that Welsh had marshaled this evidence through his continuing ties with the Board of Indian Commissioners, most especially Vincent Colyer, who accompanied him to the hearing. The two men were prepared to show that Ely Parker had pocketed money from the Bosler contract, stolen a considerable sum from the Quapaw, and delivered blankets of poor quality to the Osage.[27]

Much to Welsh's surprise, Parker would not have to face these charges alone. He had asked his friend General Norton Chipman, a highly-respected Washington attorney, to represent him, and the committee had agreed. Chipman was best known for prosecuting General Henry Wirz, the Confederate commander of Andersonville, the notorious prison in Georgia where thirteen thousand Union soldiers had died. Calling both Union soldiers who had survived their imprisonment and former Confederates who had worked at the prison, Chipman had demonstrated that Wirz had played a part in the frightening cruelty of Andersonville. Beyond the disease, malnutrition, and violence that marked life in the camp, Wirz was charged with murdering prisoners by shooting them with a pistol, ordering soldiers to gun them down if they crossed the "dead line" around the camp, and unleashing dogs to hunt escapees like wild animals. Found guilty of all counts, Wirz died by the hangman's noose, the only Confederate tried and executed for war crimes.[28]

Welsh, who had assumed his many witnesses would make a case against Parker without being contradicted, was taken aback when the appropriations committee gave General Chipman the right to cross-examine those same witnesses. With Parker so distraught that he refused to leave his bed during the first week of testimony, Chipman proved an able defender of his absent client. The committee turned first to witnesses who claimed that the Quapaw were defrauded of one-third of a $90,000 payment paid to them in October 1870. When it became clear that Commissioner Parker had no direct role in the matter, the committee turned back to the main charge against him. Vincent Colyer and Felix Brunot, the secretary and chairman of the Board of Indian Commissioners, came forward to assert that Parker had never consulted any board member before signing the contract with Bosler, nor had he ever allowed

General Norton Chipman. Chipman brought the same skills to bear defending Commissioner Ely Parker that he used to prosecute General Henry Wirz, the Confederate commander of the Andersonville Prison. COURTESY OF THE LIBRARY OF CONGRESS.

any commissioner to inspect the beef, flour, and other purchased foodstuffs. Colyer also complained that Parker had paid $8 apiece for inferior blankets shipped to the Osage.

Chipman went after the credibility of both commissioners by asking if either of them had ever brought these matters to Parker's attention. Both men said no. He further confused Brunot by asking him if he truly believed that unpaid volunteers like him were the supervisors of the Indian service and not the commissioner of Indian affairs, who had been appointed by the President. Brunot was unable to say with certitude who ran the Indian service. He became even more confused when Chipman asked him if he and his fellow commissioners had discussed troubles in the department among themselves, yet never spoke to Ely Parker. Yes, responded a befuddled Chairman Brunot.[29]

While Chipman did a good job of dismantling witnesses, Parker knew he could not stay at home forever in his sickbed. One week after the hearings had opened, he came before the committee for questioning. Welsh led the way by asking repeatedly how much Parker had bought for the Indians the previous summer, what he had purchased through private contracts as opposed to public bids, and whether the Board of Indian Commissioners had inspected the items. Parker provided memos showing his purchases, through both the Bosler contract and other agreements negotiated through open bids. He admitted that he had never asked the board to inspect or approve any of these purchases. However, he had sought their help in moving the appropriations bill for the Indian Office through Congress. Welsh responded by asking him if he had checked into the lowest prices for cattle, searched for temporary funding, or worried about how agents would handle the flood of supplies coming their way. Welsh also pummeled Parker with more than a dozen questions about freight charges for shipping goods to the Indians along the Upper Missouri. Through it all, Parker repeatedly answered that there was nothing out of the ordinary in the rates charged or protocol followed for purchasing and delivering goods to the tribes in an emergency.

Unable to elicit any admission of guilt from Parker, Welsh turned the questioning over to General Chipman, who took his client step by step through the previous summer. Parker explained how he had negotiated a contract to supply the agencies on the Upper Missouri at what he considered reasonable rates per pound for every item: 6½ cents for beef, 25 cents for bacon, 28 cents for coffee, 18 cents for sugar, 8 cents for salt, 15 cents for soap, and 85 cents for tobacco. He also paid $2 a bag for flour. The rates he paid for transporting these items were just as reasonable, he said. Parker admitted that he had not consulted the Board of Indian Commissioners but instead followed his usual practice of inviting the board to inspect the purchase of dry goods as annuity payments to the tribes. When Congressman Beck of Kentucky asked him whether the emergency on the Upper Missouri had required a "contract of this magnitude," Parker, who had remained calm until this point, became agitated. He explained that there were many agencies along the river, all in the heart of the Sioux Country. A failure on his part to supply the tribe, whom Parker described as neither friendly nor altogether hostile, would have been disastrous. If he could supply the Sioux for just three months during this emergency, and later set up more regular shipments to the tribe, he could keep the peace.[30]

As the questioning continued over several hours, Parker never wavered in his explanation of why he had negotiated the contract with Bosler. Once he was finally dismissed, the committee turned back to the issue of the defective blankets sent to the Osage. The mere mention of poor-quality goods delivered to a tribe brought to mind countless stories of corruption in the Indian service. If the Osage had received defective blankets, then somewhere down the long chain from their purchase to their delivery, corrupt officials or traders had sold the good blankets, pocketed the cash, and sent inferior ones to the tribe. Never saying this openly, Welsh brought witnesses forward who worked in dry goods companies in New York and Philadelphia. As he questioned them, he tried to prove that Parker had paid too much for blankets of poor quality and that better ones could have been purchased at far lower prices.

Chipman went to work quizzing the same witnesses to ferret out the actual complaint that the Osage had about their blankets. He discovered that the problem had nothing to do with graft in the purchasing or delivery process. Instead, the Osage were upset that one bale, out of an order valued at close to $8,000, contained blankets that were not the brilliant scarlet that the tribe desired. Chipman got the witnesses to admit that although the blankets were the wrong color, they were still of high quality. He next asked what had caused the problem. Had some blankets been dyed the wrong color? Was something wrong with their weave that caused the dye to darken the blankets? Had one bale of the wrong color been sent west among the many bales of the scarlet ones? No one knew what had happened. However, one thing became clear as Chipman quizzed the witnesses: no agent, Indian chief, or commissioner, including Vincent Colyer, who reported the matter to Welsh, had ever informed Parker that there was a problem with the Osage's blankets.[31]

As the hearings continued throughout the last week of January, the details behind the $90,000 payment to the Quapaw became clearer. General James Blunt, the man who had received one-third of the payment, appeared before the committee to defend his actions. A Civil War veteran who had led tribes in the Indian Territory against the Confederacy, Blunt described himself as a lawyer, businessman, and farmer. Despite his reputation for making shady deals in Kansas, his current home state, he claimed that the Indians trusted him and often came to him for advice. The Quapaw had specifically asked him to help win compensation from Congress for the destruction of their land during the Civil War. They offered him one-half of whatever they received, but Blunt told them he would take just one-third. In response to witnesses who claimed he had spent upward of $16,000 to push the compensation bill through Congress, Blunt swore that this money had not been paid out in bribes but instead equaled the expenses he had incurred helping the tribe. When officials of the Interior Department delivered $90,000 to the Quapaw last fall, he took his share of $30,000 with tribal leaders happily looking on.[32]

If he could not prove that Parker had bought inferior blankets for the Osage or robbed the Quapaw of the compensation due them, Welsh was sure his next witness would reveal the depth of the man's corruption. He was James Bosler, the trader who had signed the contract to provide beef and other foodstuffs for the Indians on the Upper Missouri. But no matter how hard Welsh tried to implicate him in wrongdoing, Bosler maintained that everything was aboveboard in the contract. He denied Welsh's insinuation that he and Parker were old friends who had made many deals together. Instead, the contract signed on June 15, 1870, was the first he had ever negotiated with the commissioner of Indian affairs. He said that Parker had told him there was an emergency in the West. He needed cattle, flour, and other items including bacon and tobacco sent immediately to agencies on the Upper Missouri. Bosler said he could not deliver the items all at once as Parker wanted, but no contractor could send so much food to the tribes so quickly.

He made a counteroffer to deliver the goods on three separate dates in July, August, and September. He understood there would be a delay in payment because Congress had failed to pass an appropriations bill. Bosler signed the contract knowing he would probably be paid well after the items were delivered and that there was even an outside chance that he would never be paid. Bosler admitted that he charged higher than the average price for beef, but not because he, Parker, or anyone else had pocketed the difference. Instead, the extra 2 cents a pound went to pay for the personnel he took on to fulfill the contract, including drivers and hired hands who cared for the cattle, along with any damages he might have to pay because of stampeding herds or Indian raids.[33]

While Welsh's questioning of Bosler revealed no surprises, Chipman's cross-examination of the witness uncovered some disturbing insights into the true motivation behind the charges brought against Parker. Bosler told of a private meeting he had recently had with Welsh. The former commissioner assured him he had nothing personal against him, nor did he have anything against the president, although he admitted that he could not understand Grant's misguided devotion to the Seneca Indian he chose to run the Office of Indian Affairs. His target had been Parker all along, and he had tried to remove him from office for two years. Bosler now repeated the terrible things that Welsh said about Parker at their meeting:

He spoke of General Parker, and said that his connection with those parties in New York was not very creditable, and further that the general was the representative of a race only one generation removed from barbarism, and he did not think that he should be expected to be able to withstand the inducements of parties who were his superiors in business.... He asked me in the same connection, if I had ever seen General Parker drunk; and he said that in New York he had been "feasted and wined"; and he was satisfied that General Parker did not have the moral courage to withstand temptation. He said that he had gone to Secretary Cox and told him the condition of the affairs, and the manner in which they were treating Parker, and asked Secretary Cox if he thought (Cox) could withstand inducements of that kind, and that Secretary Cox said he did not believe he could.[34]

On the same day that Bosler gave his damaging testimony against Welsh, President Grant finally made a move in support of Parker. He had been noticeably silent about the accusations against his commissioner of Indian affairs, not giving a public statement or writing any private letter to Parker on the matter. But on January 31, he provided evidence that Parker was doing an excellent job managing the Indian service. He forwarded the records of the Ocmulgee council to Congress, including Parker's reports to the Interior Department and the proposed constitution, which Grant heartily endorsed. Although he never mentioned Parker by name, the president's praise for the council's work clearly showed his support for the commissioner. The council, as Grant explained in his cover letter to Congress, was clear proof that the Indians were becoming "self sustaining, self relying, Christianized and Civilized." The implication was clear: Grant's Indian policy was working with Parker's support.[35]

Despite Grant's backhanded praise for his commissioner, the testimony of the next witness, Jacob Cox, the former secretary of the interior, did little to support Grant's notion that his Indian policy was a success because of Parker's management. He even seemed uncertain whether Parker was actually in charge of Indian affairs. At first he denied knowing anything about the Bosler contract, but then he admitted that Parker had told him he was dealing with an emergency on the Upper Missouri. When Chipman asked him point-blank who ran the Indian service, meaning the commissioner of Indian affairs or the Board of Indian Commissioners, he expected Cox to answer, "Parker." Cox, however, could not say. Only when Chipman pressed him did he answer that Parker held the ultimate decision-making authority and often had to make decisions without consulting anyone. Welsh, who could not let Cox's answer go unquestioned, asked under what circumstances a contract valued at $362,000, which was his estimate of the Bosler deal, should ever be negotiated. Cox replied, "If the Indians were starving." In a last attempt to impugn Parker, Welsh asked more directly whether the president, rather than the commissioner of Indian affairs, should have had the ultimate decision-making power in this emergency. Cox answered with a resounding yes.[36]

After the former secretary finished his testimony, Welsh worried that his previous witnesses had not sufficiently damaged Parker. Starting late in the afternoon of January 31 and continuing until February 6, he brought more people forward to try to prove that Parker was an incompetent who had paid exorbitant prices for transporting cattle from Texas to the Upper Missouri. But every trader, agent, and official he interrogated answered that the prices were fair given the emergency situation. Welsh dropped this line of questioning after asking Walter Burleigh, the Dakota Territory's delegate to Congress, what would have happened if cattle had not been delivered to the Indians. "They would steal," he answered. Starvation had caused all the Indian Wars, Burleigh asserted, adding that the Indians could only be controlled "if their bellies were full."

Failing to prove that Parker had paid too high a price for transporting cattle, Welsh returned to the money paid out to the Quapaw. He recalled Joseph Williamson, the clerk from Secretary Cox's office who had paid out $90,000 to the Quapaw. Asked why he had failed to intervene when General Blunt demanded a third of the money, Williamson answered that Cox had told him, "If the Indian throws his money into the Arkansas or makes any other disposition of it, you will not be held responsible." Finally, still trying to show that money had changed hands between Bosler and Parker, Welsh questioned clerks who worked for Jay Cooke and Company. They presented every check paid to Bosler, but when asked if any drafts had been made out to Parker, their answer was "Not one."[37]

On the final day of the investigation, neither Congressmen Sargent or Beck, who had both participated in the questioning, or Congressman Lawrence, who had rarely spoken, made any closing statement. Instead, the committee turned the floor over to Welsh. Despite this honor, Welsh could hardly contain his frustration. He sarcastically thanked the committee for allowing Parker to be represented by an attorney, which gave him "ample time" to prepare his case, and listening patiently to his many witnesses. When he finally turned his attention to Parker, he ignored his main arguments and instead echoed the opinion of Secretary Cox. If there really had been an emergency among the tribes on the Upper Missouri the previous summer, then President Grant, and not his commissioner of Indian affairs, should have intervened and ordered the army to deliver food to the Indians.

Having launched his opening salvo, Welsh next attacked Parker for what he said were the commissioner's many missteps in managing the Indian service. Parker had clearly violated the July 15, 1870, appropriations bill, which acknowledged the Board of Indian Commissioners as supervisors of the Indian service. Parker had specifically broken the law by failing to allow the commissioners to inspect the blankets sent to the Osage and, even worse, by keeping them in the dark about the secret contract negotiated with Bosler. If they had been a party to either action, knowing the public trust placed in them to root out corruption in the Indian service, they would never have sent defective blankets to the Osage or paid 6½ cents a pound for cattle worth 4½ cents. Nor would they have paid higher than the going rates for flour, salt, sugar, coffee, tobacco, bacon, or soap. Furious that Parker was continuing to usurp the authority of the Board of Indian Commissioners, Welsh had submitted a bill to the appropriations committee demanding that the Office of Indian Affairs make no purchases for the Indians until the board had examined and approved them. "Surely the tax-payers will not be satisfied by anything short of this," he added.

Worried that Chipman had proved that Parker had written the contract with Bosler before the July 15, 1870, appropriations bill was passed, Welsh brought up another law, which he had failed to mention at the hearing but now said the commissioner of Indian affairs had also broken. On March 2, 1861, Congress had made it illegal for government departments to negotiate a contract for services to be immediately filled without first advertising publicly for bids. Commissioner Parker had ignored this law when he made the supposedly bloated contract with Bosler. He had foisted cattle, along with flour and other items, on agencies that did not need them. Contrary to Parker's testimony, there had been no emergency. Welsh accused the commissioner of Indian affairs of having had a sinister motive in sending so much food up the Missouri. By so doing, Parker had damaged the nation's efforts to civilize the Indians by making them dependent on the government for food, which they should be raising for themselves. After mocking the committee members one last time for allowing Parker to be represented by an attorney, he urged them, after reading through more than two hundred pages of evidence, to come to the same conclusion that he had when he penned his letter to Secretary Delano last November. "From your intelligent and earnest consideration of the case," he added in a final flourish, "I feel confident that the cause of Indian civilization will be promoted, therefore the sole object I had in revealing the alleged wrongs to the Secretary of the Interior will be accomplished."[38]

Before he began his closing statement, General Chipman delivered a letter to the committee written by his client. In a simple statement, only two paragraphs long and no more than a thousand words in length, Parker defended the actions he had taken to prevent starvation among the Indians of the Upper Missouri in the summer of 1870. He added that through it all, he had "spared no pains, no sacrifice of personal convenience and pleasure, to discharge" his duty as the commissioner of Indian affairs faithfully. He concluded with the following declaration:

> I do not claim that I have made no mistakes, for that is more, I think, than can well be claimed by any public officer; but Mr. Chairman, I do say, and I speak it in as solemn a manner as I am capable, and to this extent I have already sworn, that I have never profited pecuniar[i]ly, or indeed otherwise, by any transaction in my official capacity while I have been serving as Commissioner of Indian Affairs.[39]

Chipman then launched his closing argument by accusing Congressmen Sargent, Lawrence, and Beck of acting as a jury rather than a House committee. He asserted that throughout the many weeks of testimony, not one shred of evidence had been produced showing Ely Parker guilty of anything. Nothing had linked Parker to the payout of the Quapaw's money to General Blunt or to the bale of dark blankets sent to the Osage. On the most serious charge, that Parker had negotiated a contract without advertising for public bids, the reasons for the commissioner's actions were abundantly clear. By failing to pass the appropriations bill for the Indian service, Congress had created an emergency situation on the Upper Missouri. Without Parker's action, starvation would have driven the Indians to violence. If he had done nothing, he would now stand condemned for launching a bloody Indian war on the northern plains. Chipman also asked how a man, acting in an emergency in June 1870, could be condemned for violating a law passed a month later. He added that the 1861 statute brought up by Welsh specifically stated that a government department could write contracts without taking public bids in an emergency, and the Supreme Court had declared this practice constitutional.

It was now Chipman's turn to address the committee sarcastically. He claimed that never had he heard so much oratory expended on the price of cattle. After a parade of witnesses and weeks of testimony, nothing was proven except the fact that Ely Parker paid a fair price for high-quality cattle in the midst of an emergency to prevent starvation among the Indians. Chipman laid out letters from several agents in a near panic during the weeks leading up to the July 1 deadline. Given the circumstances, the prices that Parker agreed to pay for cattle and other supplies were not exorbitant. The same could be said about the transportation costs incurred in delivering these goods to the tribes. The Northwest Transportation Company, which was hired to deliver supplies along the Missouri, made no profit from the transaction but merely broke even. However, the most amazing testimony came when clerks working for Jay Cooke said no checks related to the Bosler contract had ever been written to Ely Parker. Instead of attacking the commissioner of Indian affairs, Congress should be thanking him for helping the Indians in a desperate situation and keeping the peace on the northern plains.

Chipman then opened a second line of defense for his client. He declared unabashedly that William Welsh, the wealthy private citizen who had instigated this sham hearing, had done so because he despised Ely Parker. He had, in fact, expended an enormous amount of time and effort trying to besmirch Parker's character and remove the commissioner of Indian affairs from office. The one-time head of the Board of Indian Commissioners, who had been appointed to help the tribes, despised the Indian whom President Grant had chosen as the commissioner of Indian affairs. Working secretly with the man who had replaced him, Vincent Colyer, a supposedly upright gentleman, Welsh had set out to ruin Parker's good name. He lied not just to the House committee but also to the press and through the press to the American people.[40]

Beyond hating Parker and working for his removal, Chipman claimed that Welsh also had another goal in mind: he wanted to strip the executive branch of its remaining authority over the Indian service. If he could humiliate Parker and convince Congress that it should hand supervision of Indian affairs to the Board of Indian Commissioners, his evil purpose would be accomplished. He would have singlehandedly ruined not just Commissioner Parker's career but also Grant's Indian policy along with it. Chipman concluded his stirring defense of his client with only one regret: the committee had not allowed him to provide testimony that Welsh had lied to the Indians while investigating the Bosler contract. Claiming he was on a special mission for the president, Welsh did his best to turn the tribes against the two men who were helping them the most. He had also bribed officials to testify against Parker to remove the commissioner from office.[41]

Despite the voluminous testimony gathered during the investigation, the committee quickly came to its conclusions. Parker had not profited in any way from the contract he had negotiated with Bosler. However, the commissioner should not have made the deal in the first place. Instead, he should have consulted with Grant. Agreeing with Secretary Cox, the committee ruled that only the president had the authority to send goods to Indians in an emergency situation. The three congressmen also stated that Grant should have ordered the army to feed the tribes on the Upper Missouri. Despite their recognition of the president's authority, the committee had little sympathy for Grant. They might not be able to remove his friend Parker from office, but they could strip the executive branch of its remaining control over the Indian service. The committee recommended that the Board of Indian Commissioners, and not the commissioner of Indian affairs, be acknowledged as the supervisor of the Indian service.[42] To accomplish this, the committee recommended that Congress pass Welsh's bill verbatim:

> That hereafter no payments shall be made by any officer of the United States to contractors for goods or supplies of any sort furnished to the Indians, or for the transportation thereon, or for any buildings or machinery erected or placed on their reservations, under or by virtue of any contract entered into with the Interior Department, or any branch thereof, on the receipts or the certificates of the Indian agents or superintendents for such supplies, goods, transportation, buildings, or machinery, until such receipts or other vouchers shall have been submitted to the executive committee of the Board of Commissioners appointed by the President of the United States.[43]

One month after the committee completed its report, Congress passed Welsh's recommendations with only two changes. Officials could pay up to 50 percent of contracts before submitting them to the Board of Indian Commissioner's executive committee for "examination, revisal and approval." The interior secretary would then "sustain, set aside, or modify" the executive committee's recommendations. Even with these qualifications, the board was now officially responsible for reviewing "without delay" all purchases of the Indian service. Another change constricted the executive branch's power over Indian affairs. The system of treaty making between the president and the tribes established in Washington's time was abandoned through a rider attached to the appropriations bill for the Indian service.[44]

Before passing the rider, Congress had argued for several days whether to end the treaty system. In the Senate, the main debate centered on the legal status of the tribes. Should they still be considered sovereign nations, in which case the treaty system should be maintained? Or had they lost their original independence, and therefore should new kinds of agreements be written with them? While some argued that the Cherokee, Creek, Choctaw, Chickasaw, and Seminole in the Indian Territory governed themselves like nations, most senators believed that other tribes had fallen into a degraded condition and therefore could no longer be considered independent states. Representatives in the House agreed and added that once the rider was adopted, the tribes should be considered "dependent domestic communities" with whom the government must write "contracts," not treaties. Congressmen in both chambers also argued, as they had since the previous summer, about the duties assigned in the Constitution regarding Indian affairs. More specifically, which chamber had the ultimate authority: the Senate, which approved treaties with the tribes, or the House, which initiated appropriations for the Indian service? More cynical members asked this question a different way. Which at this moment held the real sway over Indian affairs: the Constitution or the all-powerful Republican Party, which could do whatever it liked with the tribes?[45]

William Welsh, along with the Board of Indian Commissioners, especially Chairman Brunot, and philanthropists like Bishop Whipple, cared little for the intricacies of the debate in Congress. Instead, they cheered the decision of Congress to end the treaty system. They had frequently condemned their own government for treating the tribes like foreign nations. Dismissing Grant's worries that treaties provided guns to warlike Indians, they had argued instead that these agreements wrongly considered the Indians capable of understanding the terms of the documents that the chiefs signed. They likewise could not comprehend how anyone who was trying to civilize the Indians could negotiate with the tribes as if the Indians were already civilized.[46]

Grant himself had recommended ending the treaty system, but on the assumption that army officers would run the nation's superintendencies and agencies. As the commander in chief, he would maintain total control over the Indian service because he had total control over the army. Once this power was stripped from the executive branch, he never participated in the subsequent debates about the legal status of the Indians or the sovereignty of the tribes. He might have described the Indians as wards of the nation or state, but he did not understand this in any strict legal sense. To Grant, the phrase meant that most of the Indians of the Far West were in desperate trouble, and the government had to protect them until they became American citizens. He, in turn, defined citizenship in the simplest terms: to be an American citizen meant living under the nation's laws, including the Constitution with its many protections, and participating fully in the political and economic life of the country, including voting in elections and owning private property.[47]

President Grant never guessed how ending the treaty system would strip the government of an effective tool in dealing with the Indians. Through treaties, reservation boundaries were determined, annuities were established, and a working relationship was set up between the executive branch and tribal leaders. When Congress abandoned the system, Grant proposed no new mechanism to replace it. He instead decided to rely on executive orders to carry out his plans. He would, in fact, write forty orders related to the Indians during the rest of his presidency, mainly to establish or modify reservations. He could still use the army, but only to round up wandering bands that attacked settlers or refused to move onto their reservations. With the ending of the treaty system, the tribes also lost much of their power. They no longer had an effective means of winning concessions from the American government; they would have no direct say in matters that affected them.[48]

Although Parker was relieved he was found not guilty of Welsh's charges, he could do little to stop the unraveling of Grant's Indian policy. Another blow came when opposition to the Ocmulgee Constitution arose among the Cherokee. They not only rejected the document but also strongly opposed the president's dream of making them American citizens. They wanted no part of bringing the Indian Territory into the United States. Such a path would destroy Indian law and tribal hegemony. The Cherokee were prepared to come to Washington within the year to tell Grant face-to-face how much they disliked his ideas. They were convinced that most Indians wanted no part of America or its citizenship. They were equally certain that they could keep the forces working against them, including railroad companies and immigrants poised on their borders, from destroying their sovereignty.[49]

Even more trouble came when dozens of Arpaiva and Pinal Apache were massacred on April 30, 1871, in the Arizona Territory near Camp Grant on the San Pedro River. Chief Eskiminzin had led his people to the place two months earlier, hoping Lieutenant Royal Whitman, the post's commander, would feed them. Whitman set up a temporary reservation and supplied the Apache with food in exchange for their help with hay and barley harvests on the surrounding farms. When their numbers increased to over five hundred, and the nearby creek ran dry, Whitman gave them permission to move a few miles upriver near the mouth of a large canyon. People living in Tucson, just fifty miles away, were horrified at the prospect of so many Apache gathering nearby. They blamed the Indians for continuing to raid towns and ranches throughout Arizona and also faulted President Grant for his policy of "fattening up the savages," who then attacked unsuspecting citizens. Early on the morning of April 30, a company of local American and Mexican civilians, along with a large party of Papago Indians, raided the Apache camp. In less than an hour, close to 150 men, women, and children and their dogs lay dead. The Papago clubbed many people to death and shot the rest full of arrows. Survivors who tried to escape up the canyon walls were gunned down by the Americans and Mexicans. The few children taken captive were later sold into slavery in Mexico.

An angry President Grant condemned the attack as nothing less than cold-blooded murder. He dispatched W. C. C. Crowley, a California district attorney, to Tucson to prosecute all those involved in planning or carrying out the raid. He also sent General George Crook to Arizona to restore order. In an earlier time, he might have sent the commissioner of Indian affairs along with Crook, but he refused to do so now. Instead, he named Vincent Colyer, who had supported Welsh's attacks on Ely Parker, as his special emissary to investigate what had happened. Colyer had little sympathy for the many participants in the "Camp Grant Massacre," as the nation's newspapers called the event. Blaming them for Arizona's troubles, he organized a new reservation for the Apache at the massacre site and ignored anyone who tried to stop him. The local populace thoroughly despised Colyer, who, in their opinion, had no understanding of how everyone in Arizona, including Americans, Mexicans, Papagos, Maricopas, and Pimas, had suffered at the hands of the Apache.[50]

While sympathetic to Indians, even the much-hated Apache, Grant was determined to defend his fellow citizens if attacked. When warriors raided settlements in Arizona, claiming they were avenging the Camp Grant Massacre, he ordered Crook to stop them. He also listened to the people of Arizona when they demanded the ouster of Colyer. He sent General O. O. Howard, the former director of the Freedmen's Bureau and a well-known Indian sympathizer, in his place to bring peace to the territory. Within a year, Howard was able to settle many Apache on a new reservation at San Carlos. The few Americans who were placed on trial for their actions in the massacre were acquitted.[51]

Commissioner Parker may have been disappointed that he was not allowed to play any part in restoring peace to Arizona, but he did not let this interfere with his duties in the Indian Office. He instead did his best to work with the now much more powerful Board of Indian Commissioners. Initially, this was not difficult, since the commissioners were interested only in seeing vouchers after goods were purchased. They had no desire, at least throughout the first half of 1871, to buy the goods themselves. They likewise audited just 50 percent of the purchases made for the Indians. However, everything changed in June, when Vincent Colyer learned that Parker had ignored a contract that the Board of Indian Commissioners had negotiated to transport goods. Parker had hired a different company that promised to ship the items at a cheaper rate. Colyer went in person to Secretary Delano's office to complain about Parker's mishandling of contracts. He demanded that Delano question Parker immediately in his presence. Delano called the commissioner of Indian affairs into his office. When Parker admitted he had changed the contract, arguing that the requirements attached to the appropriations bill did not go into effect until July 15,

Delano told him never again to countermand a decision of the Board of Indian Commissioners. He had to have the board's approval for purchasing goods for the Indians, including their transportation cost.

President Grant, who had never clarified the lines of authority in the Indian service since Parker testified before Congress, made no attempt now to support his beleaguered commissioner. Instead of worrying about Indian affairs, he had spent much of 1871 resolving a long-standing foreign policy issue on the world stage and dealing with a private scandal closer to home. The British, after lengthy negotiations with Grant's State Department, had finally agreed to pay for damages done to American shipping by vessels such as the *Alabama*, which had been built in their country for the Confederacy. According to the Treaty of Washington, which the Senate ratified in the spring of 1871, the *Alabama* claims, as the damages were collectively known, would be decided by an international tribunal in Geneva, Switzerland.[52]

At the same time, Grant's oldest child, Fred Dent, a senior at West Point, finally graduated after being involved in numerous scandals. Hated by his professors and fellow cadets for demanding special treatment as the president's son, Fred had made a name for himself as the campus bully. He was accused of harassing James Webster Smith, the first black cadet at West Point, on the grounds that "no colored boy" had the right to attend the prestigious academy. Another incident brought him before a congressional committee at the very moment that the investigation into Parker got under way. Fred had allegedly ordered scantily clad underclassmen to spend the night outside in the shivering cold. Grant stood by his son, even making sure he was given an extended furlough after his graduation so he could make a grand tour of Europe. The president disappointed many of his supporters, who accused him of doing everything in his power to protect his son but little to defend Smith and the other cadets whom his son had terrorized.[53]

While Grant remained fiercely loyal to his own child, he seemed to have lost whatever compassion he once felt for Parker. With no support from the president, and now facing the possibility of the Board of Indian Commissioners overriding his every decision, Parker had no choice but to resign. He wrote to his old friend Ulysses, who was now even more distant than he had been during the House investigation and after the Camp Grant Massacre. He said that he had done everything in his power to support the president and his Indian policy, but he could not function as the commissioner of Indian affairs if this meant he was merely a clerk of the Board of Indian Commissioners. Grant accepted his resignation, saying little to Parker beyond thanking him for his eight years of faithful service. "Your management of the Indian Bureau has been in entire harmony with my policy," Grant wrote, "which I hope will tend to the civilization of the Indian race."⁵⁴

Although they parted amicably, Grant and Parker did not remain close friends. Parker moved with his wife to Connecticut and found himself completely cut off from the president's inner circle. For his part, Grant saw no way to stop the undoing of key points of his Indian policy. He still hoped that he could achieve his goals through the work of missionaries now serving in the Indian service and the dedication of the Board of Indian Commissioners. Although both Felix Brunot and Vincent Colyer, the chairman and secretary of the board, had helped William Welsh's crusade against Ely Parker, Grant continued to support them. He even told George Stuart, who earlier had demanded that the commissioners be allowed to open the annuity goods already packaged for the tribes and had thus initiated the long process leading to Parker's departure, that his next commissioner of Indian affairs would "have the full confidence of the board."

The gulf between Grant and Parker grew even wider as Welsh kept up a steady stream of intrigue against them. Welsh now claimed that he actually sympathized with Parker. The commissioner's downfall had come about through Parker's own "conviviality." Welsh also resented the fact that Parker and his much younger wife, Minnie, were frequent guests at parties among Washington's high society. He complained that Parker's "fashionable wife" had made him the "prey of astute and polished augurs." He even spread a false rumor that Chipman had at first refused to defend Parker. The president had to bribe Chipman to take the case by offering him the post of secretary of the District of Columbia. But Welsh still struggled to understand why Grant was so fond of Parker. He considered the relationship an "infatuation" on the president's part that stemmed from the odd prospect of "an Indian civilizing his brethren."

Even though the investigation in the House had exonerated Parker, Welsh still believed him guilty. He wondered how Ulysses Grant could ever have been so devoted to a man, as Welsh had once described him, just a generation removed from savagery. In a letter to Grant published in newspapers in 1875, Welsh openly brooded about the friendship. "Your protection of Gen. Parker when he was convicted of misfeasance or malfeasance as Commissioner of Indian Affairs, and of those who had control of that office," he mused, "seems wholly unaccountable except on the hypothesis that love in you is blind." As he struggled to understand the relationship between these two men, Welsh could at least take comfort in the fact that he, along with Congress, had thoroughly disrupted the carefully laid plans of Grant and Parker.⁵⁵

6. A Sea of Change

In the months following the departure of Ely Parker from the Office of Indian Affairs, Ulysses Grant dismissed the many complaints coming his way about his Indian policy. When he learned that Red Cloud was unhappy, specifically because Protestant missionaries had overrun his country and his tribe's agency had been built too far away, he was not overly concerned. The promises in the Treaty of Fort Laramie would be fulfilled. Once things settled down in the West, which Grant estimated would take another thirty-five years, the Powder River Valley and the Black Hills would still belong to the Sioux. After the Camp Grant Massacre, when angry soldiers in the Arizona Territory accused the president of favoring the Apache over them, he answered that nothing could be further from the truth. "It is not proposed," he explained to their commander Major General John Schofield, "that all the protection shall be for the Indians." If the Apache stopped raiding settlements and moved to their designated reservations, the army would protect them. But if they refused to "put themselves under the restraints required," the United States would punish them. When the now more powerful Board of Indian Commissioners fretted that Grant was contemplating harsher methods against the tribes, he assured them, "Such a thing has not been thought of."[1]

Although his commissioner of Indian affairs had been hounded from office, and Congress had stripped the executive branch of much of its authority over the Indian service, the president still believed his policy was well on its way to succeeding. He was certain about this because, no matter what scandals had rocked his administration, his goals for the tribes remained unchanged. The Indians were still coming onto reservations, where agents would watch over them until the day they entered the American mainstream as citizens of the United States. Grant had developed this "peace policy," as his approach was nicknamed in the press, to end the bloodshed on the western frontier. He admitted that his approach required tremendous forbearance on the part of settlers, politicians, and soldiers, especially when Indian warriors went on the attack. But nothing would ever make him doubt that he had come up with the best policy for handling the western tribes. Grant explained this most forcefully in an October 1872 letter to George Stuart, who remained on the Board of Indian Commissioners: "I do not believe that our Creator ever placed different races of men on this earth with the view of having the stronger exert all his energies in exterminating the weaker." The only thing that had changed in his "humanitarian" approach was the method used to execute it. Instead of army officers implementing his plans, "various societies of Christians" had now been assigned the task. "If the present policy toward the Indian can be improved in any way," he added, "I will always be ready to receive suggestions on the subject."[2]

With Parker now gone, the job of defending Grant's Indian policy fell to Henry R. Clum, the temporary commissioner of Indian affairs. A former Union army officer from Wisconsin who had distinguished himself at the Battle of Malvern Hill, Clum believed that the president's policy remained on track, despite the recent turmoil in the Office of Indian Affairs. Preferring to emphasize the positive, Clum argued that most Indians welcomed Grant's approach. After centuries of mistreatment, they finally had a friend in the White House. They likewise placed their trust in the many men of "good standing and moral character" whom the president had appointed to run superintendencies and agencies throughout the West. Admitting that although some tribes, including the Apache, Kiowa, and Comanche, remained hostile, the vast majority of Indians accepted the goals of civilization and citizenship that Grant had set for them. Again looking on the bright side, Clum reminded his fellow Americans that Congress, whose members so often opposed the president, had recently authorized $100,000 for educating the Indians.[3]

Francis A. Walker, the man Grant appointed to be the permanent commissioner of Indian affairs in November 1871, provided an even more thorough defense of his policy. An economist and statistician first hired by the government to complete the 1870 census, he was determined to ferret out the reason why Americans seemed to have suddenly turned against the president's approach. He blamed the growing opposition on Ely Parker's testimony before the House Committee. Parker had admitted that the government spent over a quarter of a million dollars on beef, flour, coffee, sugar, salt, and soap to keep Red Cloud's Oglala from going to war. If Parker's testimony was true, the president seemed to care more about placating hostile tribes than helping "well-disposed" ones. His policy had nothing to do with peace but everything to do with bribery.

Walker even agreed with Grant's critics that the president did not treat all the tribes the same way. Hostile Indians were handled more carefully than peaceful ones but, in his opinion, for good reasons. If Grant let the more violent tribes starve, then the entire frontier would be plunged into a brutal war. Countless settlers would be slaughtered while hundreds of "outlying settlements would disappear in a night." All the soldiers currently enlisted in the army would not be enough to save them. Grant would have to recruit another hundred thousand men to cordon off the frontier from Indian attacks. It might be an "undignified business," Walker said, but Grant's "feeding system" had kept at bay the powerful Sioux of the Dakota Territory; the roving bands of Blackfeet and Assiniboine in Montana; the wild Cheyenne, Kiowa, Comanche, and Arapaho of the Indian Territory; the cruel Apache of Arizona and New Mexico; and the countless bands of Indians in Washington and Oregon. "With wild men, as with wild beasts," Walker explained disdainfully, "the question whether in a given situation one shall fight, coax, or run, is a question merely of what is easiest and safest."[4]

While Grant's approach might have offended the morally upright, Walker maintained that the president's policy was finally ending the countless wars in the West. Perhaps in the process, Grant did coddle the worst savages on the frontier. Perhaps he was "tardy" in "applying the scourge" to wild bands that left their reservations and murdered settlers. But hopefully, in just two short years, the Sioux would be completely at peace with the United States. In three more summers, the tribes living in Colorado, Utah, Arizona, and New Mexico would also be at peace. By then, the nation's burgeoning towns, farms, and railroads would form an "intractable" barrier around the tribes. Any Indian still foolish enough to resist the power of the United States would necessarily have to come onto a reservation just to survive. However, Walker admitted that Grant's policy would bring "imperial greatness" to the United States but "incalculable loss" to the Indians. To help the "original owners of the soil," a paraphrase of Grant's inaugural address, he recommended that the government establish a tribal endowment with dividends distributed regularly until every Indian had transitioned to the "white man's road."[5]

Commissioner Walker insisted, too, that civilizing the Indians still lay at the heart of Grant's carrot-and-stick approach. Unlike many who believed the Indians were past saving, since savagery was bred into their very nature, the president never doubted that the Indians could live as modern men. Eventually, after the tribes remained long enough on their reservations, they would transform outwardly and inwardly. They would wear the white man's clothes. They would attend church, send their children to school, and even elect their own kind to public office. Walker reminded his fellow Americans that Grant's policy had already accomplished what many long deemed impossible. By his estimate, a quarter of a million Indians, or at least five-sixths of the three hundred thousand living in the United States, were now "civilized" or "partially

The Cherokee were a good example of the former, while the Santee exemplified the latter. By Walker's estimate, only seventy-eight thousand could be considered "wholly barbarous," with the wild Pawnee of the plains being an excellent example.

Walker identified one more fact about President Grant's Indian policy that had been largely ignored: Grant's approach was similar to the original Indian policy of George Washington. Just like Grant, the nation's first president had placed the Indians beyond the farthest frontier. If warriors attacked American settlements, Washington sent armies against them. If they accepted the boundaries around their territory, he left them alone and looked forward to the day when the two peoples would merge as one. However, Walker noted, there was one main difference between the policies of Washington and Grant. Eighty years before, the American government considered the tribes as nations on a par with England, France, and Spain. The legal identity of Indians rested in their belonging to a particular tribe. But now Congress had ended the treaty system, declaring in the process that tribes could no longer be considered nations. Therefore, the Indians had no official status. President Grant provided the only way out of this legal limbo by setting the Indians on a course toward American citizenship.[6]

While Grant's successive commissioners of Indian affairs defended his policy as steady and clear-sighted, the Board of Indian Commissioners felt no compulsion to agree. In their opinion, a great deal had changed and all for the better. Congress had just granted the commissioners the authority to approve and inspect every purchase made for the tribes. They could refuse to pay for goods deemed too expensive or poor in quality. They were also empowered to audit the records of the entire Indian service. They technically had final approval over the appointment of future commissioners of Indian affairs since the president had promised that none would serve without the board's consent. They had demanded the removal of all soldiers from the Indian service and the end of the treaty system, and Congress had agreed. But most important, they had accomplished the single greatest change in Grant's Indian policy by recommending that Christian missionaries be appointed as agents on all reservations. When Congress backed Grant into a corner on this issue, tying his hands by forbidding soldiers to serve as agents, the president accepted the board's suggestion that "Christian societies" take their place. In the opinion of the board members, they had provided the mechanism for the "civilization and Christianization" of the Indians sadly lacking in Grant's original Indian policy.[7]

Because of the increase in their powers, the commissioners organized their activities in a more formal way. The main function of their three-member

Executive Committee would now be to conduct a yearly audit of spending in the Office of Indian Affairs. Starting just weeks after the congressional investigation into Parker's contract with Bosler had ended, the committee spent nine months reviewing 1,136 vouchers paid by the Indian service. The work was so overwhelming that the committee's first chairman, George Stuart, along with his colleagues Nathan Bishop and Edward Tobey, hired several clerks to help with the task. After examining payments for goods and cash outlays totaling $5,240,729.60, the committee rejected vouchers valued at $153,166.20 on the grounds that the purchases were unnecessary, too expensive, or made without the consent of the board. Stuart and his fellow committeemen found the process so exhausting, however, that they asked Congress to relieve them of this arduous task. Their request was firmly denied on the grounds that auditing the Indian service had been one of the primary reasons for establishing the Board of Indian Commissioners in the first place.[8]

To get a firmer grasp on all the spending, the board set new rules for the Purchasing Committee. Its four members would meet with the commissioner of Indian affairs and set regular dates when together they would purchase and inspect goods for the tribes. The committee also came up with a new method for reviewing bids. Previously, the Office of Indian Affairs kept samples on hand and expected the winning bidders to match these in type and quality. Now merchants vying for contracts to supply the Indians would have to provide samples to the government. Once contracts were handed out, an auditor hired by the Purchasing Committee would make sure the delivered products matched the samples. The committee would also make certain that advertisements for bids were widely distributed in newspapers in New York, Philadelphia, Boston, Cincinnati, Chicago, and St. Louis, along with Rapid City, Iowa, the main supply center for the Dakota Territory. This would ensure that the most reputable merchants and manufacturers came forward to supply the Indians.[9]

Continuing the practice established when they were first appointed, the commissioners met at the start of each year to schedule their upcoming inspection tours. At the annual meeting, they decided which commissioners would visit which reservations. As the commissioners traveled throughout the country, their task was to evaluate whether the tribes were well fed and well clothed and how much progress the Indians had made in raising food for themselves. The commissioners were also to determine which Indians were ready to own land privately through allotment. They had to interview as many people as possible, including tribal leaders, Indian agents, soldiers, local business owners, and teachers. They were to be ever on the lookout for signs that the tribes were being mistreated. They were to inspect any schools on the reservations and judge to what extent the children, known as "scholars," were actually learning and how their education might be improved. They also were to audit all the records of the superintendencies and agencies and report any discrepancies, along with their other observations, in annual reports to the secretary of the interior. The commissioners likewise stayed in contact with James Harlan, an Iowa Republican and the chairman of the Senate's Committee on Indian Affairs, who sympathized with their efforts to take control of the Indian service away from the executive branch. Finally, they undertook special assignments in the West, including investigating causes of unrest and negotiating agreements with the tribes, at the request of the president.[10]

The newest official task assigned to the Board of Indian Commissioners was its responsibility to recommend missionaries to work among the tribes. Even before the president had decided to use missionaries in place of soldiers in the Indian service, the board was at work recruiting Christian denominations for the cause. Vincent Colyer called the secretaries of the nation's missionary societies to a meeting at the YMCA Headquarters in New York City shortly after Congress banned soldiers from serving as superintendents or agents. The secretaries of the missionary boards of the Presbyterian, Methodist, Baptist, Dutch Reformed, Episcopal, American Episcopal, and Congregational churches were at first reluctant to take on such a great responsibility. So was the secretary of the American Board of Commissioners for Foreign Missions. Colyer received a more positive response from the Catholic Church. A devout Protestant himself, he had refused to invite any Catholics to the preliminary meeting but received word from Dr. W. F. Cady, the chief clerk in the Office of Indian Affairs and himself a Catholic, that the Catholic clergy were willing to participate.[11]

Secretary Cox had asked the board to make formal requests to the denominations to join the process in the summer of 1870. The secretaries of the many mission societies, while agreeing to take on the task of "civilizing and Christianizing" the Indians, asked for more specifics. Where were Christian missions and schools already located, and which denomination would go to what agency or reservation? When no one in the Indian service provided this information, the commissioners turned to Secretary Colyer, who had traveled extensively in the West. An accomplished artist, Colyer drew a map of the United States and painted in various watercolors to identify which denominations would go where. In January 1871, at the first formal meeting of the various faiths with the newly appointed interior secretary Columbus Delano, the many-colored map was accepted without question. Delano thanked the mission societies for their participation and assured them that they would be allowed to run the agencies without any interference from the administration. However, President Grant would have the right to dismiss any agent for bad behavior or for purely political reasons. Delano told the missionary societies that they must accept these decisions without complaint.[12]

For the moment, the only person at the meeting who had any concerns about the process was the Jesuit priest Pierre-Jean de Smet. Born in Belgium in 1801, Father de Smet had worked among the Indians across the Mississippi since 1838, when he established Saint Joseph's Mission for the Pottawatomi at Council Bluffs in the Iowa Territory. From there, he traveled north into the Sioux Country. While he was deeply impressed with the character of the Sioux, he urged them to stop warring against their fellow Indians. In 1840, after Iroquois living among the Flathead and Nez Perce in the Pacific Northwest asked for "black robes," or Catholic priests, to live among them, de Smet made his way across the Rocky Mountains to minister to their needs. On his way back to Missouri, he visited still more tribes, including the Crow, Gros Ventre, and Coeur d'Alene. A year later, he returned to the country of the Flathead, where he established Saint Mary's Mission on the Bitterroot River in Montana. He later went on the first of many trips to Europe to raise funds for his missions and to recruit Sisters of Notre Dame to help him educate Indian children. In 1844, he came back along the Columbia River and later founded another mission near Fort Vancouver. Two years later, he went alone into the country of the Blackfeet to persuade the tribe to stop attacking their fellow Indians.

The fearless Jesuit soon became a legend among all the western tribes. He was a big man, weighing over two hundred pounds. He never carried a gun but defended himself when he had to with his fists. The Indians were impressed that unlike Protestant ministers, he had no wife and children to support. He also dressed in a black cassock, which distinguished him from other settlers. Father de Smet seemed in no hurry to convert them to modern ways but instead spent time with them, listening for long hours to their troubles and telling them stories of his own faith. He did not teach them from a book like Protestant missionaries but instead used colorful symbols. He employed a pictorial catechism that highlighted the truths of the faith, especially the path to salvation through the Church and its sacraments.[13]

By the 1850s, mainly through his books on his travels among the Indians, de Smet came to the attention of the American government. Officials in both the War Department and Office of Indian Affairs recruited him to attend councils with tribes throughout the West, hoping that his presence would help the negotiations. He usually did whatever the government asked, attending councils starting in 1851 at Fort Laramie and continuing up through the mid-1860s in Utah and Nevada. He always claimed he was apolitical, caring nothing for earthly

A Sea of Change

power but only for the welfare of the Indians. However, de Smet consistently refused to help the United States with the Sioux because he believed there was no excuse for the terrible way Americans had treated them. But finally, in 1867, after traveling with General Sherman and the Peace Commission, he rode off on his own to meet with Red Cloud. He urged the chief to make peace with the United States at Fort Laramie in 1868. Even as his health faltered, de Smet remained active, visiting the missions he had established among the Sioux.[14]

When he was called to Washington in early 1871, Father de Smet could not help but be depressed at the administration's plans. After working among the Indians for so many years, he found President Grant's decision to send missionaries among the western tribes both misguided and mistimed. He felt only "deep grief" at the thought of Protestant laymen, most of whom had no experience with the Indians, racing west across the Great Plains. "In the whole of this affair," he wrote to his superior Archbishop Francois Blanchet in Oregon City, "the Indians have not been consulted as the religion they deserved to belong to."[15] The tribes might be on the road to citizenship, but for the moment they had no right to freedom of religion. This greatly bothered de Smet, since he believed most tribes would want Catholic priests to work among them. He was just as troubled by the fact that Grant's administration seemed to assume the Indians were without religion, when nothing could be further from the truth. They believed in a Great Spirit who controlled every event in their lives, both good and bad. The Great Spirit's "medicine," meaning his mysterious and all-powerful influence, was everywhere, and not even President Grant, with all his drive and determination, could sway it.[16]

Through his long experience, Father de Smet had learned the Indians were not blank slates waiting to be written over with the white man's customs. They were a difficult people who were "fickle" and in constant motion yet at the same time conservative and unbending. Every time he entered an Indian village, the men and women raced up to him to attend mass, take communion, and have their children baptized. But while many embraced Christianity, they still practiced their old religion. Every grown man carried a medicine bag containing symbols of the magical powers that helped him in life. De Smet did not condemn this practice or any part of tribal medicine, since these rituals had long served the Indians in their daily struggle for survival. In fact, he believed their "immemorial customs" were so powerful that they would never give them up, even if the government demanded they do so. While clinging to superstitions might make them seem inferior or even savage, this was simply not the case. They were a highly intelligent people, capable of learning anything, but who likewise considered their traditions "paramount."[17]

A Sea of Change

De Smet believed that Protestant missionaries, who had led sheltered lives back east, would be shocked at the morality of the western tribes. Violence was a way of life in their world. Every day, men had to hunt and kill to survive, and this mentality affected their behavior. Small quarrels often erupted into spontaneous murders. There was no court system where an Indian could redress the wrongs done to himself or his family. His only recourse was vengeance against those who had harmed him. The tendency toward violence was made worse by liquor. De Smet was fond of saying that no people were more docile when sober and more violent when drunk than Indians. Even if missionaries banned liquor at their agencies, they would still be shocked at the behavior of Indian men toward their women. A man counted himself lucky if he had many daughters, since he could trade them for horses, a far more valuable possession. Marriages were rarely permanent, with men and women frequently changing partners. Polygamy was not uncommon. De Smet also worried that Protestant missionaries assigned to agencies could never tolerate the many superstitions of the Indians. Nor could they master their difficult languages and dialects. Most terrible of all, how could they confine these restless people within the boundaries of a reservation? He knew many Indians who became "melancholy and morose" if they stayed in one place for only a few months at a time.[18]

What would become of his beloved Indians? This was the ultimate question that had troubled de Smet for nearly forty years. As a young man, he was certain he could make a difference in their lives. He could even help them survive the press of Americans all around them. Long ago, when the Flathead had first asked him about these people, he had said that they were as numerous as the blades of grass on the prairies. They were powerful, too, and as swift moving as the buffalo herds on the plains. Influenced by the imagery of the tribes, he described the United States as a warrior eagle who would one day rule the continent from sea to sea. But de Smet still believed that the Indians could live in peace with the Americans. They could secure a place for themselves in the West as fur traders. It might take two or three generations for both sides to get used to each other, but the adjustment would take place.

After the discovery of gold in California and more strikes throughout the Rockies, however, Father de Smet began to lose hope. Settlers now came west with a speed never before seen. He could not help but be anxious for the tribes with countless people heading their way. "The treasures concealed in the heart of the mountains will attract thousands of miners from every land," he told Archbishop Blanchet, "and with them will come the dregs of civilization, gamblers, drunkards, robbers and assassins." As hard as he continued to work among the Indians, de Smet worried that his effort would not be enough to save the

Indians from destruction. How could a handful of priests and nuns prevent the "unhappy war" that was spreading from the Rocky Mountains back across the central plains? The one power that could stop the war, the American government, brought only misery to the Indians. Between its corrupt agents and the broken promises of its many treaties, the United States cheated, robbed, and swindled the tribes to the point of extinction.[19]

By the time Father de Smet met with the other missionaries in Washington in 1871, he no longer believed it was possible to stop the warrior eagle's people from destroying the Indians. His missions were already under siege from settlers who demanded that they be closed for harboring savages. American life now moved at an "inexorable" speed, and President Grant's good intentions could not stop it. There was no denying the fact that one civilization, with a few hundred thousand people barely surviving as hunters, had to give way to a more advanced civilization with its millions of people living in huge cities, all surviving on products made in factories, and traveling on iron horses that moved faster than any buffalo herd. At seventy years of age, de Smet looked back at America's conquest of the West and the "spoliation" of the Indian way of life as a great drama in its final act. For the moment, de Smet's only hope was that President Grant would allow Catholic missionaries to remain on the reservations where they were already working. But even this would not long delay the inevitable destruction that lay ahead: "The curtain will soon fall on the poor and unhappy remnants of the Indian tribes and they will henceforth exist only in history."[20]

Vincent Colyer ignored the concerns of Father de Smet, preferring instead to follow the colors he had already painted on his map of the agencies. He likewise refused petitions from the Osage and Pottawatomi in Kansas, the Sioux in the Dakota Territory, and tribes living along the Umatilla River in Oregon for "black gowns" to run their agencies. He decided that Quakers should continue their service at sixteen agencies in Kansas, Nebraska, and the Indian Territory. Methodists would take the lion's share of agencies, fourteen of them spread out in a great arc from California, Oregon, Washington, Idaho, and Montana back east to Michigan. Baptists, Presbyterians, and Episcopalians would care for close to half of all the Indians, nearly 106,000 people at twenty-two agencies. Baptists and Presbyterians would run four agencies in the Indian Territory and ten more in Nevada, Utah, Arizona, New Mexico, and Idaho. Most agencies in the Sioux Country, eight in all, would go to Episcopalians. Catholics would serve only at the Flathead Agency in Montana, the Grand River and Devil's Lake Agencies in the Dakota Territory, and a few more places in Oregon and Washington. The Dutch Reformed Church was given the difficult task of maintaining five agencies for the Apache, Navajo, Pima, and Maricopa. Eight more agencies were distributed among the Congregationalists, Unitarians, and Lutherans, along with one for the American Board of Commissioners of Foreign Missions. (See Appendix B.)[21]

Within a year of appointing denominations to the various agencies, Colyer admitted he had made a few mistakes. The Nez Perce Agency, first given to Catholics, was reassigned to Presbyterians at the tribe's request. At the same time, control of the Umatilla Agency was taken away from Presbyterians and granted to Catholics after local Indians demanded that the Jesuits who had worked among them for six years be allowed to return.[22] Just as important, Colyer, along with the rest of the commissioners, understood at last the magnitude of the tasks assigned to the new agents. They were solely responsible for teaching the Indians, who were mainly hunting and gathering peoples, how to farm, raise livestock, build homes, sew the white man's clothes, pray in church, and attend school. They must also make sure that all the goods and annuities due to the tribes were safely delivered and, by so doing, end the corruption in the Indian service.[23]

One of the biggest problems right from the start was finding decent men willing to take on these difficult tasks. According to the standards set by the board, agents had to be morally upright and preferably married. They had to be willing to risk their lives and those of their families on a frontier where murder and mayhem were common. They had to spend their days turning the ideal of "civilizing and Christianizing" Indians into reality, and all this had to be accomplished with little pay and few resources beyond what the religious denomination that ran their agency could provide. Finding laborers to help the agents, especially blacksmiths who were hard-working and interpreters who were truthful, was next to impossible. No wonder so many agents had lost their way in a world that offered little respite from work but many enticements to wrongdoing, including liquor, gambling, and licentiousness.[24]

Far worse than all this, according to the commissioners, was the fact that the Indian Ring, the amorphous web of graft and bribery rampant in the Indian service, would not simply disappear with the arrival of missionaries in the West. Decent agents were merely being sent into the midst of corrupt activities like lambs to the slaughter. Even the most moral man would feel the pressure of "communities living about him," which were only "interested in defrauding the people committed to his care, in every endeavor to thwart him, and threatened with removal by men of influence." The ring's power reached everywhere, defrauding the tribes of land, money, and goods. According to the commissioners, its efforts were helped along by the prevailing attitude that the "Indians have no rights that a white man must respect, any more than wild beasts that roam the forest." Its leaders were all too obvious in their main goal: they must "secure the lands that belong to the Indians." Sadly, money seemed to be the only thing that mattered to anyone across the Mississippi, from the innermost circle of the great invisible ring to the poorest settlers struggling to survive on the central plains. Even the Board of Indian Commissioners could only come up with a monetary solution to keeping the agents honest: their pitiful annual salary of $1,500 had to be raised.[25]

The board never looked past the corruption in the Indian service to see the whirlwind of changes reshaping the West in the way that Father de Smet had done. All these changes made life difficult for the Indians and the agents who served them. The speed of change brought to the West by the warrior eagle, as Father de Smet described America, picked up noticeably during President Grant's first term in office. Miners, whom de Smet had first seen transforming the landscape in 1849, never stopped coming, especially as strikes were made up and down the Rockies. One of the biggest came in 1870, when miners discovered an even deeper vein of pure gold and silver in Nevada's Comstock Lode, already deemed the most valuable strike in history. Three years later, a still richer vein, nicknamed the Big Bonanza, was found a hundred feet deeper. Although the ore in both veins could be extracted only with heavy equipment paid for by wealthy capitalists, news of these strikes sent waves of hopeful miners across the Great Plains toward Nevada. The fact that they had to trample through country belonging to many Indian tribes mattered little to anyone. While only a handful of miners became wealthy, the promise of quick riches led the rest to search for the next bonanza. Rumors swirled that it would come in the Black Hills of the Dakota Territory in the country of the Sioux.[26]

This wealth pouring out of the western mountains made it imperative that the United States complete the Transcontinental Railroad swiftly. Just two months after Grant was inaugurated, workers at Promontory Point in the Utah Territory drove the last golden spike into a silver-wrapped laurel tie, thus uniting the Union Pacific and Central Pacific Railroads between Kansas and California. Ulysses Grant had looked forward to this moment when serving as the general of the army. He hoped that once the Transcontinental Railroad was completed, conflict between the Indians and his fellow citizens would come to an end. People and goods would travel safely back and forth across the center of the nation, leaving the rest of the northern and southern plains to the tribes.

Grant failed to realize that the first transcontinental line would not be the last. The Kansas Pacific Railroad, originally planned as a trunk line of the Union Pacific, was already under construction. Within a year, its tracks would reach Colorado. The Atchison, Topeka, and Santa Fe, now also heading west across the plains, would arrive at La Junta, Colorado in 1873, and then send a branch northwest to Salt Lake City and another southwest through New Mexico and Arizona to its final terminus in Sacramento. Two more transcontinental lines, the Northern Pacific connecting Minnesota to the Columbia River and the Southern Pacific connecting Texas and California, likewise began construction during Grant's first term.[27]

However, by the time he was sworn in as president, Grant understood that the many transcontinental lines would not simply transport people back and forth across the nation. They would also bring them directly into the central section of the nation to live and work. Cattle ranchers in Texas were the first to realize that high profits could be made in the Great Plains. Starting in 1869, they drove their herds north from Texas to the current endpoints of railroads in Missouri and Kansas. Here the cattle were loaded onto cars and transported to stockyards in Kansas City, St. Louis, and Chicago. During Grant's presidency, millions of cows, calves, and steers would make the long drive from Texas to cattle towns such as Abilene on the Kansas Pacific Railroad and Dodge City on the Atchison, Topeka, and Santa Fe. A cycle of abundant rainfall provided ample grass for the grazing herds as they trekked northward. Entrepreneurs were soon inspired to set up ranches closer to the railroads. In the process, the Great Plains, long dismissed as the Great American Desert, fit for only Indians and buffalo, suddenly became desirable country not just for raising cattle but also for farming.[28]

The huge swath of dry, arid, and treeless land at the center of the nation had long appeared hostile to agriculture. Even so, the dream of settling the last unbroken frontier on the American continent had helped propel the nation into the Civil War. Northern farmers and Southern slaveholders fought each other in Kanas long before the first shot was fired at Fort Sumter. As Ulysses Grant battled Confederate armies from Shiloh to Vicksburg, Congress, now dominated by Northern politicians, passed the Homestead Act to open the Great Plains to settlement. American citizens, or immigrants determined to become citizens, who were heads of households or at least twenty-one years of age and had never taken up arms against the United States, could each stake out 160 acres. If they made improvements on their claim and paid a small required fee, the land would be theirs in five years. If settlers were willing to pay $1.25 an acre, they could own their land in six months. Men and women, white and black, native born and immigrants all were entitled to free land in the West. As railroads crisscrossed the Great Plains, farmers and the many workers who supported them poured in. Trains also brought lumber to build homes, barns, and fences, along with steel plows, reapers, and threshers, to help conquer America's last frontier.

A Sea of Change

Starting in Grant's first term and continuing to the end of the nineteenth century, more land was opened for settlement in the United States than in the entire period since the founding of Jamestown. Over 521,000,000 acres were occupied, of which slightly more than half was placed under cultivation. Of the land handed out by the government, close to 100,000,000 acres were made available to six hundred thousand individuals through the Homestead Act. Another 140,000,000 acres were granted to states, while 181,000,000 acres went to railroad companies that sold land on either side of the tracks to settlers. Another 100,000,000 acres were sold at government land offices. Indian land provided an extra 100,000,000 acres. Whether through homesteading, railroad companies, or preemption, the dream of owning free or cheap land on the Great Plains launched a massive migration from the surrounding states and the rest of the world. An army of settlers from the North, freedmen from the ruined South, immigrants from Ireland, Great Britain, Germany, Russia, Poland, and the Hapsburg Empire, including Czechs and Austrians, intermingled with people from Mexico, Central and South America, and China.[29]

While the Board of Indian Commissioners failed to consider the immense changes under way in the West, the Indians well understood them. Their devastating impact on the buffalo was particularly clear. As soon as the Union Pacific was laid across the plains, the buffalo refused to cross back and forth over its tracks. They instead divided into northern and southern herds. Soldiers stationed in the West along with people traveling on the Union Pacific made a sport of shooting at the southern herd. Many travelers enjoyed gunning the animals down from the trains as they passed. At first the killing went on at a slow place, since no one except the Indians saw any value in the tough, woolly hides of the buffalo. But in 1873, a Philadelphia tannery perfected a method for turning buffalo skins into workable leather. Offering $1 to $3 per hide, the company, whether intentional or not, launched the wholesale destruction of the buffalo, turning a sport into a slaughter. Now professional teams of sharpshooters headed onto the plains and killed up to fifty buffalo a day. They stripped the hides off the animals, loaded the skins onto wagons, and hauled them back to the nearest railroad, leaving the carcasses to rot in the sun and endless wind.

When Ulysses Grant launched his campaign for reelection in 1872, the slaughter of the southern herd was reaching its climax. Within two years, the herd would be on the brink of extinction. The buffalo, on which the Comanche, Kiowa, Cheyenne, Arapaho, and so many other tribes depended, were dying not by the tens or hundreds of thousands, but by the millions. Congress tried throughout Grant's first term to pass bills that would ban killing buffalo on public lands except for the purpose of using their meat for food and hides for

A Sea of Change

Shooting buffalo on the line of the Kansas Pacific Railroad. The American public learned about the destruction of the buffalo in the "Far West" through images in the popular press like this drawing, from the June 3, 1871, edition of *Frank Leslie's Illustrated Newspaper*. COURTESY OF THE LIBRARY OF CONGRESS.

robes, two practices critical to the Indians' survival. However, the bills all died in committee. On January 5, 1874, with the situation growing ever more desperate in the West, Congressman Greenburg Fort of Illinois introduced a bill in the House of Representatives outlawing buffalo hunting by anyone but Indians. Fort's legislation passed the House and the Senate and headed to the White House for the president's signature. Grant killed the bill with a pocket veto on the grounds that no good could come from allowing the Indians to live in the past. Later attempts to pass legislation levying heavy taxes on buffalo hides or banning hunting by anyone but Indians went down to defeat in Congress.[30]

The slaughter would take longer on the northern plains, but the extinction of the buffalo there was just as certain. Ten years after the southern herd had disappeared, the great northern herd was practically gone. Eyewitnesses remembered seeing the last buffalo, eighty thousand in all, heading down the Yellowstone River and crossing the border into Canada. Even in the terrible winter of 1884, the last survivors never headed toward the warmer south, preferring to die in the frozen north. There was only one flicker of hope that the buffalo might return someday. According to an Indian legend, a Kiowa woman had seen a mountain open up in the Yellowstone River Valley, allowing about thirty buffalo to enter before closing behind them. Locked in this mountain, the buffalo were still alive, the Indians believed, and might one day come back to keep the Lakota and Yankton, the Northern Cheyenne and Arapaho, the Crow, the Blackfeet, and all the other tribes alive.[31]

Like the Indians, Ulysses Grant recognized the transformation under way in the West, but unlike them, he welcomed the changes. Everything that was happening, from the greatest triumph to the worst tragedy, had a purpose in creating a better future for all Americans. As the president, he was determined to do everything in his power to extend settlements into the most "remote districts of the country." To accomplish this, he signed bills into law providing greater opportunities for landownership in the West. Recognizing the problem of farming on the treeless plains, Grant signed the Timber Culture Act in 1873, which gave an extra 160 acres to homesteaders who planted trees on one-quarter of their land. The trees were to provide lumber for homes, barns, and fences, while also acting as breaks against the unending wind. Four years later, he approved the Desert Land Act, which allowed married homesteaders to claim 640 acres of land and single men half that amount in the arid country beyond the hundredth meridian, where rainfall was sparse. Settlers could also buy the land in three years for $1.25 an acre if they showed proof that they had reclaimed, irrigated, and cultivated it. Like every president since Washington, Grant looked forward to the western territories becoming states. He fought for Colorado's admission into the United States against politicians who had delayed its entrance for more than a decade. He finally succeeded when Colorado entered the Union as the thirty-eighth state in 1876.[32]

Ulysses Grant saw no contradiction between his support for the westward march of American civilization and his Indian policy. Even though the United States would soon fill up the continent, this did not mean, as Father de Smet thought, that the Indians were doomed to disappear. He would protect them on their reservations, sustain them with generous supplies, and allow them to adapt to the modern world closing in all around them. If at times the Indians left their reservations, attacked settlements, and refused to make peace, Grant believed his nation was powerful enough not to strike back at every offense. Americans must be patient and give the Indians time to transform into self-supporting farmers. He entered the nation's highest office believing soldiers were the best people to help the tribes make this transition. Even after missionaries took their places at agencies throughout the West, he still believed the ultimate goal of his Indian policy would be fulfilled. The tribes would not be, as Father de Smet predicted, reduced to a memory but instead would take their rightful place as citizens of the United States.

After he won his second term, Grant described his plans for the Indians in even greater detail. As he explained in his fourth State of the Union address, written for Congress in December 1872, he was more determined than ever to establish a working government in the Indian Territory. He considered this goal an "important complement to existing Indian policy." With Americans racing westward and demanding every last acre for themselves, Grant worried that the tribes would be driven into the "less desirable portions of the public domain." The only solution was to move all the tribes to the Indian Territory. "There is no other location now available," Grant explained, "where a people who are endeavoring to acquire knowledge of pastoral and agricultural pursuits can be as well accommodated as upon the unoccupied lands in the Indian Territory."

He hoped that all three hundred thousand Indians would live there someday. The government would stake out farms of the "proper size" for members of tribes already living in the territory and grant these farms as fee simples, meaning that their titles could be passed down to descendants. The remaining land would be divided among the tribes that moved there from elsewhere in the West. Only in this way could the Indians be protected from the worst frontier types who wanted to rob them of their last remaining land. Safe and secure in the Indian Territory, the tribes would have time to "become sufficiently advanced in the arts of civilization to guard their own rights." He had also not given up the hope that the Indian Territory would enter the Union as a new state governed by and for the tribes.[33]

On March 4, 1873, in a bitterly cold wind and with temperatures falling below freezing, Ulysses Grant stood on the steps of the Capitol to take the oath of office for his second term as president. Refusing an overcoat and once again wearing a plain black suit, he calmly read his address to the shivering crowd. In his first inaugural, one statement about the "first occupants of this land" had stood out. But in this speech, he went far beyond describing his hopes for the Indians and now spoke of his vision for peace in the entire world. He saw God's hand at work in the rapidly changing technology of the day. "I believe that our Great Maker is preparing the world, in His own good time," he explained, "to become one nation, speaking one language, and when armies and navies will no longer be required." He then related specifics in his grand vision, particularly for the country he would continue to govern for the next four years. Harmony would be restored between the North and the South. The nation's currency would be strengthened by tying its value to gold. Railroads would spread across the land, providing affordable transportation for the people and a huge internal market for business. America would live in peace with her neighbors, exporting enough goods on the oceans of the world to pay for every import. As profits poured in to the nation's manufacturers, working people would not be forgotten. Amid this burgeoning wealth, the "elevation of labor" would be secured.[34]

After laying out his dreams for his country, Grant spoke of the Indians. Acknowledging that many people still wanted a "war of extermination" against the tribes, rather than accepting his "humane course" toward them, he asked how an advanced people like the Americans, who were "pursuing commerce and all industrial pursuits," could willingly destroy a weaker people. This not only would be "wicked" but would also demoralize the entire nation. Grant urged his fellow Americans to realize that their civilization, which was blessed with so many advantages, should be "lenient toward the Indian." Although the Indian was capable of terrible atrocities, the injustices he had long suffered had to be "taken into account and the balance placed to his credit." Instead of calling for the extermination of the tribes, which would be an "expensive" proposition if undertaken, Americans should ask themselves, "Can not the Indian be made a useful and productive member of society by proper teaching and treatment?" Grant answered the question by asserting that if Indians were welcomed into the national experience, "we will stand better before the civilized nations of the earth and in our own consciences for having made" the offer. Remaining true to the policy he had crafted years before, he pleaded with the people and Congress to help him: "All these things are not to be accomplished by one individual, but they will receive my support and such recommendations to Congress as will in my judgment best serve to carry them into effect. I beg your support and encouragement."[35]

Although important aspects of his Indian policy had been overturned, Grant believed his approach was on the brink of achieving lasting peace in the West. The wars against the Sioux, Comanche, Kiowa, Cheyenne, and Arapaho had come to an end. Even the great Apache chief Cochise had finally brought his people onto a reservation. There was every reason to believe the calm that had prevailed during his first term would continue for the next four years. For the moment, as the weather grew warm in the spring of 1873, the only trouble in the West was among the Modoc in Oregon. This small tribe had been sent to live on the same reservation as their enemies the Klamath. When they could bear it no more, they fled back to their homeland in northern California.

Here in the rugged country of lava beds left by an ancient volcano, gullies filled with sagebrush, and mountains covered with pine forests, the Modoc resisted every effort to bring them back to Oregon. The president had finally decided, just weeks before his second inauguration, to offer the tribe a compromise:

he would send commissioners among them with a proposal that the tribe could settle on a reservation of their own along Oregon's Pacific coast. He had no doubt that the Modoc would accept the offer, and thus the peace he had first envisioned when he worked out his Indian policy with Ely Parker would continue forever. Grant had no idea of the tragic struggles that lay ahead. The fighting with the Modoc would mark the beginning of a series of Indian wars that would become as legendary as the Civil War, which had made him famous.[36]

7. War on the Far Horizon

*U*lysses Grant could be optimistic about his Indian policy because he believed he was saving the tribes from certain destruction. He might support the many miners, railroad workers, cattle drivers, and farmers heading into the Great Plains. He might even accept the slaughter of the buffalo as a necessary step toward the future. But he did so with the certainty that the "original occupants of this land" would play an integral part in the new world being created. There would be no exterminating the Indians under Grant's watch, even though many Americans still called for it. He would stand between the tribes and the onslaught of his own civilization. However, he would not treat the Indians like museum pieces forever caught in the past. Instead, he expected the tribes to transform themselves even as he watched over them. They must become exactly like the people who crisscrossed the country on trains, tore up the mountains for gold and the prairie sod for farms, and killed the buffalo for sport or profit. He knew the transformation would not be accomplished during his presidency. Still, he was convinced that the course he had set for the Indians would continue even after he left office. The final goal would eventually come true. Somewhere in the distant future, when another man served in the nation's highest office, every Indian would be a citizen of the United States.

Never once in all his planning did President Grant wonder whether the Indians agreed with him. Nor did he ever consider how unhappy they might be contemplating the future he had laid out for them. That many would escape from their reservations and take up the warrior life again was completely astounding to a man who, like other successful generals, had come to hate war. Grant never stopped sympathizing with the Indians, believing that his own people had grossly mistreated them, but he could not understand why anyone would turn down the opportunities he offered them. Every Indian man, woman, and child was worth saving, but not their traditional way of life. Unlike the Board of Indian Commissioners and missionaries appointed to run the reservations, he did not believe that the tribes had to abandon their habits overnight. They should be given time, a generation or two, to become modern people who supported themselves like everyone else in America. Even if they were slow in coming onto the reservations or periodically bolted from them, he would not immediately retaliate. But if a point came when they had resisted his plans too violently or for too long, he would hit back as hard as any commander ever had in any war. He would use the army, which he had once hoped would bring peace to the West by managing the Indian agencies, as a whip to defeat the tribes who wanted no part of his dreams for their future.

At the start of his second term, the Modoc became the first tribe to rise up against Grant's dreams. As long as they could remember, they had made their home near Tule Lake in northern California. Everything they needed to survive was close by. They used tules, the long reeds that grew ten feet tall along the lakeshore, to build their homes and to weave baskets. Higher up in the Cascade Mountains, where the peaks were often covered in snow, their homes were made of sod. They fed their families by gathering berries, nuts, and the bulbs of the quamash plant, which settlers knew as Indian hyacinth. Like other tribes living near them, they collected the seeds of the yellow water lilies that grew in the marshes of their homeland. With wildlife plentiful, the Modoc also lived by hunting and fishing. For food, they took ducks, geese, and swans from the surrounding lakes and larger animals such as elk, antelope, and deer in the foothills of the Cascades. They also fished for salmon and trout in the many streams. They used the fur of wolves, coyotes, badgers, fox, wildcats, and rabbits to make clothes, moccasins, and blankets.[1]

With the exception of their mortal enemies the Klamath, the Modoc lived peacefully with other tribes. But trouble came into their lives when pale-skinned creatures arrived in their country in the early 1840s. At first the Modoc were terrified that the Great Spirit had sent these frightening beings to punish them, but they soon realized that these were merely humans like themselves. The many white people tramping over their land had come from the east searching for gold in the mountains and land for farming and raising their cattle. The Modoc overcame their initial fear of these odd-looking strangers and traded with them. The tribe welcomed the never-ending supply of bread, flour, coffee, tea, bacon, and blankets that the emigrants always seemed to have loaded in their wagons. But it did not take long for the two peoples to clash. The bloodiest fighting broke out in March 1852, when white people killed more than forty Modoc who had come to a peace parley. Six months later, the Modoc retaliated by attacking a wagon train on the eastern edge of Tule Lake at a place known ever after as Bloody Point. The soldiers, who rode to the rescue too late, found the bodies of men, women, and children hacked to pieces and strewn along the shoreline for close to a mile.[2]

War on the Far Horizon

Skirmishes between the Modoc and the increasing number of American settlers continued for twelve more years. Finally, in October 1864, when General Grant and his troops were bogged down in the trenches around Petersburg, Virginia, President Lincoln sent commissioners among the Modoc, Klamath, and Snake to offer peace. They asked the tribes to give up their traditional homeland from Goose Lake in the east, across the Lost River Valley in the center, to the Cascade Mountains in the west. In exchange, the three tribes would be given a joint reservation just north of Upper Klamath Lake. For the thousands of acres that they surrendered, the tribes would receive $80,000 paid in installments over fifteen years. Another $35,000 would be paid in a lump sum, which the tribes could use to buy supplies for setting up farms. No white people, except those involved in the Indian service, would be allowed onto the Klamath Reservation. However, roads and trains could be built across it. For their part, the three tribes promised never again to drink any liquor or attack white people or other Indians.[3]

The Modoc did their best to fulfill the promises they had made in the treaty. They moved to the reservation, where they built cabins and laid out their farms. But they could not get along with the Klamath, who remained their enemies. The Klamath constantly harassed the Modoc, stealing lumber and raiding their crops and livestock. Complaints to the local Indian agent did little good. Every time the Modoc were moved to another part of the reservation, the Klamath were never far behind. Many Modoc fled back to their ceded lands, only to be coaxed back onto the reservation with promises of protection. Finally, in 1870, a young chief named Kintpuach, better known as Captain Jack, led two hundred Modoc home to the Lost River Valley. Fighting soon broke out between Captain Jack's followers and settlers who had staked claims on their land in their absence. Alfred Meacham, whom Ely Parker had kept on as Oregon's superintendent of Indian affairs, begged the Grant administration to find a new reservation where the tribe could live in peace. However, because of the turmoil in the Indian Office when missionaries took over for soldiers at agencies throughout the West, and later when Congress investigated Commissioner Parker, no one answered him.[4]

President Grant could not long ignore the rising tensions in the Pacific Northwest. Complaints about Modoc warriors committing the same kinds of crimes that the Klamath had once committed against them came in from California and Oregon, two states that had voted for Grant in the 1868 and 1872 elections. The president thought appointing Thomas B. Odeneal, the clerk of Oregon's legislature, as the state's new superintendent of Indian affairs might ease tensions in the region. But Odeneal had no sympathy for the Modoc and was determined instead to move them back to the Klamath Reservation. When negotiations with

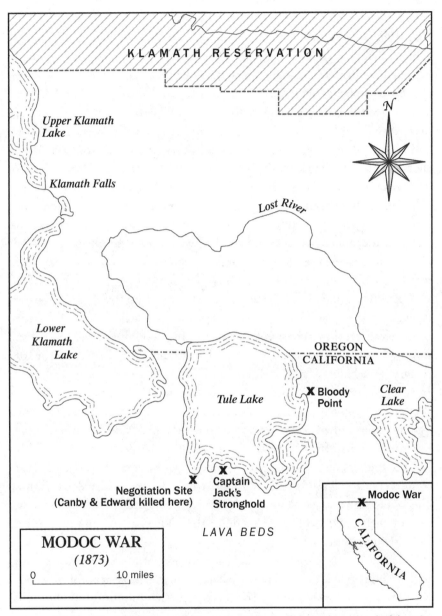

Modoc War (1873). The map shows both the traditional homeland of the Modoc and the Klamath Reservation from which Captain Jack and his people escaped. COPYRIGHT © ROBERTA STOCKWELL, 2018.

the tribe failed, he demanded that local military commanders forcibly remove the tribe from California to Oregon. Three weeks after Grant's reelection, he directed the army to bring the Modoc back to the reservation. The officers welcomed the order, believing a mere "show of military force" would convince the Indians that they should return to Oregon. No one, including the president, expected the trouble with the tribe to develop into an all-out war.[5]

On November 27, 1872, Major John Green, the commander of Fort Klamath, at the western edge of the Klamath Reservation, arrived at Captain Jack's village in the Lost River Valley. He had come with a large body of soldiers, militiamen, and concerned citizens to negotiate the tribe's return to Klamath Lake. When shots rang out, leaving a handful of soldiers and Indians dead, Green hurried back to his post, while Captain Jack and his people fled toward Tule Lake. Each side blamed the other for starting the fight. Green claimed that the Modoc had come armed to the teeth with no intention of making a deal. Defending his tribe, Captain Jack countered that Green's soldiers were already drunk when they rode into his village and never stopped drinking throughout the negotiations. But no matter who fired first, the Modoc War was under way.[6]

Captain Jack and his few dozen warriors killed at least twenty settlers before fleeing into the Lava Beds, a one-hundred-square-mile landscape of flattened black volcanic rocks just south of Tule Lake. The Modoc knew every fissure and ravine of the barren place and used it to their advantage. The soldiers sent after them, now including Major Green's 1st Cavalry, Lieutenant Frank Wheaton's 21st Infantry Regiment, and California and Oregon militiamen, could not dislodge the Modoc from the place they named Captain Jack's Stronghold. The worst fighting came on January 27, 1873, when the combined American forces moved into the Lava Beds from three directions. Fighting in a deep fog that would not lift, the soldiers found themselves pinned down by rifle fire coming at them from every direction. By late afternoon, thirty Americans lay dead, with no one having seen a single Modoc all day during the fighting. The Indians stayed hidden in the Lava Beds, gunning down the soldiers at will and suffering no casualties of their own.[7]

Little did the soldiers know that the tribe fought bravely not just because of their impregnable position but also because of the mysterious Ghost Dance, which had spread among them. They battled the army in the certain hope that the future belonged to the Indians and not the white man. Wodziwob, a Paiute prophet living in the Nevada Territory, taught his followers that if they did the Ghost Dance faithfully, moving around and around in a great circle until they fell down in a trance, they would see their dead relatives again. A dreamer and visionary, he predicted that a great earthquake or perhaps a fire would swallow up or burn all the white people and leave the earth to the Indians. Wodziwob also preached that a great train was coming from the east, filled with all the Indians who had ever lived. They would arrive soon to take their places beside the living members of the tribes. The earth would be restored to what it had been before settlers came west. All the animals would return, too, and the prairies and mountain valleys would be covered with a carpet of flowers. Life would be as it had been before any miner, railroad man, or farmer had tramped through the Indian country.[8]

Grant could not understand why the Modoc, Paiute, and so many other tribes throughout the West preferred to live in the past rather than embrace the future he offered them. Nor could he comprehend that behind the growing resistance to his plans lay a vision of the future just as powerful as his own. He still sympathized with the Indians, however. He was convinced that soldiers at Fort Klamath had done something to instigate the Modoc War. He made this point in late January 1873 during a meeting with Secretary Delano and William Belknap, his secretary of war, who had taken over the post when his friend John Rawlins died of tuberculosis. He ordered army officers in the Pacific Northwest to do nothing that would further antagonize the Modoc. They must avoid all military engagements until peace commissioners could meet with the tribe. Grant appointed as commissioners General Edward Canby, the top army commander in the region; Alfred Meacham, Oregon's previous Indian superintendent; Jesse Applegate, a famous Oregon pioneer and former Indian agent; Judge A. M. Roseborough; and Samuel Case, the acting agent at the Siletz Agency. He also sent along Frank Riddle, a local settler, and his Modoc wife, Winema, a cousin of Captain Jack, to act as interpreters. They were to offer the Modoc their own reservation along an eighty-five-mile stretch of Oregon's Pacific coast between Cape Lookout in the north and Cape Perpetua in the south.[9]

Canby, a West Point graduate and veteran of both the Mexican and Civil Wars, accepted the role of chairman of the peace commission, but he chafed at Grant's accusation that his soldiers had instigated the Modoc War. The orders to use his soldiers sparingly "to protect citizens, and, if possible, avoid war," which had come directly from the president by way of General Sherman, especially infuriated him. If Grant thought the army had caused the Modoc War, then he was sadly mistaken. "I have been very solicitous that these Indians should be fairly treated," Canby explained to Sherman, "and have repeatedly used military force, lest they might be wronged." He had acted exactly as Grant had hoped his soldiers would behave toward the Indians. He tried to be their protector, not their persecutor. In Canby's opinion, the Modoc would have gone to war no matter how perfectly the army had treated them. The tribe would have gunned down anyone, soldier or civilian, who tried to force them from their homeland. At the mere approach of an army, the Modoc would have gone down into the crevices of the Lava Beds or up into the mountains to escape. From either place, they would have kept up a steady fire on the soldiers sent to dislodge them. The Modoc were so determined to stay in their own country that they had even attacked two trains in a desperate bid to secure ammunition.[10]

As much as he disagreed with the president, Canby would follow his orders. He would join his fellow commissioners and their interpreters, go to the Modoc Country, and investigate what "difficulties and hostilities had led to the war in the first place." He would get a message through to Captain Jack that no harm would come to him if he stopped fighting. Canby planned to work with the Modoc leader to devise a plan for restoring calm and preventing further hostilities. He would offer the tribe their own reservation on Oregon's Pacific coast. If the tribe decided that another location was preferable, Canby would notify the administration and let the president decide where they should live. Through it all, Canby would follow Grant's clear instructions that the army must use "no more force or violence" than "absolutely necessary and proper" to end the war. As Grant had ordered, Canby would treat the Modoc respectfully, to honor both their demand for a better home and the president's wish to end the slaughter.[11]

The Modoc were determined to hold out in the Lava Beds as long as possible, but they soon broke under the strain of the siege. Captain Jack's fellow chiefs pressured him to turn down every peace offer or promise of a reservation except in the Lost River Valley. After weeks of negotiating with Elijah Steele, a local judge whom the Modoc trusted, the tribe still refused to meet with the commissioners. They were hostile enough in the preliminary meetings that Steele warned Canby of their possible treachery. He recommended calling off the negotiations, fearing they would end in tragedy. But Grant would not hear of it. He told Canby to keep trying. If any commissioner doubted the wisdom of the president's orders, then the general was to replace that man. After Applegate and Case resigned, Canby asked Dr. Eleazer Thomas, a Methodist minister, and Leroy Dyer, the agent at the Klamath Reservation, to join the peace commission.

On April 2, 1873, Captain Jack finally agreed to meet with General Canby, his fellow commissioners, and their two interpreters about a mile west of the Lava Beds. Everyone noticed how agitated the Modoc chief appeared when he entered the tent where the negotiations were to be held. He seemed incapable of freely discussing the proposals set before him. The commissioners guessed that the other Modoc leaders were making it difficult for Captain Jack to negotiate a deal. They were, in fact, so hostile that Canby's top cavalry officers warned him not to go to the next round of negotiations scheduled for 11 A.M. on Good Friday,

April 11, 1873. Canby agreed that the Modoc seemed dangerously unpredictable, but he decided to head to the negotiation tent anyway with Meacham, Thomas, Dyer, and the Riddles at his side.

The commissioners brought no weapons to the meeting, but Captain Jack, along with his top advisors, Boston Charley, Schonchin John, Black Jim, Bogus Charley, and Hooker Jim, all arrived heavily armed. They demanded a new reservation at a place called Hot Creek. General Canby refused to answer, but Alfred Meacham said, "I will ask the Great Father at Washington for you people." Captain Jack responded by walking up to Canby, raising his pistol, and shooting him directly in the face. Bogus Charley then tripped him and slit his throat. The Modoc immediately turned their rifles on Reverend Thomas, who died instantly, and Meacham, who collapsed seriously wounded. Dyer and Frank Riddle ran from the tent, while Winema stayed behind to protect Meacham, who was still alive. The Modoc stripped all three men of their clothing and possessions, scalped Canby and Thomas, and were just about to scalp Meacham when Winema cried out, "The soldiers are coming! Go quick, all of you!" The Modoc fled from the tent at her cry, which she had made to save Meacham's life.[12]

The army, now under the command of Major Green, descended on the Lava Beds in pursuit of Captain Jack and his followers. Although more determined than ever to dislodge them from their stronghold, the soldiers were no more successful than they had been before. Sporadic fighting dragged on through May, with every skirmish played out in the nation's newspapers. Outrage over the treachery of the Modoc was front-page news across the country. Canby's murder stirred the nation, as a reporter from the *Boston Evening Telegraph* explained it, like "no other event has done since the death of President Lincoln."

From New York to California, the sentiment was the same: Captain Jack and his chiefs had to be hunted down and executed. The only disagreement was over whether the rest of the Modoc should also be exterminated. Western newspapers generally called for the death of every last Modoc, while eastern papers, including the *New York Times*, which had faithfully defended Grant's Indian policy, argued that only the hostile ones should be wiped off the face of the earth, while the rest should be imprisoned. For the moment, the nation seemed able to agree on only one thing: President Grant's Indian policy had failed, either because, as western papers claimed, he coddled the savages right up until the moment they went on the warpath or because, as eastern papers argued, he paid lip service to peace while planning for war all along.[13]

On June 3, 1873, the army finally captured Captain Jack. Soldiers found him hiding in a cave in the Lava Beds unable to move. He said that after months of being on the run, his legs had simply given out. If not for the president's orders,

General Edward Canby. Canby, who headed Grant's peace commission to the Modoc, became the first and only general to die in an Indian War in the American West. COURTESY OF THE LIBRARY OF CONGRESS.

he might have been shot dead then and there, along with his top aides and all the women, children, and old people of his tribe. Grant decided that Captain Jack, along with the few Modoc leaders who had survived the war, namely Boston Charley, Schonchin John, Black Jim, Brancho, and Slolux, should be tried by a military court. The rest of the Modoc were to be treated as prisoners of war. Grant had asked Attorney General George Williams, one of the authors of Oregon's Constitution, who had also served as a senator from the state and a justice on Oregon's Supreme Court, for advice on whether this was legally possible. Williams assured him that the Modoc leaders could be tried in a military court just as Captain Henry Wirz, the Confederate commander of the Andersonville Prison, had been.

The trial of Captain Jack and the other Modoc leaders began at Fort Klamath on September 3, 1873. The six men were charged with murdering Canby and Thomas in violation of the rules of war and assaulting peace commissioners under a flag of truce. They were found guilty on all counts and were sentenced to die by hanging on October 3. Most Americans were thrilled at the verdict and looked forward to the execution of the Modoc chiefs as fitting justice for their crimes. But when the fateful day arrived, they were stunned to learn that Grant had commuted the sentences of Brancho and Slolux to life imprisonment on Alcatraz Island. He had done so on the recommendation of army officers who believed that the two young men were merely soldiers doing their duty and had no involvement in planning the murders of the commissioners. While Grant allowed some Modoc to return to Klamath Lake, he ordered the rest to new homes in the Indian Territory.[14]

Although the Modoc War had ended, the debate over how Grant's Indian policy had contributed to the revolt of Captain Jack's people went on. Western newspapers blamed the tribe's rebellion on Grant's leniency toward all Indians. Eastern newspapers ridiculed Grant's "peace policy" as nothing more than a mask worn by a warmonger. Columbus Delano stepped into the fray on the president's behalf. He had defended Grant during his reelection bid and continued after the execution of the Modoc leaders. He was especially incensed that anyone could question the motives of a man who had suffered so much for his country. Had they forgotten Paducah and Shiloh, Vicksburg and Chickamauga, the Wilderness and Appomattox? he asked. To suspect Ulysses Grant of having anything less than the best interests of his country at heart when dealing with the Indians was nothing short of treason in Delano's view.

Calling Grant's approach the "peace policy," Delano summarized its purposes in five points to try to silence critics who condemned it as too lax or totally duplicitous. First, the president placed the Indians on reservations to protect them from the worst elements of frontier life and to allow American civilization to expand into the remotest parts of the country. Second, Grant promised to guard the Indians only so long as they behaved peacefully. If they caused the kind of trouble the Modoc had, then he would punish them harshly. Third, once the Indians settled on their reservations, food, clothing, shelter, and any supplies they needed to become self-supporting farmers would be theirs for the asking.

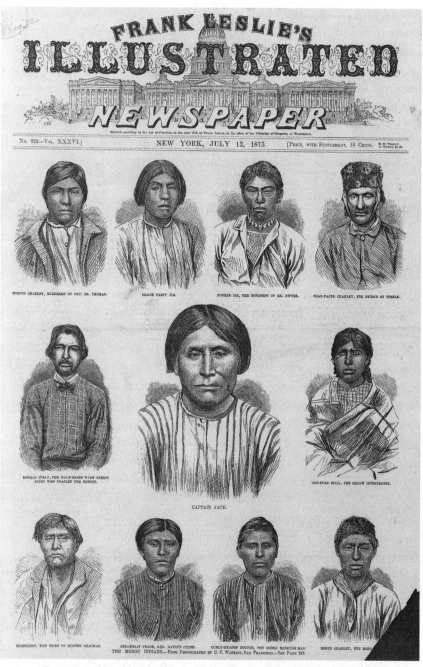

Captain Jack and his followers. The men, front-page news when they went on trial for attacking General Canby and his fellow commissioners, are shown on the July 12, 1873, cover of *Frank Leslie's Illustrated Newspaper*. COURTESY OF THE LIBRARY OF CONGRESS.

While this might seem burdensome to taxpayers, Delano assured his fellow Americans that the expense was worth it. As always, he compared the cost of supplying the tribes on reservations with the cost of fighting wars against them. While the budget for the Indian Office was $5,000,000 a year, the army spent $1,000,000 apiece, plus the lives of twenty soldiers, for every warrior killed.

For his final two points, Delano emphasized the religious character of Grant's Indian policy. Ignoring the fact that the president originally wanted army officers to run the Indian service, Delano argued that Grant had the best reasons for appointing devout Christians to the reservations. As agents, they would distribute goods purchased for the tribes without making any profit on them. As teachers, they would establish churches that taught the Christian faith and its moral values. They would show the wild tribes still roaming the plains, who seemed incapable of letting go of the past, that a civilized life was preferable to a savage one. Leading by example, through the decency of their lives, these people would help Grant achieve the main goal of his policy: American citizenship for all the Indians.[15]

Delano did not claim that everything was sweetness and light on the frontier. There was violence in the West, and Ulysses Grant, who had seen horrific brutality in his own military career, understood this better than anyone. However, Delano blamed the press for exaggerating the amount of violence in the West. Most of the trouble, Delano argued, took place in the Arizona Territory and the Texas Panhandle, where small parties of Indians attacked isolated ranches, stole cattle, and even carried off a few settlers. There was, in fact, more violence on any given day in a big city like New York than in western places. Just as important, the Indians causing trouble in the West were small in number compared with the 180,000 Indians who supported themselves as farmers and the 80,000 more who were attached to their local agencies. Renegade bands might light up the nation's headlines, but they never had the backing of their chiefs or tribes. The vast majority of Indians wanted to live in peace. They agreed with Grant's policy, despite the many criticisms launched against it by Indian sympathizers and haters alike. As Delano had explained on the campaign trail in 1872:

> Let those who, from lack of correct information, are incredulous; let those whose desire for punishment or revenge has been aroused by exaggerated accounts of Indian depredations; let those who wish to change the present policy in order to renew again a host of faithless agents and contractors to plunder the ignorant savage, and rob him of the aid and beneficence of the Government; and, finally, let those who desire war that they may reap the rich profits which its large and necessary

expenditures afford, ponder these facts, and answer before God and a Christian nation whether they will, if they can, destroy the present policy of peace, justice, and progress, and restore the former system of cruelty, robbery, inhumanity, war, bloodshed, and crime.[16]

Delano's words rang hollow in the summer of 1874, when another Indian war broke out, this time along the Red River Valley on the southern plains. Comanche, Kiowa, and Cheyenne warriors, who did not find life on the reservations carved out for them in the Medicine Lodge Treaty as idyllic as Delano described it, attacked buffalo hunters at a trading post near Adobe Walls on the Canadian River in the Texas Panhandle. Led by the daring Quanah Parker, the son of Peta Nocona, a Comanche chief, and Cynthia Ann Parker, a white girl captured in Texas when she was nine, they fought believing the promises of Eshatie, an Indian prophet, who told them that the white man's bullets would never harm them. Attacking the outpost at dawn on June 27, 1874, Parker, along with hundreds of warriors, all on horseback, arrayed in war bonnets, and armed with guns, lances, and buffalo hide shields, swooped down on the few stores and saloon that made up the post.

At first they fought recklessly, crashing their horses into the doors and smashing every window. They retreated only when the twenty-eight men and one woman at the post fired back at them with deadly accuracy. After assaulting the place two more times, circling around the post's lone street and shooting at its defenders, the warriors fled back into the surrounding Staked Plains. Many Indians were killed by rifle fire from the buffalo hunters, who took aim at them across the plains through the telescopic lenses of their long-range guns. Parker was knocked from his horse when a bullet hit his powder horn. He was saved by a warrior who helped him back onto his mount, and together they raced away. Parker left fifteen warriors, countless Indian horses, and only four Americans dead behind him.[17]

Grant, who had been merciful toward Captain Jack's Modoc, at least in the beginning, had no intention of forgiving the Comanche, Kiowa, and Cheyenne warriors for their attack on Adobe Walls. Instead, the army would move swiftly against them. Since he was away from Washington for the summer, Grant left the planning of the campaign to Sherman, still serving as the nation's top general, and Sheridan, the army's second in command, who worked out of his headquarters in Chicago. They were to confer with Columbus Delano, William Belknap, and Edward Parmelee Smith, the new Commissioner of Indian Affairs, to develop a strategy that would quickly defeat the rebellious chiefs and their many followers. They must also find a way to protect every Indian who preferred peace to war. By late July, the five men, after meeting in person or communicating through

Quanah Parker. Parker was less than thirty years old when he led Comanche, Kiowa, and Cheyenne warriors in the Red River War.
COURTESY OF THE LIBRARY OF CONGRESS.

letters, had come up with a twofold strategy. Soldiers already stationed on the southern plains would hunt down warriors in the Red River Valley. Chiefs who wanted no part of the bloodshed would be told to hurry with their people to the nearest agency, where they would be registered as peaceful. Roaming bands that refused to come into the agencies would be marked down as hostile. The Indians had to make up their minds quickly or else they would be caught in the web of the long columns of soldiers marching toward the Red River.[18]

General Sheridan developed the military plan for defeating the Indians. Five columns would head for the Comanche, Kiowa, and Cheyenne fighters like spokes moving toward the center of a great wheel. Colonel Nelson Miles would lead four companies of the 5th Infantry and eight companies of the 6th Cavalry toward the southwest out of Fort Dodge in Kansas. Just below Miles's column, Lieutenant Colonel "Black Jack" Davidson would bring the 10th Cavalry, along with several companies of the 11th Infantry, west from Fort Sill in the Indian Territory. Lieutenant Colonel George Buell would lead more companies of the 9th and 10th Cavalries, plus soldiers from the 11th Infantry, up from Fort Griffin in Texas on a sharp diagonal from the southeast. To Buell's left, Colonel Ranald Mackenzie's 4th Cavalry, along with hundreds of infantry, would march north from Fort Concho. The final spoke on the wheel would come directly from the west: Major William Price would lead four companies of the 8th Cavalry due east from Fort Bascom in the New Mexico Territory.[19]

As the soldiers made their way toward the Red River Valley, tribes throughout the southern plains recognized a clear change in the government's treatment of them. Until recently, when small parties of warriors had left their reservations and raided nearby settlements, Grant had never called out hundreds of his soldiers in retaliation. The Quakers who served at agencies throughout the Central Superintendency were just as restrained. They never punished the majority of peaceful Indians for the actions of a few hostile bands. But after the attack on Adobe Walls, these attitudes disappeared overnight. Indian chiefs were now treated with little respect by the many soldiers marching through their country.

The Comanche leader Pearuaakupakup, better known as Big Red Meat, experienced this firsthand when he tried to register his people as peacefuls. He had joined Quanah Parker in the fight at Adobe Walls, but two months later, when his people were starving, he brought them into Fort Sill. He expected the agents to forgive him and feed his followers. However, he was turned away on the grounds that the deadline to register had passed. The chief led his band to the Anadarko Agency on the Washita River, where hundreds of Indians from many different tribes were waiting for food. Rather than welcoming Big Red Meat, as they would have done before the attack on the buffalo hunters, officials demanded that the Comanche leader surrender as a prisoner of war. Instead, he opened fire on them before fleeing back to Parker's side, taking many disgruntled warriors and their families with him. They left behind four agency workers and sixteen Indians dead in this second battle of the Red River War.[20]

The next major fight came early on the morning of August 30, when Colonel Miles's column of cavalry and infantry approached the headwaters of the Red River. Three days previously, after coming upon a well-traveled Indian trail,

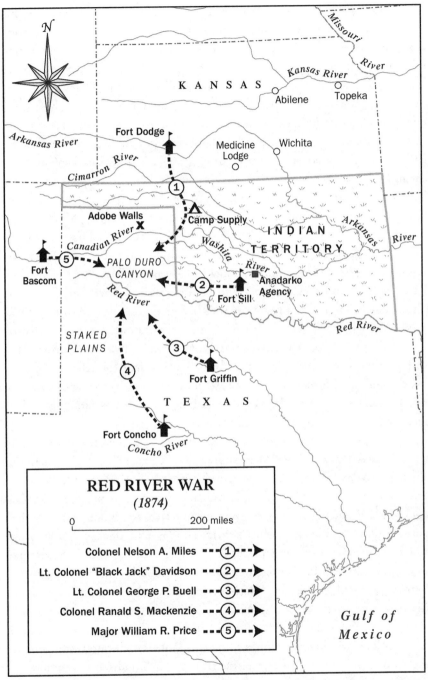

Red River War (1874). The map shows the convergence of General Philip Sheridan's five columns on the Red River Valley in northern Texas in 1874.
COPYRIGHT © ROBERTA STOCKWELL, 2018.

Miles had ordered his supply train to stay behind while he and the rest of his troops set off in pursuit of what he hoped would be a large party of warriors. Exhausted after traveling sixty-five miles in just two days, Miles's soldiers took up their march on the thirtieth shortly before dawn. Four hours later, they were suddenly attacked by hundreds of well-armed Comanche and Kiowa warriors. When the soldiers, after fighting into the afternoon in the searing heat, were on the brink of succumbing to the foe, Miles ordered his one howitzer and two rapid-firing Gatling guns wheeled into position. Once the artillery opened fire, the Indians retreated back toward their camp with Miles's cavalry pursuing them. They killed seventeen warriors, captured most of their supplies, and might have overtaken the enemy completely if not for the fact that with little food or water to sustain them and no fodder for their horses, they could go no farther.[21]

Skirmishes between the Indians and the army continued back and forth throughout September. On the ninth, the supply train now making its way toward the stranded column of Colonel Miles was attacked near the Washita River by five hundred Comanche and Kiowa warriors. They were led by the Kiowa chiefs Satanta and Big Tree, who had just been released from a Texas prison where they had served time for raiding American settlements. With little more than a hundred men at his command, Captain Wyllys Lyman ordered the thirty-six wagons in the supply train formed into a circle for defense. Then for five days, he and his men held off the attacking warriors, who dug in for a long siege around the wagons. Finally, after killing only five soldiers, the Indians retreated back toward Palo Duro Canyon.

Another skirmish took place on September 12 between the south fork of the Canadian River and the Washita. At dawn, 125 warriors attacked Sergeant Zechariah Woodall and the five men under his command. The small party was on its way back to Camp Supply in the Indian Territory with messages from Colonel Miles. Woodall had ordered everyone to retreat to a buffalo wallow. Here in the shallow, muddy ditch, which provided no cover, they held off the warriors, who raced around them on horseback and shot at them at will. From sunup to well past sundown, the six men took aim at the Indians with rifles and pistols. Finally, as the night grew ever darker with the moon hidden behind clouds, the warriors moved off, leaving one soldier dead and three severely wounded.[22]

The final major battle of the Red River War took place on September 28, when Colonel Mackenzie's troops attacked a large Indian camp stretching for three miles in Palo Duro Canyon. He stunned the hundreds of warriors and their families living there by sending his men straight down the canyon walls to attack them. Most of the Indians got away, but they left behind over a thousand horses. While the warriors remained determined to fight on, they could hardly do so once Mackenzie's soldiers killed the horses captured in the canyon. This was a tragedy from which even the most daring chiefs and their bravest warriors could not recover. What the death of so many prize mounts failed to accomplish, the brutal winter finished. With deep snow covering the plains for months at a time, the soldiers retreated back to their posts while small parties of Indians slowly made their way to Fort Sill, now under the command of Colonel Mackenzie. In the spring of 1875, the Red River War officially came to an end when, on June 2, Quanah Parker brought four hundred of his people, along with fifteen hundred horses, into the post to surrender.[23]

No soldiers or officials were waiting to negotiate a treaty with Parker and the other defeated chiefs. Just as Grant's leniency had evaporated, so had the treaty system, a fact of which many Indians were unaware when they came into Fort Sill the following winter and spring. Instead of being welcomed into councils, they were herded into stone corrals that served as outdoor jails. They were stripped of their rifles, lances, bows and arrows, shields, and even their buffalo robes. Colonel Mackenzie took their horses and sold them for just $4 apiece but promised to use the profits to buy livestock for the tribes. Once their imprisonment was up, most of the Comanche, Kiowa, and Cheyenne were sent to reservations in the Indian Territory. Their leaders were treated more harshly. Like Captain Jack, they were tried before military tribunals. However, this time there would be no executions. Their punishment would be life imprisonment in jails in Texas or Florida. By the time the trials were over, sixty-seven Comanche, Kiowa, and Cheyenne leaders were sentenced, including Satanta and Big Tree. Quanah Parker, who now became a leading advocate of Grant's Indian policy among his people, was the one chief not tried by a military court.[24]

Despite winning the support of the defeated Comanche leader, the president once again came under attack by the nation's press. The main arguments were similar to the ones made during the Modoc War. Many newspapers criticized Grant for being too kind to the Indians in the first place. He had failed to round up warriors and punish them severely as soon as they left their reservations. A few papers, which were more sympathetic to the Indians, mocked the word *peace* in association with Grant's policy. They accused the president of having been bent on war ever since he had assumed office. He had been just as determined to wipe out the Indians as his two top generals, Sherman and Sheridan, the commanders to whom he had abdicated all responsibility during the Red River War.[25]

The job of defending Grant's Indian policy now fell to Edward Parmelee Smith, the new commissioner of Indian affairs. After Francis Walker resigned the post in 1872 to accept a teaching position at Yale, the president asked the

American Missionary Society to recommend a trustworthy man to replace him. He wanted someone with no ties to politicians who might manipulate him and also someone who would faithfully implement his policy. The society chose Reverend Edward Parmelee Smith, a Congregational minister from Massachusetts who first came to national prominence as an active member of the Christian Commission during the Civil War. He had dedicated his postwar career to helping both the freedmen and the Indians. Most recently, he had served as an Indian agent in Minnesota.[26]

Appointed in 1873, Reverend Smith came to the Indian Office with no fawning respect for Ulysses Grant. Smith agreed with the president's many critics who claimed he had exhibited a "mistaken leniency" toward the tribes. Although Grant had threatened to punish Indians who left their reservations to murder, rob, and kidnap settlers, he never did, at least not until Quanah Parker's warriors attacked the buffalo hunters at Adobe Walls. Grant was equally culpable for failing to stop white marauders from stealing horses and cattle from tribes living peacefully in the Indian Territory. Although the government had vowed to banish white people from reservations, even writing these promises into the Fort Laramie and Medicine Lodge Treaties, Grant rarely followed through on these commitments. Crimes against Indians went unpunished and thus set off a vicious cycle of violence as warriors, angry at America's broken promises, gunned down agency officials, attacked wagon trains, and then rode off to take out their anger on unsuspecting settlers.[27]

Even though Reverend Smith criticized Grant for his many failures, he still believed that there could be no turning back from his policy, especially its fundamental belief that Indians were not savages. Through the trauma of the Modoc and Red River Wars, Grant never doubted that the Indians were decent people at heart. They might appear barbarous in their present circumstances, but if those circumstances changed, they would be as civilized as any American. The immediate problem was to get the Comanche, Kiowa, and Cheyenne away from their wild life on the southern plains and place them on tracts of land purchased from the Cherokee, Choctaw, and Chickasaw farther east in the Indian Territory. Here they could be trained as ranchers, an occupation that would hopefully be more appealing to buffalo hunters than farming. The government had to provide every family with a house, cattle, and supplies worth $250. While the government had to spend $250,000 a year for a short time on the same tribes that had wreaked havoc on the southern plains, the end result was worth it. In less than a tenth of a generation, the many painted warriors, once wrapped in feathers and riding high atop their decorated horses, who had once gunned down settlers and soldiers without mercy, would suddenly become hardworking ranchers.[28]

Smith also lauded Grant's efforts to set up a territorial government, which would include criminal and civil courts, in the Indian Territory. Tribes such as the Cherokee must no longer be allowed to block this from happening. Courts must likewise be established on all reservations throughout the West. Smith noted that when tribes were moved onto reservations, the government had not created a legal system, beyond tribal customs, to regulate them. Thus there was no law and little order on any of the reservations. Army officers had provided some control when they ran the agencies, but their authority disappeared when missionaries replaced them. The 10th Cavalry had guarded the Indian Territory, primarily by removing squatters from tribal land, but it had been ordered to Texas after the Red River War. The problem was made worse by the fact that Indians had no legal identity, especially after Congress ended the treaty system, which disallowed the recognition of tribes as nations. Smith believed that granting "qualified citizenship" to the Indians would resolve most of these issues. The president could then extend the jurisdiction of state courts onto the reservations and assign deputy marshals to police them. In turn, the Indians could hold elections to manage the new police power on their reservations.

The rule of law had to also be extended to property rights. Presently, individual Indians owned no land. Even though they were encouraged to work farms or ranches, they were not allowed to hold the deeds to these properties. The government had to find a way to allow individual Indians to own land that could not be alienated for a set term of years. They would thus have the time to learn farming or ranching without fear of unscrupulous traders buying their land out from under them. The system of distributing annuity payments in cash or goods to the tribe, rather than to individuals, also had to be abolished. The president should distribute annuities only to individuals in exchange for some kind of labor. Finally, and most important, there had to be a way for Indians who desired it to become American citizens.[29]

While he had criticized the president, Commissioner Smith had no doubt that Grant's policy was still on the way to becoming an unqualified success. Most Indians now accepted the future that Grant had laid out before them as inevitable. Smith also predicted that no tribe would ever be able to collect more than five hundred warriors to resist the president's plans. Even the mighty Sioux, who had once struck terror in the hearts of settlers and soldiers alike, were now in such a weakened state that they would never go to war again. To Smith, they were nothing more than ragged paupers who came regularly to beg for food at agencies set up throughout their country. They were so dependent on the government for their survival that they would be willing to sell the land granted to them in the Treaty of Fort Laramie, including their beloved Black Hills, and move to a new reservation on the southern plains. By thinking along the same lines as Commissioner Smith, Ulysses Grant made the greatest miscalculation of his presidency when it came to implementing his Indian policy. His error in judgment set off a horrible Indian war and revealed a fault line running between corruption in the Indian service and his own honorable intentions toward the tribes that he had been largely able to ignore.[30]

8. The Web of Corruption

*I*n his attempt to defend the president's Indian policy, Reverend Smith had painted a less than accurate picture of Ulysses Grant. Far from being a distant figure who ignored the troubles of Indians and settlers alike, he was well aware of the turmoil engulfing the West. Although he expected Commissioner Smith to handle day-to-day matters in the Indian Office, Grant still received letter after letter from people living along the frontier asking for his help. Territorial officials often complained that he had set up reservations in the wrong places. Governor Samuel Axtell of New Mexico, for example, told him that the Apache were dissatisfied living on the Jicarilla Reservation. They should be moved to the Mescalero Reservation and their former territory opened for settlement. Farmers in the Dakota Territory who lived near the Standing Rock Agency told Grant to keep the Sioux away from their homes, while tribes in the Indian Territory asked him to send soldiers to remove squatters from their land. Letters came, too, from former slaves living with the southern tribes who complained that the Indians treated them like second-class citizens. Knowing how well the president protected freedmen in the former Confederate states, they begged him to do the same in the Indian Territory. Half-breeds among the Osage, who received no respect from the full-bloods in their tribe, demanded Grant's help in winning every right and privilege owed them as Indians.[1]

Still, Reverend Smith sensed a change in Grant's attitude, but barely knowing the president, he could hardly identify what it was. Following the Modoc War, particularly after the attack on his peace commissioners, Grant had lost much of his enthusiasm for his original Indian policy. It had been a terrible shock to be serving as the commander in chief when, for the first time in American history, a general died in an Indian war. Canby's death seemed an affront to Grant's every attempt to rescue the tribes from certain destruction. He had offered the Modoc a reservation along Oregon's Pacific coast, a compromise between the tribe's demands and the expectations of the white citizens. The Modoc had responded by murdering General Canby and Reverend Thomas, scalping both men, and stripping their corpses. His patience disappeared as he ordered Captain Jack and his followers to trial and banished most of the rest of his tribe from their traditional homeland. Even though he commuted the sentences of two of the Modoc leaders, this could hardly be called merciful, since both men would spend the rest of their lives on the rock of Alcatraz. Nor was much compassion meted out to the dozens of Comanche, Kiowa, and Cheyenne chiefs who were tried and convicted for their participation in the Red River War.

Grant's new attitude could be seen most clearly in his reaction to the hunt for gold in the Black Hills. He had made the protection of the Sioux's homeland, which had been guaranteed to the tribe in the latest Fort Laramie Treaty, a hallmark of his presidency. While serving as general of the army, he had closed the three forts on the Bozeman Trail. But by the summer of 1874, with letters and petitions flooding his administration from people claiming that a bigger bonanza than the Comstock Lode lay buried beneath the Black Hills, he gave up his long-standing role as the defender of the Sioux. He raised no objections to General Sheridan's plan to send an exploring party into the region held sacred by the tribe. In July, Sheridan ordered Lieutenant Colonel George Armstrong Custer and his 7th Cavalry, along with scientists, miners, and reporters, onto the Sioux Reservation to find out once and for all if there really was any gold in the Black Hills. Just as important, he wanted Custer to scout for the best locations to build forts. Once soldiers were stationed there, they could prevent the tribe from heading south to join the tribes at war on the southern plains.[2]

Custer led more than a thousand men and a wagon train loaded with supplies from Fort Abraham Lincoln on July 2, 1874. Traveling west at the leisurely pace of four to five miles a day, the expedition took nearly three weeks to arrive at the upper end of the Black Hills. The mysterious beauty of the place became more apparent as the expedition made a sharp turn south and headed directly for it. Fred Power, a young reporter from the *Saint Paul Daily Pioneer*, tried to describe the wonder of the ridge that appeared deep blue or almost purple across the prairies covered in a burst of spring flowers. At a loss for words, he quoted the Scottish poet Thomas Campbell in his diary: "Distance lends enchantment to the view." Twenty days after starting out, the expedition finally entered the Black Hills near a place called Inyan Kara and then headed southeast toward Harney Peak.

After climbing with a small party to the peak's summit, and then camping near its base for five days, Custer ordered the wagon train due south toward the Cheyenne River. At French Creek, a shallow fork in the stream, miners traveling with him discovered the best evidence of gold in the Black Hills. They estimated that a man could make $150 a day working along its banks. Custer's men crossed the creek and camped at a place they named Alice Park. After resting there for several days, which Custer spent hunting grizzlies, they headed to Bear Butte, an outcropping of rock rising a thousand feet at the southern edge of the Black Hills. Passing by the sacred site where the Sioux and other tribes from the northern plains made frequent pilgrimages, Custer's men made the turn for home, where they arrived on August 30.[3]

Throughout the expedition, Custer sent letters to George Ruggles, the assistant adjutant general of the Dakota Territory stationed in St. Paul, filled with his observations about gold in the Black Hills. His every word was quickly telegraphed to newspaper editors across the country. He was not overly enthusiastic about the region's potential, but his reports said enough to inflame the nation's gold fever even more. "I have on my table forty or fifty small particles of gold," he wrote from French Creek on August 2, "averaging a pin head, and most of it obtained from one pan." When he passed Bear Butte on August 15, he noted more optimistically that his men had "found gold in the grass roots and from the surface of the greatest depth reached." The aside that followed contained the exact words that miners waiting on the borders of the Sioux Reservation wanted to hear: "It has not required an expert to find gold in the Black Hills, as men without former experience found it."[4] While his final report to the War Department contained a caution, his words seemed to confirm long-standing rumors about the Black Hills:

> From this it will be seen that no satisfactory or conclusive examination of the country could be made of its mineral deposits; enough, however, was determined to establish the fact that gold is distributed throughout an extensive area of the Black Hills. No discoveries, as far as I am aware, were made of gold deposits in quartz, although there is every reason to believe that a more thorough and extended search would have discovered it.[5]

Once Custer's words were sent across the country, there was no holding back the many desperate men who dreamed of winning quick riches, especially with the nation's economy still reeling from the panic of the previous year. Credit had dried up after the collapse of Jay Cooke's financial empire, which followed on the bankruptcy of the Northern Pacific Railroad. Businesses had failed throughout the nation, with unemployment rising to ever higher levels. With mines in the Rockies petering out or now in the hands of wealthy investors who could pay for the equipment needed to blast the remaining ore from the rock, Custer's letters set off a new gold rush into the sacred country of the Sioux. Within days of Custer's return to Fort Abraham Lincoln, five hundred men were ready to set out from Yankton, the capital of the Dakota Territory. They planned to go up the Missouri by steamboat to the town of Pierre and then march overland to the Black Hills. Just as many miners had gathered sixty-five miles away in Sioux City, Iowa, ready to head along the Niobrara River to French Creek. Both parties were the vanguard of still more people coming from as far away as Massachusetts and California.[6]

For the moment, Grant was still determined to use the army to keep miners out of the Black Hills. He had Sheridan direct General Terry, the commander of the army's Department of Dakota, to stop everyone coming from Yankton or Sioux City into the Black Hills. Grant told Terry to use any means at his disposal, including burning wagons, destroying equipment, and locking up miners at the nearest fort. He could even call out the cavalry to keep everyone confined in the two troublesome towns. When the citizens of Yankton learned about Terry's orders, they called a mass meeting to protest. They were furious at the generals and also at the president, who was acting as the protector of the Sioux rather than the defender of white people. The resolution they passed expressed the bitterness they felt toward the army, its commanders, and ultimately Ulysses Grant: "Resolved, that we shall exercise our rights as American citizens to go and come when and where we please without asking the consent of General Sheridan or any other military chieftain."[7]

Throughout the summer, soldiers rounded up miners in the Black Hills. This was no different from what the army had been doing for some time in the Indian Territory, where soldiers, also under direct orders from the president, had regularly removed squatters, especially farmers who every spring tried to plant their crops on Indian land. By the fall of 1874, however, Grant did not think the army could keep this up much longer, at least not everywhere. He decided that the only hope for protecting the tribes was to move them to the Indian Territory, a conclusion he reached when he traveled west in early October.

Grant and his wife, Julia, were on their way to Chicago to attend the wedding of their oldest child, Fred. They left Washington on October 3, heading first to St. Louis for an agricultural fair, before proceeding by train to the Indian Territory. Arriving on the eleventh, they passed through the reservations of the Cherokee, Choctaw, and Creek. Grant gave several short speeches to tribal councils expressing his amazement at the country that the Choctaw called Oklahoma, meaning "red people." Noting the "surpassing beauty" of the place, he was stunned at the farms that extended for miles and miles. The tribes were clearly prospering in the "soil of so rich and magnificent a country." He imagined even greater prosperity coming from cash crops like cotton, which, if cultivated, would make the Indians among the "most wealthy citizens of the United States."⁸

The president had never given up the dream of winning citizenship for every Indian, not even in the midst of the recent tragedies in the West. But he now believed this dream could come true only if all the tribes were safe in the Indian Territory. Here they would enjoy the success experienced by the "civilized tribes," and together they would take the necessary steps to bring this "beautiful country" into the Union as a new state. He did not go into detail about his plans during this visit, preferring instead to remember, somewhat wistfully, all he had attempted for the Indians: "I have always tried to see you protected in every right guaranteed you in your treaties, and while I hold my present position I shall endeavor to see that you are protected in the enjoyment of your personal and civil rights."⁹

When Grant returned to Washington, he had renewed hope that there was still a chance that his Indian policy was succeeding, at least in the Indian Territory. For the first time in his presidency, he embraced the nickname of the "peace policy," which both his supporters and critics had given his approach. As he explained in his sixth State of the Union address, written in December 1874, his approach aimed to bring peace to the West. Despite the rash of troubles in northern California, the Red River Valley, and now the Dakota Territory, he looked forward to the day when all the fighting that had plagued the frontier for centuries would come to an end. He openly discussed achieving his goal of settling all the tribes in the Indian Territory. Here they would thrive on prosperous farms, just like the Cherokee, Choctaw, and Creek were doing already. Together the tribes would build a government for their territory, which would one day enter the Union. Every Indian would also become an American citizen. The Homestead Act could then be extended to the new state and thus allow individual Indians to own land. Looking ahead, Grant worried about only one thing: once the Indians held the title to individual plots of ground, unscrupulous people might swoop in and buy the property out from under them. The Indians would have achieved American citizenship only to become penniless vagrants. He planned to solve this by adding a caveat to the Homestead Act: Indians would not be allowed to sell their land for at least twenty years, thus giving them time to establish themselves as farmers or ranchers.¹⁰

Grant's belief that all the tribes should live in the Indian Territory took on a greater sense of urgency when, in the same month that he delivered his latest State of the Union, miners broke through the cordon that the army had placed around the Black Hills. They raced to French Creek, only to be driven out by soldiers, even as others quickly took their place. By March 1875, the situation was dire enough for the president to lay out a specific plan to handle the explosive situation in the Dakota Territory. After meeting with Secretary Delano and Secretary Belknap, he decided that a "competent Geologist" must be sent into the Black Hills to confirm that gold was plentiful in the region. Professor Joseph Henry, the director of the Smithsonian Institution, recommended Walter P. Jenney and his assistant Henry Newton for the job. Assuming these two men would find "precious metals in large quantities" in the Black Hills, Grant planned to open negotiations with the Sioux to extinguish their title to the region. Before bringing their chiefs to Washington to make the deal, he planned to send an agent among them to verify their willingness to sell. Until the tribe officially surrendered the Black Hills to the government, Grant would order the army to continue removing miners and other squatters from their country. All this would be done carefully so as not to upset the tribe since, as Secretary Delano described the situation to the president, "a general war with the Sioux would be deplorable." Unlike Commissioner Smith, Delano still believed a war with the tribe was possible.[11]

As Jenney and Newton prepared to leave for the Black Hills, Grant invited Red Cloud and Spotted Tail to visit him in Washington in May 1875. John Collins, the special agent whom Grant had sent to gauge the sentiments of the Sioux, assured him that the tribe would most likely sell the Black Hills to the government. But once the chiefs arrived in the capital, the negotiations to purchase the country did not go well. In the opening meeting with Secretary Delano and Indian Commissioner Smith on May 28, Red Cloud denied knowing anything about troubles in the Black Hills or the government's desire to purchase land guaranteed to them by the Fort Laramie Treaty. He had come to Washington to complain about John J. Saville, the tribe's agent, who gave them stringy cattle, rancid pork, and moldy flour, coffee, sugar, and tobacco. Professor Othniel Marsh, a paleontologist from Yale, had met Red Cloud while searching for fossils in the Dakota Territory and had urged him to complain directly to the president. Red Cloud took Marsh's advice and laid his troubles before the Great Father, who had long been the Sioux's staunchest defender.[12]

When Red Cloud and his fellow chiefs were ushered into the White House on May 29, they found their old friend greatly changed, especially in his attitude toward them. The man who had once closed down the forts on the Bozeman Trail, and who even now was sending his soldiers against trespassers in their country, was not interested in listening to their problems. Grant even told them not to speak, but rather to listen to him. He then read a speech that on the surface showed his usual concern for the Sioux but underneath indicated only one thing: getting the Black Hills away from them. The president reminded Red Cloud and his fellow chiefs that he had long been their friend. He assured them that he had tried to do what was best for the Sioux and not just for his own people. But his words betrayed a grasping quality that the chiefs had heard from other white men, but never before from Ulysses Grant.

Because of his long-standing concern for the Sioux, the president said, he had to warn them of troubles coming their way. While the danger was not grave at the moment, it would become so soon. The Treaty of Fort Laramie, which established their current reservation, contained clauses with time limits that the Sioux had overlooked. The government had promised to clothe the tribe for thirty years but to feed them for only five years. Once that time was up, the Sioux were expected to be self-supporting, especially by farming the land. However, they were not currently feeding themselves on their own. Instead, they were obtaining most of their food at government agencies. For the last two years, Congress had paid for this food, but this generosity could stop at any moment. Grant warned the chiefs that the flow of food would definitely stop if fighting broke out between the Sioux and his own people.

Although he had tried to maintain peace, the president said, he could not do so for much longer. His restless people, who went anywhere they pleased, were now demanding to go into the Black Hills. If there were only a few of them, perhaps he could hold them back, but for every Indian, there were at least two hundred Americans, and the imbalance was growing. So many people were pouring into the Sioux Reservation since gold was discovered in the Black Hills that his soldiers could not keep them out. Fights would inevitably break out between the Indians and the miners who were overrunning the tribe's land. Soon the northern plains would be engulfed in a war without end for which neither side would be to blame.

As a friend of the Sioux, Grant wanted to prevent this nightmare. He urged the tribe to give up the Black Hills, guaranteed to them at Fort Laramie in 1868. He encouraged them to move south to a land where the climate was much better. There the grass was tall and the game, including buffalo, was plentiful. Although he did not mention the place by name, he was clearly describing the Indian Territory. Once they moved there, he would send teachers among them to show them how to become successful ranchers. He promised that he would not force them from their homeland against their will. But if they finally realized the danger coming their way and rightly decided to move, then he would do everything in his power to help them. He would even make sure that the next Great Father, meaning the man who succeeded him as president, would do the same.[13]

While they had listened politely, Red Cloud and his fellow chiefs were unimpressed with the case Grant had made. They took a copy of his speech with them on leaving the White House, even promising to study it, but they had no intention of selling the Black Hills or moving to the Indian Territory. In a later meeting with Grant on June 2, the chiefs refused to discuss another matter that the president pressed on them. Grant said that Congress wanted the Sioux to surrender their hunting grounds in Nebraska, which had been guaranteed to the tribe in the Fort Laramie Treaty. Under increasing pressure from the state's citizens, Congress was willing to pay $25,000 to the Sioux if they never hunted in Nebraska again. However, Red Cloud and Spotted Tail turned down the offer, saying they could not make an important decision like this without consulting all the Sioux in a formal council. When Grant still urged them to accept the deal, both men said they would if they were given the cash immediately. After the Indians left for home a few days later, Grant told Delano to send word after them that he would pay the Sioux an extra $25,000 if they accepted the offer. He would also send gifts, including a new horse, to every Indian who had just met with him in Washington.[14]

Grant's desperate attempt to win concessions from the tribe was roundly mocked in the nation's press. Instead of being called a peacemaker, he was now portrayed as an impostor who had been lying to the tribes all along. He had assumed the presidency claiming his new Indian policy would be more merciful than those of previous administrations. He would watch over the tribes, prevent their extinction, and protect them from harm, all the while slowly bringing them into full American citizenship. But after he tried to ply the Sioux with cash and a few extra gifts to surrender their hunting grounds in Nebraska, he seemed as much a liar as any other agent who sold food and blankets meant for the Indians and pocketed the profits. His determination to appoint a commission to buy the Black Hills from the Sioux confirmed this impression.[15]

In response to his critics, the president argued that he was acting in the only way possible to prevent a catastrophe on the northern plains, especially now that miners were crossing into the Sioux Reservation faster than the army could keep them out. Most miners continued to gather along French Creek where Custer had made his pronouncement of plentiful gold in the grass. Before long, the expedition of Jenny and Newton came to the same conclusion, reporting that Spring, Rapid, and Deadwood Creeks, along with Terry Peak, were "gold bearing." Even after all the precious metal had been taken out of the Black Hills, which the Smithsonian geologists estimated would not be any time soon, the richly timbered country of tall grass and rolling prairies was perfect for ranching.[16] Grant had made up his mind that the Sioux and the many people

The Web of Corruption

END OF THE BIG TALK AT WASHINGTON.
THE GREAT FATHER—"*Set your mark there, and 'twill be all right.*"
RED CLOUD (seeing Delano behind the President)—"*Never—except for cash!*"

Red Cloud's second visit to the White House. A less than heroic Red Cloud, shown here at the "end of the big talk at Washington," demands cash for the Black Hills instead of a check for $25,000 and the many trade goods that President Grant and a sly Columbus Delano offer him in the June 19, 1875, issue of *Frank Leslie's Illustrated Newspaper*. Grant actually offered $25,000 to Red Cloud for the surrender of the Sioux's hunting rights in Nebraska rather than for the purchase of the Black Hills. COURTESY OF THE LIBRARY OF CONGRESS.

racing west could never live peacefully side by side. The faith he had once had in such a possibility had been dashed in the Modoc and Red River Wars. The latest gold rush into the Sioux Reservation had confirmed to him just how dead this dream was. The only hope would be to appoint a commission, which Grant would choose with the help of Secretary Delano, to purchase the Black Hills from the Sioux. At some later time, the tribe could be moved to a safer location, preferably in the Indian Territory.[17]

If the pending negotiations were not enough to prove Grant a fraud to his many detractors, then the scandals currently rocking his administration, especially those impacting the Indian service, certainly were. Secretary Delano had tried for more than a year to squelch the first scandal to hit the Office of Indian Affairs since Congress investigated Ely Parker. Late in 1873, William Welsh, who had stayed in contact with the Board of Indian Commissioners, accused Edward Parmelee Smith of committing the same kind of fraud that he had once accused Ely Parker of committing. Determined as ever to ferret out the activities of the nebulous Indian Ring, he claimed to have dozens of witnesses ready to testify that Reverend Smith had canceled contracts to buy and transport goods that the Board of Indian Commissioners had already approved. He also accused Smith of negotiating several lucrative contracts without the board's approval, undoubtedly to line his own pockets. After leaking the story to the *Saint Paul Dispatch*, Welsh published a pamphlet detailing the wrongdoing of the supposedly sterling Smith. Delano challenged both Welsh and the newspaper editor to prove their charges. He called them and their supposed witnesses before a committee set up in the Interior Department to investigate the matter. After hearing from several people in February 1874 who claimed they had no knowledge of any corruption in the Indian service, Reverend Smith was exonerated while William Welsh was publicly humiliated.[18]

The outcome did not please Felix Brunot, who was still serving as the board's chairman. Like Welsh, he believed corruption ran deep in the Office of Indian Affairs. He blamed much of the trouble on the fact that the Indian service had been wrongly housed within the Interior Department. Since matters dealing with the tribes were critical to the nation, Brunot proposed establishing the Office of Indian Affairs as a separate cabinet-level department with an "officer of high ability" as its head. In March 1874, he met first with Delano and then with Grant, asking them to make a formal request to Congress to establish the Department of Indian Affairs. When both men refused, saying that such a request would never pass Congress, Felix Brunot and the rest of the original commissioners promptly resigned.

In their formal letter of resignation delivered to Grant two months later, they assured the president that they still respected the "honorable intentions" of his Indian policy. They appreciated the fact that Grant had always treated them kindly and supported their every effort to root out corruption. More important, he had done his best to save the tribes from certain destruction, even though Congress, many Americans, and the wildest "savages" worked against him. When the president refused to establish a new cabinet post for Indian affairs, however, the commissioners had no choice but to resign. They added that they were quitting because Congress had just required the board to review all purchases for the Indians in Washington, DC. None of the commissioners, who ran businesses in other parts of the country, were willing to move to the nation's capital to fulfill their duties. In their final farewell, they admitted that perhaps it was impossible after all, as Ely Parker had previously noted, for the Board of Indian Commissioners to wield power equal to but independent from top officials in the Interior Department.[19]

The wealthy men who took their places on the board were just as determined to run the Office of Indian Affairs as the departed commissioners. Clinton B. Fisk, a banker who had served as a brigadier general in the Union army and former assistant director of the Freedmen's Bureau, took over as the chairman. He was joined by Henry Hasting Sibley, the former governor of Minnesota, who was now a banker in St. Paul; Charles G. Hammond of Chicago, a founder of the Union Pacific Railroad; and William Stickney, the director of the National Savings Bank in Washington, DC. The new board members welcomed the responsibility of investigating charges of wrongdoing at several Indian agencies. Their first major assignment came in 1875, when they were given the task of organizing the investigation into the complaints of Red Cloud and Spotted Tail against their agent, John Saville.

They ultimately found no wrongdoing in the Office of Indian Affairs but recommended the removal of Saville and several contractors. However, they were not as impressed with the president as their predecessors had been. They showed their displeasure in their annual reports, which contained far more criticism of Grant's Indian policy than praise, specifically about the dangerous laxness in its implementation. First and foremost, compulsory education had not been instituted for Indian children, even though this had been promised in several treaties. Just as bad, the men of the wildest tribes were not required to work in exchange for food, although Congress had mandated it. Finally, for all the glowing talk of the future of the Indian Territory, the place remained essentially lawless.[20]

The embarrassment caused by the board's observations paled in comparison to the scandal that engulfed Secretary Delano in the summer of 1875. Delano had been facing accusations for several months that he allegedly oversaw a private slush fund for his son John, who worked in the Interior Department. According to newspaper reports, the younger Delano was receiving kickbacks from several operations in the West that his father, as the secretary of the interior, supervised. It was said that he was accepting bribes from buyers of land in the Colorado

Territory to secure their patents. The second accusation was that he had been made a partner of mines throughout the Wyoming Territory, even though he had made no investments in these businesses. Third, and most devastating, was the allegation that he had listed himself as a government surveyor on sham contracts that paid him at the rate of $10 a mile. Money for the fraudulent surveys was placed in the account of a banker friend of the Delano family in St. Paul named Mr. Merriman. Dr. Silas Reed, the nation's surveyor general, was also supposedly in on the scheme. He told Columbus Delano, his supervisor in the Interior Department, that he was "doing a good thing for John." When newspapers printed Delano's response, "Be careful to do nothing that would have the semblance of wrong," many in Congress, the wider public, and Grant's own cabinet demanded his firing.[21]

The scandal reached a fever pitch just as the president chose the members of the commission to negotiate the purchase of the Black Hills from the Sioux. Senator William Allison, a Republican from Iowa, was appointed the delegation's chair. At his side were Frank Wayland Palmer, a former Republican congressman from Iowa currently living in Chicago; Abram Comingo, a former Democratic congressman from Missouri who now practiced law in Independence; Reverend Samuel Dutton Hinman, an Episcopalian missionary to the Santee who knew the Sioux language; General Terry, who as commander of the army's Department of Dakota was already deeply involved in the troubles of the Sioux Country; Geminien Beauvais, a friend of Missouri's Democratic senator Lewis Bogy and formerly a fur trader among the Sioux; William H. Ashby, an ex-Confederate who had set up a law practice in Nebraska after the Civil War and was well respected by local politicians of both parties; Albert G. Lawrence of Rhode Island, who had served as the minister to Costa Rica during the Johnson administration; and John Collins, Grant's personal emissary to the Sioux, as the commission's secretary.[22]

With the Allison Commission on its way west in late August 1875, Grant still hoped the American people would see his attempt to purchase the Black Hills from the Sioux as honorable. He believed his formal instructions to the commissioners, delivered to them by Reverend Smith, proved his good intentions. He reminded the commissioners that these were not treaty negotiations, since Congress had abandoned the treaty system. The Sioux could not be regarded as a sovereign state; they were wards of the nation. The commissioners must therefore negotiate on behalf of the Indians as well as the United States. More specifically, they were to ask for the cession of the Black Hills with the exact borders of the surrendered country to be determined later by Grant himself. They also had to ask for the cession of the Bighorn Mountains in Wyoming, which would allow access to the Black Hills from the west. They were to offer no specific sum for either place but were instead to assure the tribes that they would receive a "fair equivalent" for the two valuable territories. Throughout the negotiations, the commissioners were to inform the Sioux that their instructions had come directly from Ulysses Grant, the Great Father himself. They had to remind them, too, that Grant was not all powerful but would have to submit any final decision to Congress.

The negotiations opened on September 20, 1875, along the White River eight miles east of the Red Cloud Agency. The Sioux had finally agreed to surrender their right to hunt in in Nebraska, but they were clearly in no mood to sell any of their territory. Red Cloud and Spotted Tail arrived with most of their people, but many Sioux bands stayed away from the council. Sitting Bull, the most influential Hunkpapa chief, said that as long as there was game to feed his people, he would never meet with the white man. The highly respected Oglala warrior Crazy Horse agreed with him and also refused to come to the council. Still, there were enough warriors present, anywhere from five thousand to ten thousand, that several commissioners, remembering what had happened to General Canby, were terrified. They refused to send their cavalry escort away, even though Red Cloud demanded their departure.

Surrounded by young men on horseback, all painted and dressed for war, the commissioners wavered in their resolve, arguing among themselves about how to approach the obviously hostile Indians. They were certain the Sioux would never sell the Bighorn Mountains to the government, but what offer would they accept? Even if they could get the top chiefs to sell the Black Hills, how would they ever get three-quarters of the adult men of the tribe to approve the sale, which was a requirement of the Treaty of Fort Laramie? Should they instead simply offer to buy the mining rights to the region? If they did, how could they ever convince the Indians that the Americans would leave their country when the gold was gone?

The commissioners finally decided to ask the Sioux to lease the Black Hills to the United States. Two days after the offer was made, the chiefs, who had gathered in separate councils to discuss the proposal, finally responded. They would gladly sell the Black Hills, but only if the government promised to supply them for seven generations. Red Cloud gave a specific list of the items that the Indians required. They must have Texas steer and the "best kind" of flour, coffee, sugar, tea, and bacon that money could buy. Their "old people" must have rice, cracked corn, dried apples, salt, pepper, soap, tobacco, and baking soda to make bread. For himself, Red Cloud must have a wagon, fine horses to pull it, and working cattle. Every Sioux family had to receive a boar, cow, bull, ram,

Sitting Bull. The Hunkpapa chief, who led the resistance to Grant's efforts to conquer the Black Hills, was both a great warrior and a visionary. COURTESY OF THE LIBRARY OF CONGRESS.

ewe, hen, and rooster. They also had to have houses like the white man's, filled with wooden chairs and bedsteads. The Sioux needed a sawmill, too, plus a mower and a scythe. Other chiefs demanded even more goods, including clothes, knives, horses, powder, and lead. Red Cloud asked for two final things from the government: Catholic missionaries had to be sent to the Sioux, replacing the Episcopalians who had previously been assigned, and the government must keep whiskey away from the tribe. Looking at the stunned commissioners, Red Cloud concluded, "Maybe you think that I ask too much from the Government, but I think those hills extend to the sky—maybe they go above the sky, and that is the reason I ask so much." Spotted Tail, putting the matter more directly, simply said, "As long as we live on this earth we will expect pay."

In response to the detailed demands of the two chiefs, the commissioners made two counteroffers. If the Sioux leased mining rights in the Black Hills, the government would pay the tribe $400,000 a year as long as the lease ran. If they sold the Black Hills, the Sioux would receive $6,000,000 paid in fifteen annual installments. No matter what the tribe decided, if Congress approved the deal, three-quarters of the adult men of the Sioux would have to sign the agreement.

After the Sioux turned down both offers, the commissioners headed home in late September, trying to understand what had gone wrong. Their biggest regret was not having brought presents with them to the council. Their high-minded contemporaries might look back cynically at negotiators in the past who offered gifts to the chiefs, but this sadly was the only way to win agreements with the Indians. The commissioners also regretted that they had met with all the Sioux instead of only a few select leaders. This, too, had been a longtime recommendation of the Board of Indian Commissioners, who believed it was more democratic to negotiate with an entire tribe rather than a handful of chiefs. But meeting with thousands of Indians, rather than just a handful, only increased the chances of not reaching an agreement. However, the commissioners concluded that no price would have been acceptable to the Sioux, since the tribe valued the Black Hills too much to sell them. They advised the president to have Congress set a fair price for the land, considering its value from the points of view of both the Sioux and the United States, and then present the decision to the tribe as a "finality."[23]

News of the commission's failure came at the very moment that Grant finally accepted Delano's resignation. Although he had failed to defend his friend Ely Parker against charges of corruption, he remained faithful to his interior secretary to the end. Delano had tried to resign for a year, but Grant had refused to accept the offer. He explained his resistance in military terms, saying that no soldier should ever retreat from the battlefield while under fire. Even now, when he finally took the resignation, he did so grudgingly, complaining that Delano had been wrongly hounded out of office by the press. In his final letter to Grant, Delano said he had tried to be a good administrator, even though his duties in the Interior Department were "laborious, difficult, and delicate." The job was simply too big for any one man. The secretary of the interior was expected to oversee the land office, patents, education, pensions, mines, and most troublesome of all, the operations of the Indian Bureau, a truly "intricate, delicate, and vexatious business."

The Web of Corruption

Delano took some comfort in the fact that Grant understood how difficult it was to manage Indian affairs in a large nation with many tribes governed by treaties that stretched back a hundred years. It was simply impossible to prevent corruption in so vast a country. With hundreds of empty miles between reservations, how could anyone expect Indian agents, who were lonely, unsupervised, and poorly paid, to remain honest? No wonder many of them gave in to temptations that even the strongest men could not resist. Delano also knew Grant realized that no matter what decision was made regarding the Indians, not everyone would be happy. There were so many competing interests within the tribes and between the Indians and the government that every decision was condemned by someone. Leaving the troubles of the Interior Department behind, and escaping the scandal involving his son, Columbus Delano retired to his farm in Mount Vernon, Ohio.[24]

Grant chose Zechariah Chandler, a Republican politician from Michigan who had recently lost his Senate seat, as the new secretary of the interior. Many considered Chandler little more than a political hack, but he surprised everyone with his zeal for cleaning house. He went to work immediately to weed out corruption. After auditing each division within the Interior Department, he fired all the clerks in the Patent Office. When he tried to do the same in the Office of Indian Affairs, Reverend Smith protested, saying that even if some of the clerks were corrupt, he could not function without them. Chandler turned for help to Grant, who advised him to lock the doors after the clerks went home at night and refuse to let them back in again.[25]

A short time later, when Reverend Smith resigned his position to assume the presidency of Howard University, Chandler recommended John Quincy Smith, a Republican from Ohio who had also lost his seat in Congress, as the new commissioner of Indian affairs. Like Chandler, Smith had no stomach for corruption in the Indian service. The two men agreed to stop paying the many attorneys who demanded money for performing services on behalf of the Indians, like General Blunt had once done for the Quapaw. If the tribes needed legal counsel, Chandler and Smith said they would get it for them in the Justice Department. While both men promised to implement Grant's Indian policy, neither had much sympathy for the tribes, especially "wild" ones like the Sioux. Chandler also disliked the more advanced Indians who refused to give up their tribal identity, while Smith introduced racially charged terms taken from the popular science of the day into departmental language denigrating the tribes. In contradiction to everything Grant had hoped to achieve, Smith wondered how the red man, "unintelligent, ignorant, and uncivilized," and thus low on the evolutionary chain, could ever rise to the level of "Anglo Saxon" civilization.[26]

The Web of Corruption

In fact, by the time Chandler and Smith were appointed, the light had gone out of Grant's Indian policy. He believed his fellow citizens had caused the turmoil in the Dakota Territory, but he sided with them in their determination to take the Black Hills away from the Sioux. In his opinion, he had tried his best to defend the tribe, but after Red Cloud and Spotted Tail refused to sell or lease the Black Hills, he could no longer protect them. He blamed younger individuals such as Sitting Bull, Crazy Horse, Black Moon, Rain in the Face, and Afraid of His Horses, all of whom lived much of the year in Montana, for disrupting the negotiations in the previous summer. If not for them, Grant insisted, older men such as Red Cloud and Spotted Tail might have made a deal with the government.

On November 3, 1875, Grant called a meeting at the White House to lay out a strategy for taking the Black Hills away from the Sioux and subduing any resistance. Generals Sheridan and Crook were present, along with Secretary Chandler and Reverend Smith, who would resign his post within the week. The president told these men that his order to evict miners from the Black Hills would remain in place, but Sheridan was to pass the word to his commanders that this order was not to be enforced. Grant also said that he would make no public pronouncement that he had abandoned this position. He defended this policy reversal on the grounds that restricting the miners had only increased their avarice and thus made the situation more dangerous. All Sioux bands wandering freely on the northern plains would be ordered to attach themselves to the Red Cloud, Pine Ridge, Rosebud, Spotted Tail, or Standing Rock Agency by January 31, 1876. If any chiefs or warriors refused to report by the deadline, Grant said, the army should launch a winter campaign against them.[27]

With no soldiers stopping them, miners flooded into the Black Hills. Overnight, the town of Custer, founded near French Creek where the 7th Cavalry first discovered gold, had eleven thousand inhabitants. Hundreds of miners headed north after another strike was made in a canyon near Deadwood Gulch. Within just a few weeks, five thousand people were living in the wild frontier town of Deadwood. The move against any Sioux not attached to an agency went just as swiftly. One month to the day after the White House meeting, Secretary Chandler ordered agents to notify Sitting Bull's Hunkpapa, along with "all other wild and lawless bands of Sioux Indians residing without the bounds of their reservation," to come into an agency by January 31. One week to the day after the deadline passed, General Sheridan received orders from the War Department to move against Sitting Bull and the other chiefs and warriors living with their people west of the Black Hills in the river valleys of Montana.[28]

Sheridan organized the army for the conflict that would become known as the Great Sioux War. He used the same plan he had implemented during the Red River War. His soldiers were to move from three directions toward the Sioux, Cheyenne, and Arapaho camps along the Yellowstone and Bighorn Rivers. Colonel John Gibbon would lead cavalry and infantry companies east from Fort Shaw and Fort Ellis. His men would come down the Yellowstone and prevent the Sioux from retreating farther south. Lieutenant Colonel Custer would bring his 7th Cavalry west from Fort Abraham Lincoln, pushing hostile bands ahead of him toward the Little Missouri River, where scouts had spotted Sitting Bull and his people. General Crook would lead a column of cavalry and infantry north from Fort Fetterman in the Wyoming Territory, pressing Sioux, Cheyenne, and Arapaho warriors toward the headwaters of the Powder River.

One of the worst winters on the northern plains in living memory disrupted the army's carefully laid plans. Only Colonel Gibbon's troops made it through the deep snow to their rendezvous point. They arrived at the juncture of the Yellowstone and Bighorn Rivers but found no Indians anywhere, even after sending out several patrols. The weather turned so terrible back east in the Dakota Territory that General Terry refused to let Custer's cavalry leave Fort Abraham Lincoln. He called the march off, too, because Sitting Bull had moved his people two hundred miles west. General Crook led his men through deep snow and freezing temperatures into the Powder River Valley. They attacked an Indian village, made up largely of Oglala and Cheyenne, but were thrown back by warriors, leaving six soldiers dead and a herd of stolen ponies lost during the retreat. He ordered his column back toward Wyoming.[29]

The harsh weather and failed attack on the Indian village were not the only problems plaguing the campaign against the Sioux. Just as during the previous summer, when the scandal around Columbus Delano overshadowed the negotiations for the Black Hills, so now shocking accusations of corruption against Secretary of War Belknap further hampered the military's efforts in the Sioux Country. News of the latest scandal to rock the Grant administration could actually be traced to the army's troubles in the winter of 1876. Lieutenant Colonel Custer, who had been prevented from heading west by his commander General Terry, took leave to go to New York City. Here he regaled his friend James Gordon Bennett, the publisher of the *New York Herald*, with rumors about Belknap's questionable management of trading posts throughout the West. According to Custer, Belknap appointed traders only if they paid him a cut of the profits. He also implicated the president's brother Orvil in the corrupt scheme.

Bennett immediately penned an editorial titled "Extravagance and Corruption in the War Department," which called for a congressional investigation into Belknap's shady dealings. Both the House and Senate, now controlled by the Democrats, agreed. Ten days after Bennett published his editorial, the House

Committee on Expenditures in the War Department opened an investigation into kickbacks allegedly coming Belknap's way. The star witness, Caleb Marsh, who shared the tradership at Fort Sill in the Indian Territory with John Evans, gave the committee enough evidence to recommend Belknap's impeachment. Marsh admitted that he had made quarterly payments to the secretary of war from profits at the trading post. He explained how Belknap's wife, Carrie, had set up the deal. She had obtained a joint tradership for Marsh at Fort Sill on the condition that he share the profits with her husband. Marsh claimed that Evans, who actually ran the day-to-day operations at the post, paid him upward of $12,000 a year. He, in turn, paid half of this amount in quarterly installments to Belknap. He estimated that so far he had paid $20,000 to the secretary of war. What made the scandal even more shocking was that because of the corruption, Evans had to raise prices at the trading post higher than any soldier, Indian, or settler could afford to pay.[30]

On March 2, 1876, just hours before the scheduled House vote on his impeachment, Belknap raced to the White House and tendered his resignation to President Grant. Ignoring the fact that he no longer worked for the government, the House voted to impeach the former secretary of war, and the Senate took up his trial. Belknap escaped a final conviction when a majority of Senators, including Democrats as well as Republicans, refused to find an official who had resigned his post guilty of any crime. But the scandal continued when Custer testified before several congressional committees about wrongdoing in the Indian service throughout the West. As he had done with Bennett, he passed along every rumor he had heard about wrongdoing at agencies and trading posts, especially how corrupt officials, including Orvil Grant, sold high-quality goods meant for the Indians, pocketed the profits, and supplied the tribes with the cheapest items they could find.

Custer's testimony added to his criticism of the president already contained in his memoir, *My Life on the Plains*, which had recently been published in the *Galaxy* magazine. In this work, Custer stated that he respected Colonel Ely Parker, a man who, in his opinion, understood that the military should be in charge of Indian affairs, but loathed the Quaker policy that Grant foisted on his first Indian commissioner. Custer could not understand how anyone in his right mind could expect missionaries to handle the likes of Sitting Bull or Crazy Horse. Custer's latest round of attacks came during a trying time for the president. Not only had Belknap resigned, but so had Orville Babcock, Grant's personal secretary. Babcock had just been acquitted of taking bribes in the Whiskey Ring scandal but faced new charges of harassing officials who investigated him. Reports also surfaced that Secretary of the Navy George Robeson had pocketed $15,000,000 in questionable contracts. With his administration awash in scandal, the president took his frustration out on Lieutenant Colonel Custer, whom he fired as the commander of the 7th Cavalry and thus as the leader of one of Sheridan's columns.[31]

But though Custer had been dismissed, Grant still believed the army's three-pronged strategy would defeat the last roving bands of Sioux, Cheyenne, and Arapaho in the Montana Territory. He took more interest in the upcoming campaign than he had demonstrated in either the Modoc or Red River War. Sheridan once again moved the army out in three directions in the spring of 1876. Gibbon would head south from his winter camp through the Bighorn River Valley, while Crook would come north from Wyoming. Terry, not Custer, would lead the third column west from Fort Abraham Lincoln. However, Custer would once again be in charge of the 7th Cavalry as part of Terry's column. He had sent a letter to the president reminding him how terrible it was for a commander to see his soldiers marching off without him. Grant, remembering his own humiliation after the Battle of Shiloh, forgave Custer and restored him to his command.[32]

Despite warmer weather, the campaign went just as badly in late June as it had in the deep snow of the previous winter. On the seventeenth, Crook's column of 1,300 men was ambushed along Rosebud Creek by three times as many Sioux and Cheyenne warriors under the command of Crazy Horse. If not for the Crow and Shoshone scouts who threw back the initial attack at the front of his column, Crook's entire force might have been massacred on the spot. Having lost nearly a hundred men killed or wounded, Crook retreated again toward Wyoming. Custer was not so lucky. Terry had sent him ahead with 600 men to scout for Indians camped along the Little Bighorn River. He was to cut off their escape to the south when Terry and rest of the column attacked from the north. On June 25, after spotting what he believed was a small village, and fearing that the Indians had discovered his trail and thus might flee, Custer decided to attack. Splitting his regiment in three, he sent Captain Frederick Benteen to search for more Indians in the ravines farther to the east, while Major Marcus Reno would cross the river and attack the lower end of the village. Custer would take the remaining 210 men into the bluffs farther west and turn south to attack the upper end of the Indian camp.

Custer realized too late that he had stumbled onto the largest gathering of Indians on the northern plains in recorded history. As many as ten thousand Sioux, Arapaho, and Cheyenne had set up a huge camp stretching for three miles along the southern bank of the Little Bighorn. At least one-third of them were warriors. The Indians had been gathering near the place they called Greasy

The Web of Corruption

Custer's Last Stand. The massacre of Custer's soldiers at the Little Bighorn, described here as *Custer's Last Charge*, came as a shock to many Americans who were just beginning the celebration of their nation's centennial in the summer of 1876. COURTESY OF THE LIBRARY OF CONGRESS.

Grass since the early spring, knowing all the while that they had to remain close together because soldiers were coming their way. Besides, this was the traditional meeting held every summer among the tribes on the northern plains. Here they attended councils to decide their future plans, hunted buffalo and visited with relatives, and most important, participated in the Sun Dance. Sitting Bull had a vision during one of these ceremonies in which he saw soldiers dressed in blue falling from the sky. He said this meant that the many Indians warriors gathered along the Little Bighorn would soon defeat the American army. The Sioux, along with their Cheyenne and Arapaho allies, thus were ready for Custer's surprise attack.

As soon as Reno's men crossed the Little Bighorn on their way toward the southern end of the Indian camp, hundreds of mounted Indians confronted them, quickly pushing the soldiers back over the river and into the surrounding hills. Many more warriors hurried to the northern bank of the Little Bighorn to take on Custer's men, who were now fleeing as fast as they could ride or run away from the Indian camp. The Indians chased the troops over the hills and ravines, shooting bullets and arrows at them and clubbing many to death. Custer and the last survivors raced up a small embankment known afterward as Last Stand Hill. According to legend, after everyone else was killed, Custer died at the hands of Crazy Horse, who shot him once in the head and again in the chest. The battle had taken no more than an hour. Four miles to the east, Reno and his retreating soldiers united with Benteen and his troops, and together they fought off the attacking Indians until Terry brought the rest of the column to their rescue two days later.[33]

Word of Custer's Last Stand, as newspapers soon described the massacre, arrived back east on July 4, 1876, the official start of the nation's yearlong centennial celebration. Grant was one of the few Americans who did not blame the Indians for the massacre of the 7th Cavalry. He held Custer personally responsible for the debacle. In a rare interview he gave to the *New York Herald*, the paper that had humiliated him over the Belknap scandal just months before, he boldly asserted, "I regard Custer's massacre as a sacrifice of troops, brought on by Custer himself that was wholly unnecessary, wholly unnecessary." In contrast to a skilled commander like General Crook, who was as "wily as Sitting Bull" and thus knew when to retreat, Custer had disobeyed Terry's orders to scout the camp and instead attacked the Indians even though he was outnumbered ten to one. Ignoring the hysteria sweeping the nation, Grant remained certain that Sheridan's strategy was working. The army would soon round up the rest of the Sioux and their allies. No matter where the tribe finally ended up, whether farther down the Missouri or in the Indian Territory, a "military barrier" would be placed around them. They would no longer be able to come into an agency for food and guns only to wander away, meet up with hostile bands from other tribes, and then attack settlers and soldiers at will. Grant promised, "All this play is to be stopped."[34]

The "play" of the Sioux, as Grant named the tribe's resistance, came quickly to an end after the Battle of the Little Bighorn. The three columns of soldiers that Sheridan had sent against them finally forced most chiefs to surrender with their people at agencies throughout the Sioux Reservation. While Sitting Bull escaped to Canada and Crazy Horse held out for another year, they were mere afterthoughts to Grant's conquest of the Black Hills, which he sought even more relentlessly after Custer's massacre. He chose George Manypenny, who had served as the commissioner of Indian affairs during the 1850s, as the lead negotiator to meet with the Sioux and get their signatures on an agreement, which Grant now defiantly called a treaty. They had no choice. They had to surrender the Black Hills to the United States. Manypenny was famous for having won

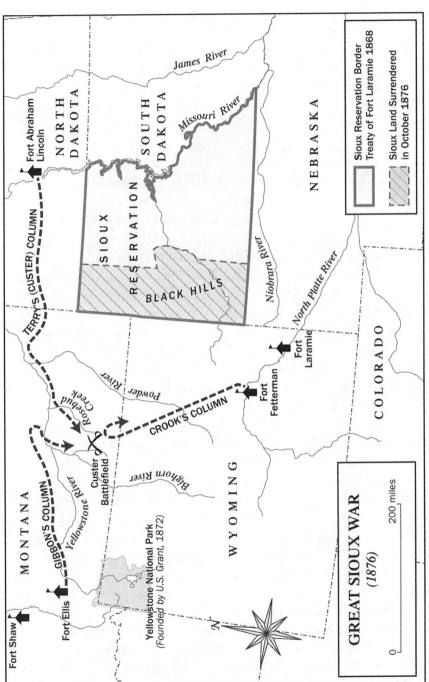

Great Sioux War (1876). The map shows the army's three-pronged strategy for fighting the Sioux in 1876, along with the reduction of the tribe's territory as a result of the agreement signed at the end of the war. COPYRIGHT © ROBERTA STOCKWELL, 2018.

land in Kansas from eastern tribes forced west as a result of Jackson's Indian Removal Act. Most had sold their land to the government in exchange for small allotments and American citizenship.[35]

With a few other commissioners at his side, most notably Bishop Whipple, Manypenny traveled in September and October 1876 from one agency to another on the Sioux Reservation to win back much of the land guaranteed to the tribe in the Fort Laramie Treaty. Manypenny would long remember sitting with his fellow commissioners, "our cheeks crimsoned with shame," as they listened to one chief after another ask how Ulysses Grant, their Great Father, could do this terrible injustice to them. A chief whose name they did not record said it best: "If you white men had a country that was very valuable, which had always belonged to your people, and which the Great Father had promised should be yours forever, and men of another race came to take it away by force, what would your people do? Would they fight?"[36]

According to the treaty, which Red Cloud and 227 chiefs and headmen of the Oglala, Brulé, Blackfeet, Hunkpapa, Upper and Lower Yankton, Sans Arc, Miniconjou, Two Kettles, and Cheyenne signed in late October 1876, the Sioux gave up the Black Hills and their claims to unceded land in Montana and Wyoming. They retained a reduced reservation in the Dakota Territory but had to promise that they would allow wagon trains to cross it unmolested. The government, in turn, promised that all the annuities due the tribe would still be paid. Every person would receive daily rations, including 1½ pounds of beef or ½ pound of bacon plus ½ pound of corn, with those same individual rations delivered to heads of households. For every hundred rations, the Sioux would also receive four pounds of coffee, eight pounds of sugar, and three pounds of beans. Schools would likewise be built for the children on the Sioux Reservation as originally promised in the 1868 Treaty of Fort Laramie.

If the Sioux wished to move to the Indian Territory, the government would provide escorts for five or more of their principal chiefs to visit the place and choose the best location for a new reservation. The tribe would also receive any help necessary to become self-supporting and thus "live like white men." The principal chiefs and the heads of families who moved to the Indian Territory would have houses built for them by the government. To improve the morals of the Indians, only married agents and other workers, along with their wives and children, would be allowed to live with the Sioux. All half-breeds, who had been labeled as troublemakers by government negotiators as well as the Board of Indian Commissioners, would be banished from the reservations. Finally, the Indians promised to abide by all the new rules and also allow a yearly census of the tribe every December.[37]

As the treaty made its way through Congress, in the late fall of 1876, Grant prepared his final State of the Union address. For the first time in eight years, he had almost nothing to say about the "original occupants of this land." He mentioned the recent troubles in the Dakota Territory in passing, blaming the commotion on the greed of miners. They were so determined to win every last ounce of gold in the West that he could never have sent enough soldiers to hold them back. He had no choice but to win the Black Hills for them. As to the Indians, he had only two things to add: his treatment of them had always been "humane," and he had finally ended the bloody conflicts that long plagued the West. That he had launched a war against the Sioux to take the Black Hills away from them, even though the sacred land had been promised to the tribe at Fort Laramie, was the unspoken truth missing between these two points.

With either Samuel Tilden or Rutherford B. Hayes on his way to the White House, Grant no longer felt the need to explain or defend his Indian policy. Nor did he try any longer to embrace the nickname of "peace policy" for his approach. After trying for years to treat the Indians with greater respect than any president had all the way back to Washington, he had nothing more to say. He could offer no reason why his plans for the Indians had come undone, no analysis of why the policy he crafted on their behalf had been impossible to implement, and no advice for future Great Fathers. After so much effort, and so many words, there was now only silence.[38]

9. A Forgotten Legacy

Despite what Grant had said in his final State of the Union address, peace did not reign in the West, for the Indian Wars were far from over. Just before he left office in March 1877, Grant demanded that the Nez Perce give up their traditional homeland in Washington's Wallowa Valley and move to an arid reservation in the Idaho Territory. By year's end, with President Hayes now serving as the new Great Father, a Nez Perce leader named Inmuttooyahlatlat, better known as Chief Joseph, fled with his people from the desolate place. The Nez Perce raced more than a thousand miles along a circuitous route toward Canada before surrendering to General O. O. Howard just short of the border. The Ponca, a tribe from the northern plains who had been forced onto a reservation in the Indian Territory in the last days of Grant's presidency, died there in record numbers from hunger and malaria. The Northern Cheyenne, who were moved south to the Indian Territory after the Great Sioux War, bolted from their reservation with another army pursuing them. The Ute battled soldiers in Colorado, while the Bannock fought them in Idaho. Geronimo and his Apache bands kept up their resistance for another ten years before finally surrendering in 1887. Three years later, during another terrible winter of deep snow and freezing temperatures in the Dakota Territory, soldiers at Wounded Knee Creek murdered hundreds of Sioux whose only crime was believing, like the Modoc once did, that they could meet their dead relatives in a Ghost Dance.[1]

Ignoring the troubles in what remained of the Indian country, Grant likewise never looked back at how his actions may have contributed to the continuing unrest. He knew that he had come into office with a coherent plan to save the tribes from extermination. They would be placed on reservations where the army would protect them from harm. Here the American government would supply their every need and wait patiently for the day when they transformed themselves into hardworking farmers and ranchers. Even when his plans to have the army manage the reservations were overturned, and he assigned missionaries to take their place, he never gave up the dream that one day the Sioux, Cheyenne,

Arapaho, Comanche, Modoc, Navajo, Apache, and all the other tribes would become citizens of the United States. They would be the equals of people like himself who could trace their families back to colonial times, the many immigrants pouring into the country each day, and the descendants of African slaves whom he had helped set free as the commander of the Union army.

Facing great resistance from Congress and the Board of Indian Commissioners, as well as his own citizens, Grant came to doubt that Indians could live safely on reservations with the press of settlers around them. There was simply too much hostility and resentment on both sides. Americans had to have their mines, railroads, ranches, farms, and towns wherever they pleased no matter what Indians had to be moved out of their way. If warriors struck back at them, they had to avenge every person killed, every child taken, and every outpost burned to the ground. The Indians were just as determined to retaliate against their losses. Grant saw the outlines of the hopeless conflict most clearly after the Modoc gunned down General Canby and Quanah Parker's warriors attacked the buffalo hunters at Adobe Walls. His new awareness drove him to launch the Great Sioux War and lay the groundwork for conflicts that played out after he left the White House.

Ultimately, Grant decided the only solution was to move all the tribes to the Indian Territory. Here they would learn to live as the white man, the common expression of the day for the expected transformation of the Indians. However, he did not believe that this meant stripping every ounce of what it meant to be an Indian away from the tribes. For Grant, the change that had to occur was primarily in their livelihood. The days of the Sioux hunting buffalo and antelope, the Modoc and Klamath gathering the seeds of the water lily, and the Apache raiding and killing on the desert floor were over. If the tribes finally accepted this inevitability and moved to the Indian Territory, then they could farm, ranch, or set up any kind of business they wanted. They could send their children to school to learn how to support themselves in the modern world, just as he had learned to make a living as a soldier, farmer, and storekeeper. Most important, once the tribes were safe in the Indian Territory, they could take the even greater step of governing themselves, first as a territory and then as a state in the Union that he had saved as a general in the Civil War.

Yet all this was forgotten immediately after Ulysses Grant left office. If politicians or scholars took the time to remember his plans for the Indians, they reduced their discussion to two main issues: First, was Grant's "peace policy" truly peaceful? Second, what motivated him to establish a "Quaker policy" that placed the Society of Friends in charge of the reservations? As to the first question, Grant's Indian policy was generally dismissed as hypocritical for talking peace while prosecuting the most memorable Indian wars in American history, including those against the Modoc, the Comanche and their allies, and especially the Sioux. No one considered the reflection that had gone into his policy, even before he assumed office, nor did anyone analyze its continuing development as his original goals met resistance along the way. Similarly, his plan to use the army to run the Indian service, for reasons that he clearly stated in speeches early in his presidency, was ignored.

The fact that Grant appointed Quaker agents as a courtesy at the start of his administration, and later chose missionaries to run reservations only after Congress banned soldiers from government positions, disappeared from both contemporary studies and historical narratives about his presidency. From the time he left office until quite recently, Grant remained a "circumstantial" reformer at best or a clueless tool of powerful forces he could not control at worst. Even contemporary historians, who have tried to evaluate his Indian policy more positively, particularly noting its similarities to his defense of the freedmen, still wrongly assume he turned first to the Quakers, rather than to the army, to help him rescue the far western tribes from certain destruction.[2]

For his part, Grant showed no interest in debates over how he treated the Indians. He stopped explaining and defending his policy after the Great Sioux War. When he penned his *Personal Memoirs*, he wrote a few details about his family's history, his early life, and his sympathy for the Indians he met as a young soldier, but he spent most of the book remembering every last detail of his time fighting in the Civil War. In some ways, this was only fitting, for at the end of his presidency, after serving as the most powerful civilian leader of his country, he became a soldier once again as he fought the Sioux, Cheyenne, and Arapaho for control of the Black Hills. The man who was so tired of war when he assumed office, and who wanted to treat the Indians with the respect that they had not known since the founding of his nation, took up the sword again after so many of his plans for them had failed.

Although Ulysses Grant wrote nothing more about his Indian policy in his memoirs, the debate over the "Indian question" and where the Indian service should reside went on after he set off on a world tour in the spring of 1877. Talk of moving the Office of Indian Affairs from the Interior Department back to the War Department had been going on since before Grant became president. While Grant's every attempt to make this move failed, including a final try at the start of the Great Sioux War, many current and former army officers continued making the same arguments. Soldiers were already stationed throughout the West. They were experienced in Indian warfare, but more important, they knew the Indian country and the Indian character better than anyone. Their well-regulated supply system could be easily adapted for delivering goods to the tribes with little chance of graft. A soldier also had his "military reputation and commission" to keep him in line. By contrast, a civilian was merely a "temporary officer of the government" and for all practical purposes "exempt from trial and punishment for misconduct." A soldier, unlike a civilian, could be convicted for conduct "unbecoming to a gentleman, or prejudicial to good order." Placing the office back in the War Department, where it had been in the early years of the nation, would thus resolve the Indian question.[3]

The Board of Indian Commissioners, along with growing numbers of reformers who styled themselves as friends of the Indians, blocked every attempt to place soldiers in charge of reservations. They were just as adamant in their arguments for keeping the Indian service in the Interior Department, despite the many scandals that came to light during Grant's presidency, as those advocating military control of the agencies. The Indians, "with scarcely an exception," were opposed to the army. The thought of soldiers running reservations brought images to mind of Colonel Custer's raid on Black Kettle's camp on the Washita River and General Howard's army stalking Chief Joseph's Nez Perce through the northern Rockies. The mere possibility of soldiers heading onto reservations was enough to set off more resistance and more wars. If anything, the move would slow the advancement of the tribes. Furthermore, it was cheaper to continue using missionaries as agents because they were steadier individuals than soldiers who were prone to drunkenness and immorality. Since Indians were learning the value of land as private property, the Interior Department, which oversaw the Land Office, should remain in charge. Finally, far from being exemplary characters, most soldiers had a corrupting influence on every Indian who came near them, especially the women.[4]

By the 1880s, when the wars on the frontier were finally over, public opinion came to sympathize with the Indians far more than with the army. They were now seen as the victims of soldiers and the government that had sent the army west. Much of the change in opinion could be credited to Helen Hunt Jackson's bestselling book, *A Century of Dishonor*. Published in 1881, Jackson's work, subtitled *A Sketch of the United States Government's Dealings with Some of the Indian Tribes*, laid the blame for centuries of conflict on government leaders, including the presidents, and not the Indians. Jackson, the wife of a wealthy banker who managed the Denver and Rio Grande Railway Company, had begun her work after learning in 1879 about the sufferings of the Ponca on the reservation that Grant had established for them. Bishop Whipple, who wrote the preface, set the tone for the book and the subsequent calls for reform that the work inspired. He mocked Grant's peace policy as "little more than a name" and dismissed the president who had appointed him to the Sioux Commission as the last in a long line of politicians who had robbed, cheated, and murdered the Indians. The only good Grant had done for the tribes came when he inadvertently appointed Christian missionaries to run the reservations. These good people had replaced not just soldiers but also the beat of the medicine drum and scalp dance with church bells calling everyone to worship the one true God in heaven.[5]

Jackson took up the story of the suffering Indians by describing the injustices done to seven major tribes. The Delaware had befriended William Penn, welcoming his settlers to their new colony, only to be pushed westward from the Atlantic into the bloody ground beyond the Ohio. The Cheyenne had gone wherever the government ordered them to go, only to be massacred at Sand Creek and the Washita River. The mighty Ulysses Grant himself had pushed the Nez Perce from the beautiful Wallowa Valley, the Sioux from the Black Hills, and the Ponca from the northern plains to the malaria-infested swamps of the Indian Territory. His successors were even now driving the Winnebago from their homeland in the northern forests and the Cherokee from the farms they had worked so hard to establish in Oklahoma. Jackson agreed with Bishop Whipple that the "one bright spot in the dark record" of America's mistreatment of the Indians, including Grant's presidency, could be found in the Christian missionaries who toiled selflessly among the tribes. In her opinion, a befuddled President Grant had done nothing to help the Indians beyond sending a few commissioners to check up on the tribes during his first year in office.[6]

After demanding that her nation stop cheating, robbing, and breaking its promises to the tribes, Jackson laid out reforms that the government must institute immediately to save the tribes from ruin. Indians, whom she described as noble creatures, must be made citizens of the United States as "fast as they are fit." This must be done quickly for their own protection, since many currently lived on reservations where there was no rule of law to prevent crime and no courts to settle disputes. Until the day that all Indians were declared citizens of the United States, they had to be granted "every right and particular in which laws protect other 'persons' who are not citizens," including the right to own land as individuals, not merely as members of tribes.[7]

Helen Hunt Jackson went on to found the Boston Indian Citizenship Association to promote her reforms. She won the support of many former abolitionists, including Harriet Beecher Stowe, who established the Connecticut Indian Association. These organizations were soon joined by the Women's National Indian Association, set up with the support of the wealthy Mrs. John Jacob Astor, and the Indian Rights Association, organized by Herbert Welsh, a nephew of William Welsh. All the groups, along with the Board of Indian Commissioners, which continued to serve in successive administrations, quickly agreed on their mutual goals. Even though politicians had caused much misery for the Indians, the government still controlled the reservations. The reformers would therefore petition Congress and the White House to adopt their recommended reforms. Indians must be made citizens of the United States so they could enjoy the same rights to life, liberty, and the pursuit of happiness. Most especially, they had to be able to own property, a right guaranteed to all Americans, including the right to own land individually. Their tribal identity, which limited their ability to develop as individuals, must be weakened or denied altogether. The reformers also demanded the establishment of trade schools where Indian children could learn the skills they would need to function in the modern economy. Courses at these schools must be taught in English with an emphasis on American patriotism built into the curriculum. To break their ties to tribal traditions, these institutions should be boarding schools set up in a central place on a reservation or preferably at a great distance off the reservation.[8]

As soon as *A Century of Dishonor* was published, politicians in the nation's capital, both Republicans and Democrats, came under increasing pressure from the American people, who had made the book a bestseller, to enact the proposals of Jackson and her many followers. They, in turn, reduced the reformers' demands to just one policy: allotment. In December 1881 in his first State of the Union address, President Chester Alan Arthur formally proposed granting allotments of land to individual Indians. He recommended that the deeds to these allotments should be inalienable for twenty to twenty-five years to ensure the "permanent advancement" of the Indians. Arthur assured his fellow Americans that Indians who still clung to outdated tribal traditions would gladly settle down as farmers once the government gave them their own land.[9]

Six years later, on February 8, 1887, President Grover Cleveland signed An Act to Provide for the Allotment of Lands in Severalty to Indians on the Various Reservations. Better known as the Dawes Act in honor of its main architect, Senator Henry Dawes of Massachusetts, the law allotted 160 acres to heads of Indian households, 80 acres to single adults and orphans eighteen or older, and 40 acres to orphans under eighteen. Indians had four years to stake their claims, after which the secretary of the interior would choose the land for them. The government would hold the deeds for twenty-five years before giving them to individual Indians. Every Indian who accepted an allotment would automatically become an American citizen.[10]

Over the next thirty years, allotment and citizenship were invariably entwined in laws passed on behalf of the Indians. In 1891, the Dawes Act was amended to grant allotments in varying quantities on reservations that did not have enough land for Indians in the amounts prescribed in the original law. If Indians were given land more suitable for ranching than farming, the amount of their allotments could be doubled. Seven years later, the Curtis Act, named after its author, Kansas congressman Charles Curtis, a descendant of several tribes who had been raised on the Kaw Reservation, applied the Dawes Act to the "Five Civilized Tribes," which had been exempted from the original bill. Besides dividing the reservations of the Cherokee, Choctaw, Chickasaw, Creek, and Seminole among individual members of the tribes, the change also overturned their government, law, and courts. In 1906, the Burke Act, also known as the Forced Patenting Act, gave the secretary of the interior the authority to force Indians to accept allotments. In 1924, if there were still any Indians who had not become Americans by way of allotment, the Indian Citizenship Act granted it to them.[11]

The dream of citizenship that Ulysses Grant long held for the Indians had been fulfilled through the efforts of people like Helen Hunt Jackson, who forgot that Grant was the first president to advocate for this reform. However, the price paid by the tribes for citizenship was much steeper than Grant had originally calculated. He had envisioned a slow pace for the process, which the tribes would set themselves on their own reservations or in the Indian Territory. However, the reformers believed the Indians had to be hurried into a future not of their own making so that they might thrive in it. The price demanded of them was letting go of every last vestige of being an Indian, including breaking tribal ties and giving up much of their land. That millions of acres on reservations would not be allotted due to the small numbers of Indians living on them, but would instead be sold to non-Indians, was a fact not lost on the many politicians, business leaders, and average citizens who supported allotment. By 1924, the fervent drive for allotment and citizenship stripped the Indians of ninety million acres of tribal land. This included most of the Indian Territory, which was thrown open for sale to the wider public in 1889 and entered the Union as the state of Oklahoma in 1907.[12]

During the mad dash for allotment and the subsequent promise of citizenship, the reformers constantly praised the people they were trying to save. Yet their insistence on breaking all tribal ties, dividing up the reservations, and training children to forget their heritage betrayed an underlying disgust with all things Indian. They never asked themselves why wiping out every tradition was a requirement for Indians to participate fully in American society. However, during the final push for citizenship, a new group of reformers did raise this question. They were part of a growing movement that defended Indian civilization as worthy of both study and practice. Many were Sioux who had grown up in their tribe's last days of freedom on the northern plains before war broke out for the Black Hills. They agreed with Helen Hunt Jackson and her supporters that the Indians were a noble people but asked why the very things that made them so had to be destroyed. Their close family ties, the rhythm and purpose of their everyday lives, and their keen sense of the sacred were worth saving and not repressing, whether through allotment, the breakup of the tribes, or Indian boarding schools.

Born on the Santee Sioux Reservation in 1868, Charles Eastman, known among his people as Ohiyesa, led the way in promoting American Indian culture. His family sent him east to study at Dartmouth College, where he became a doctor. He later worked at the Pine Ridge Reservation, where he witnessed the Wounded Knee Massacre. In defense of his people, he lectured throughout the country and wrote numerous books about their traditions. The most notable, titled *The Soul of the Indian*, was published in 1911 and revealed that the Sioux were far from savages. They learned early in life, especially from their mothers, how to recognize the "Great Mystery," or the divine presence of the Creator, which bound all life together. Luther Standing Bear, an Oglala also born in 1868, long remembered Custer's attack on his people at the Little Bighorn. His 1931 memoir, *My Indian Boyhood*, explains that Indian men were not bloodthirsty animals. Instead, they were carefully trained as hunters and warriors from boyhood to sustain their people within the circle of life. A year later, the stories of Black Elk, another Oglala who fought at the Little Bighorn and later survived Wounded Knee, were gathered together in *Black Elk Speaks*, a work destined to become a classic. This memoir stands to this day as a moving testament to the deep spirituality and visionary power of the Sioux.[13]

All these works were part of a reform movement meant to elevate awareness of the values of Indian civilization, which had been forgotten in the drive to make the tribes part of the American mainstream. These books were not the first to be written in this vein, however, for they followed in the footsteps of a book penned in the previous century. In 1851, Lewis Henry Morgan, a New York lawyer who had immersed himself in the culture of the Iroquois, published the first serious study of a major tribe ever written in American history. *The League of the Ho-dé-no-sau-nee or Iroquois* describes the history of the Mohawk, Onondaga, Cayuse, Oneida, and Seneca, their matrilineal social structure, and their complex government, a true federation founded on a constitution, that allowed five enemy tribes to join together as one great nation, which dominated the Northeast until displaced by another powerful confederation, the United States of America. What made the book even more remarkable was the person to whom the book was dedicated, a Seneca Indian whom Morgan had met while

A Forgotten Legacy

Savagery to "Civilization." Cartoonist Udo (Joseph) Keppler, a supporter of American Indian culture and an honorary Seneca chief, reminded suffragettes in this drawing from the May 16, 1914, edition of his satirical magazine *Puck* that their rights lagged far behind those of "savage" Iroquois women. The words on the banner clearly express this sentiment: "We, the women of the Iroquois, own the land, the lodge, the children, ours is the right of adoption, of life or death; ours the right to raise up and depose chiefs; ours the right of representation at all councils; ours the right to make and abrogate treaties; ours the supervision over domestic and foreign policies; ours the trusteeship of the private property; our lives are valued again as high as man's." COURTESY OF THE LIBRARY OF CONGRESS.

browsing in an Albany, New York bookstore. This young man had a wealth of information which served as the foundation of Morgan's seminal study. His tribal name was Hasanoanda, but most people knew him as Ely Parker, the scholar, lawyer, and engineer who would one day serve as Ulysses Grant's military secretary and his first commissioner of Indian affairs. He had been able to enter the white man's world while still remaining proud of his heritage.[14]

After resigning his post in 1871 and moving away from Washington, Ely Parker still looked out for the interests of the Tonawanda Seneca, but he lost touch with his old friend Ulysses Grant. He saw Grant only two more times after leaving office. Parker came to Philadelphia in December 1879 to join other surviving members of Grant's military family in greeting the president on his return from his world tour. The following October, Parker visited Grant in

New York. His purpose was to give Grant a copy of the surrender terms he had drafted at Appomattox along with the pen he had used. But beyond these two short meetings, he never saw Grant again. When the former president lay dying in the summer of 1885, Parker came often to visit, but Grant's son Fred always turned him away.[15]

Unlike Grant, who did not reflect on the successes or failures of his Indian policy, Parker could not help but look back. He never understood why Grant had defended Delano and Belknap, when they were obviously guilty, but stood silently by when he was wrongfully accused. In the end, Parker blamed the president's neglect on the change that came over him once he was surrounded by wealthy and powerful men in the White House, such as the Board of Indian Commissioners, top cabinet officials who took bribes, and the many miners who dreamed of fortunes yet unmade in the Black Hills. Parker often described the transformation of Grant in biblical terms, blaming him for "taking unto himself of false and strange gods who at last ruined him utterly." But to Parker, what was most terrible was the fact that the Indian policy, which the two friends had crafted so carefully, started out well but ended badly.

Like Grant, and just as he and the Tonawanda Seneca had done, Parker wanted all Indians to become an integral part of the American body politic. Every plan he and the president had established was meant to accomplish this fact. The tribes would be saved from extermination. They would be placed on reservations, where they could slowly get their bearings in a changing world and build a better future for themselves. Like Grant, he spoke in terms of civilizing and Christianizing the Indians, but neither man believed this meant stripping everything away from the Indians, including their history, language, customs, land, and tribal identities. Much more than Grant, he came to regret the decision to replace army officers with missionaries in the Indian service. In his opinion, most of these missionaries worked too hard to wash the Indians clean of their traditions. Even worse were the reformers who rose up after Grant left office, demanding allotments that diminished the reservations, broke up the tribes, and left families in ruins. Until the day he died in 1895, Parker hated what had become of Grant's original purposes. The Indians had survived and were well on the way to becoming citizens of the United States, but the price they had paid was too high.[16]

Parker might have been surprised to learn that a growing interest in tribal culture led to calls for changes in the nation's Indian policy in the 1920s. Authors such as Charles Eastman (Ohiyesa), Luther Standing Bear, and Black Elk, along with anthropologists, artists, ethnographers, poets, and scholars of religion, who were all fascinated by native traditions, demanded greater respect for the civilization of the tribes. They were joined by many Americans who were outraged at the efforts of President Warren G. Harding's administration to take control of the Pueblo Reservation in New Mexico to profit from the tribe's water and mineral rights. Calvin Coolidge, who assumed the presidency when Harding died, put a stop to these plans, and in 1926, his Interior Department set up a committee to investigate living conditions on all reservations. The final report, *The Problem of Indian Administration*, better known as the Merriam Report in honor of Lewis Merriam, the Harvard lawyer who chaired the committee, provided 850 pages of shocking testimony about the suffering among the nation's Indians. On average, they were far poorer and much sicker than other Americans. The report blamed this condition primarily on allotment, which had given small plots of ground to individual Indians without providing the resources necessary to develop the land or pay taxes on it. Much of the sickness among the Indians could be traced to diseases such as tuberculosis, which children contracted in the boarding schools they were forced to attend.[17]

The next president, Herbert Hoover, had greater sympathy for the Indians than many of his fellow Republicans. When he was a child, after his parents had died, he became the ward of the Quaker Indian agent Lawrie Tatum. He later lived for a time on the Osage Reservation in the Indian Territory where his uncle, also a Quaker, was the agent. As president, Hoover worked to resolve several problems identified in the Merriam Report. He slowed the allotment process and irrigated reservations that had been established in arid country. But the real reform in the nation's Indian policy came when Franklin D. Roosevelt was elected president in 1932. Promising a New Deal for the Indians, he chose John Collier, a former social worker and leading voice in the movement to respect Indian culture, as his commissioner of Indian affairs. Together, they were as determined as Grant and Parker had once been to help the Indians. They laid out their plans on the revolutionary assumption that it was possible to be an American citizen and still remain a member of a tribe.

Upon the advice of Secretary Collier, who had come to believe that the best in Indian culture could reinvigorate the broken civilization of the modern world, Roosevelt signed an executive order in 1933 disbanding the Board of Indian Commissioners. All matters related to the Indians were now back under the control of the commissioner of Indian affairs. While members of the board had made less of an attempt to take full control of the Indian service after Grant left office, they had become ever more adamant that all vestiges of Indian culture must disappear forever. The long-standing drive to eradicate all tribal traditions finally came to an end when Roosevelt worked for passage of the Indian Reorganization Act. Approved in 1934, the law allowed the Indians

A Forgotten Legacy

to reorganize as tribes and establish governments based on constitutions for their respective nations.

Just as important, allotment officially came to an end. Land could no longer be taken away from the tribes without their full consent. The secretary of the interior was authorized to hold land in trust for the Indians and to establish new reservations for them. The act also set up a loan program for the economic development of reservations and gave tribal members preference in hiring throughout the Bureau of Indian Affairs. Beyond the passage of this important law, Roosevelt's administration encouraged the Indians to reinvigorate their culture, which would no longer be considered less valuable than any other strand in the American mosaic. Through his many reforms, Roosevelt assumed the role of chief executive over the nation's Indian affairs that Grant had once hoped to attain. Grant's bid to take control slipped away almost immediately after he appointed the Board of Indian Commissioners, which Roosevelt finally dismissed.[18]

Despite his failure, Grant deserves to be remembered as the man who stood between the twin peaks of Andrew Jackson, the president who pushed the tribes out of his nation, and Franklin D. Roosevelt, the president who welcomed them back in. During a time marked by great prejudice and violence, Ulysses Grant believed the Indians must not only be saved but brought into the odyssey of all the people who were citizens of the United States as they moved together toward an ever-brighter future. If he had ever looked back on his efforts, he might have agreed with Black Elk, who failed in his attempt to rescue the Sioux, about why the best dreams often do not come true, at least not right away. As Black Elk surmised, "It is hard to follow one great vision in this world of darkness and of many changing shadows. Among those shadows, men get lost."[19]

Acknowledgments
Appendixes
Notes
Bibliography
Index

Acknowledgments

I am most grateful to my sister Roberta Stockwell, an artist and professional cartographer, for the maps she created for this book. She is an excellent writer and editor in her own right and provided valuable insights and encouragement to me along the way. I am also thankful to my little friends Jamie and Adam, who supported me during this project. I must thank, too, my friend Dr. William Pederson, the director of the International Lincoln Center at Louisiana State University–Shreveport, for recommending me as an author to the editors of the *Papers of Ulysses S. Grant*. He is a great scholar and dedicated teacher, who truly deserved his recent award from the state of Louisiana as Humanist of the Year. I appreciate the staff of the Research Division of the National Archives who finally found the Records of the Board of Indian Commissioners after much prodding on my part. Thanks, too, to Sylvia Frank Rodrigue, the executive editor at the Southern Illinois University Press, for her patience and encouragement, as well as to Dr. John Marszalek, the executive editor of the Grant Papers, and Dr. Timothy Smith, who teaches at Mississippi State University, for their thoughtful review of the manuscript. Finally, I am grateful to my graduate school professors, W. Eugene Hollon and William Leckie, both accomplished scholars of the American West, who taught me to appreciate every aspect of this complex odyssey that lies at the heart of our national experience, and to my late father, John Stockwell, who loved history, including the story of the settlement of the American West, especially the railroads, which provided so many opportunities for our Irish ancestors who came to this country seeking freedom and a better life.

Appendix A: Army Officers Appointed to the Indian Service, 1869

Civilian appointees are italicized.

Washington Superintendency
Superintendent Brevet Colonel Samuel Ross

Indian Agency/Reservation	Indian Agent or Subagent
Makah Agency	Brevet Captain Joseph H. Hays
S'Klallam Agency	Lieutenant Colonel Joseph M. Kelly
Yakima Subagency	First Lieutenant James M. Smith
Quinaielt Subagency	Brevet Major Thomas H. Hay
Duwamish Subagency	Brevet Captain George D. Hill

Oregon Superintendency
Superintendent *Alfred B. Meacham*

Indian Agency/Reservation	Indian Agent
Umatilla Agency	Lieutenant W. H. Boyle
Warm Springs Agency	Brevet Captain William W. Mitchell
Grande Ronde Agency	Captain Charles Lafollette
Siletz Agency	*Benjamin Simpson*
Alsea Subagency	Lieutenant F. A. Battey
Klamath Agency	*Lindsey Applegate*

California Superintendency
Superintendent Brevet Major General J. B. McIntosh

Indian Agency/Reservation	Indian Agent or Subagent
Round Valley Reservation	First Lieutenant J. S. Styles
Hoopa Valley Reservation	First Lieutenant J. Lewis Spalding

Appendix A

California Superintendency (*continued*)

Indian Agency/Reservation	Indian Agent or Subagent
Tule River Reservation	First Lieutenant John H. Purcell
Mission Indians	J. Q. A. Stanley (special agent)

Nevada Superintendency
Superintendent H. G. Parker

Indian Agency/Reservation	Indian Agent or Subagent
Paiute Agency	Captain R. N. Fenton

Arizona Superintendency
Superintendent Brevet Colonel George L. Andrews

Indian Agency/Reservation	Indian Agent or Subagent
Pima Villages	Levi Ruggles
Colorado River Agency	John Fuedge

Utah Superintendency
Superintendent Brevet Colonel J. E. Tourtellotte

Indian Agency/Reservation	Indian Agent or Subagent
Uintah Valley Agency	First Lieutenant George F. Graffam

New Mexico Superintendency
Superintendent Major William Clinton

Indian Agency/Reservation	Indian Agent or Subagent
Navajo Agency	Captain F. T. Benton
Cimarron Agency	E. B. Dennison
Abiquiu Agency	First Lieutenant J. B. Hanson
Mescalero Apache Agency	First Lieutenant A. G. Hennisee
Southern Apache Agency	First Lieutenant Charles E. Drew
Pueblo Indian Agency	First Lieutenant Charles L. Cooper
Special Agency	First Lieutenant George E. Ford

Colorado Superintendency
Superintendent *Edward M. McCook*, governor of the Colorado Territory

Indian Agency/Reservation	Indian Agent
Middle Park Agency	Daniel C. Oakes
Southern Agency	Lieutenant C. T. Speer

Wyoming Superintendency
Superintendent *J. A. Campbell*, governor of the Wyoming Territory

Indian Agency/Reservation	Indian Agent
Fort Bridger Agency	*Luther Mann Jr.*
Shoshone and Bannock Agency	Captain J. H. Patterson

Idaho Superintendency
Superintendent Colonel De L. Floyd Jones

Indian Agency/Reservation	Indian Agent
Bannock and Shoshone Reservation	Colonel De L. Floyd Jones
Nez Perce Indian Agency	Second Lieutenant J. W. Wham
Fort Hall Agency	First Lieutenant W. H. Danilson

Montana Superintendency
Superintendent Lieutenant Colonel Alfred Sully

Indian Agency/Reservation	Indian Agent or Subagent
Flathead Indian Agency	Brevet Major Alvin S. Galbreath
Gros Ventres and River Crow Agency	A. S. Reed
Blackfoot Agency	Lieutenant William B. Pease

Dakota Superintendency
Superintendent *John A. Burbank*, governor of the Dakota Territory

Indian Agency/Reservation	Indian Agent or Subagent
Yankton Agency	Captain W. J. Broatch
Ponca Agency	Brevet Major William H. Hugo
Fort Berthold Agency	Captain W. Clifford

Appendix A

Dakota Superintendency (*continued*)

Indian Agency/Reservation	Indian Agent or Subagent
Crow Creek Agency	First Lieutenant William H. French, Jr.
Cheyenne Agency	Captain George M. Randall
Whetstone Agency	Captain De Witt C. Poole
Grand River Agency	Brevet Major J. N. Hearn
Santee Sioux Agency	Dr. Jared W. Daniels

Northern Superintendency
Superintendent *Samuel M. Janney*

Indian Agency/Reservation	Indian Agent or Subagent
Santee Agency	Samuel M. Janney
Omaha Agency	E. Painter
Winnebago Agency	Howard White
Pawnee Agency	Jacob M. Troth
Ottoe Agency	Albert L. Greene
Great Nemaha Agency	Thomas Lightfoot

Central Superintendency
Superintendent *Enoch Hoag*

Indian Agency/Reservation	Indian Agent or Subagent
Sac and Fox Agency	Albert Wiley
Chippewa and Christian Indian	Joseph Romig
Kickapoo Indian Agency	John D. Miles
Pottawatomie Agency	L. R. Palmer
Delaware Agency	John G. Pratt
Shawnee Agency	Reuben L. Roberts
Kaw Agency	Mahlon Stubbs
Osage River Agency	James Stanley
Neosho River Agency	G. C. Snow
Arapaho and Cheyenne	Brinton Darlington
Wichita and Comanche Agency	Lawrie Tatum

Army Officers Appointed

Southern Superintendency
Superintendent Brevet Major General W. B. Hazen

Indian Agency/Reservation	Indian Agent or Subagent
Cherokee Agency	Brevet Major John N. Craig
Choctaw and Chickasaw Agency	Captain G. T. Olmstead
Creek Agency	Captain F. A. Field
Seminole Agency	Captain T. A. Baldwin

Independent Agencies
Superintendent (None)

Indian Agency/Reservation	Indian Agent or Subagent
Chippewa Agency	Brevet Captain J. J. S. Hassler
Lake Superior Agency	Brevet Lieutenant Colonel John H. Knight
Michigan Agency	Brevet Major General James W. Long
Green Bay Agency	Lieutenant J. A. Manley
Oneida Agency	Captain E. R. Ames
Special Agency (Stray Bands)	D. A. Griffith (army rank unlisted)
Sac and Fox Agency in Iowa	First Lieutenant Frank D. Garratty

Appendix B: Christian Missionaries Appointed to the Indian Service, 1871–72

The superintendent positions were eliminated in 1873, after which all agents reported directly to the commissioner of Indian affairs.

Quakers (Hicksite)

Agency	Indian Agent	No. of Indians	Location
Great Nemaha	T. Lightfoot	313	Nebraska
Omaha	E. Painter	969	Nebraska
Winnebago	Howard White	1,440	Nebraska
Pawnee	Jacob M. Troth	2,447	Nebraska
Otoe	A. L. Green	464	Nebraska
Santee Sioux	Joseph Webster	965	Nebraska

Quakers (Orthodox)

Agency	Indian Agent	No. of Indians	Location
Pottawatomie	J. H. Morris	400	Kansas
Kaw	Mahlon Stubbs	290	Kansas
Kickapoo Indian	R. W. Miles	598	Kansas
Quapaw	Hiram W. Jones	1,070	Indian Territory
Osage	James Stanley	4,000	Indian Territory
Sac and Fox	Albert Wiley / John Hadley	463	Indian Territory
Shawnee*	—	663	Indian Territory
Wichita	Jonathan Richards	1,250	Indian Territory
Kiowa	Lawrie Tatum	5,490	Indian Territory
Upper Arkansas	John D. Miles	3,500	Indian Territory

* The Shawnee Agency closed after most of the Shawnee moved to the Cherokee Reservation in the Indian Territory or the Sac and Fox Reservation in Iowa.

Baptist

Agency	Indian Agent	No. of Indians	Location
Cherokee	John B. Jones	18,000	Indian Territory
Creek	F. S. Lyon	12,300	Indian Territory
Walker River	C. A. Bateman	6,000	Nevada
Paiute	C. F. Powell	2,500	Nevada
Special	G. W. Dodge	3,000	Utah

Presbyterian

Agency	Indian Agent	No. of Indians	Location
Choctaw and Chickasaw	T. D. Griffith	16,000	Indian Territory
Seminole	Henry Breiner	2,398	Indian Territory
Abiquiu	J. S. Armstrong	1,920	New Mexico
Navajo	W. F. Hall	9,114	New Mexico
Mescalero Apache	A. J. Curtis	830	New Mexico
Tularosa	O. F. Piper	1,200	New Mexico
Moquis Pueblo	W. D. Crothers	3,000	Arizona
Nez Perce	J. B. Montieth	2,807	Idaho
Uintah Valley	J. J. Critchlow	800	Utah

Catholic

Agency	Indian Agent	No. of Indians	Location
Tulalip	E. C. Chirouse	3,600	Washington
Colville	W. P. Winans	3,349	Washington
Grand Ronde	J. B. Sinnott	870	Oregon
Umatilla	N. A. Cornoyer	837	Oregon
Flathead	C. S. Jones	1,780	Montana
Grand River	J. C. O'Connor	6,700	Dakota
Devil's Lake	W. H. Forbes	720	Dakota

Appendix B

Methodist

Agency	Indian Agent	No. of Indians	Location
Hoopa Valley	D. H. Lowry	725	California
Round Valley	H. Gibson	1,700	California
Tule River	C. Maltby	374	California
Yakima	J. H. Wilbur	3,000	Washington
Skokomish	E. Eells	919	Washington
Quinaielt	G. A. Henry	520	Washington
Warm Springs	J. Smith	626	Oregon
Siletz	J. Palmer	2,500	Oregon
Klamath	L. S. Dyer	4,000	Oregon
Blackfeet	W. F. Ensign	7,500	Montana
Crow	F. D. Pease	2,700	Montana
Milk River	A. J. Simmons	19,755	Montana
Fort Hall	J. N. High	1,037	Idaho
Michigan	George I. Betts	9,117	Michigan

Dutch Reformed

Agency	Indian Agent	No. of Indians	Location
Colorado River	J. A. Tonner	828	Arizona
Pima and Maricopa	J. A. Stout	4,342	Arizona
Camp Grant	E. C. Jacobs	900	Arizona
Camp Verde	J. W. Williams	748	Arizona
White Mountain	James E. Roberts	1,300	Arizona

Congregational

Agency	Indian Agent	No. of Indians	Location
Green Bay	W. T. Richardson	2,871	Wisconsin
La Pointe	Selden N. Clark	5,150	Wisconsin
Chippewa of the Mississippi	Edward T. Smith	6,455	Minnesota

Protestant Episcopal

Agency	Indian Agent	No. of Indians	Location
Whetstone	D. R Risley	5,000	Dakota
Ponca	W. E. Gregory	735	Dakota
Upper Missouri	H. F. Livingston	2,647	Dakota
Fort Berthold	J. E. Tappan	2,700	Dakota
Cheyenne River	T. M. Kones	6,000	Dakota
Yankton	T. G. Gasman	1,947	Dakota
Red Cloud	J. W. Daniels	7,000	Dakota
Shoshone	James Irwin	1,000	Wyoming

American Board of Commissioners for Foreign Missions

Agency	Indian Agent	No. of Indians	Location
Sisseton	M. N. Adams	1,496	Dakota

Unitarian

Agency	Indian Agent	No. of Indians	Location
Los Pinos	C. Adams	3,000	Dakota
White River	J. S. Littlefield	800	Colorado

Christian Union

Agency	Indian Agent	No. of Indians	Location
Pueblo	J. O. Cole	7,683	New Mexico
Neah Bay	E. M. Gibson	604	Washington

Lutheran

Agency	Indian Agent	No. of Indians	Location
Sac and Fox	Leander Clark	273	Iowa

Appendix B

Total Number of Indians by Denomination

Denomination	No. of Indians
Methodist	54,473
Baptist	40,800
Presbyterian	38,069
Protestant Episcopal	26,929
Catholic	17,856
Orthodox Quaker	17,724
Congregational	14,476
Christian	8,287
Dutch Reformed	8,118
Hicksite Quaker	6,598
Unitarian	3,800
Foreign Missions	1,496
Lutheran	273
Total	238,899

Total Number of Agencies by Denomination

Denomination	No. of Agencies
Methodist	14
Orthodox Quaker	10
Presbyterian	9
Protestant Episcopal	8
Catholic	7
Hicksite Quaker	6
Baptist	5
Dutch Reformed	5
Congregational	3
Christian	2
Unitarian	2
Foreign Missions	1
Lutheran	1
Total	73

Notes

Ulysses S. Grant: A New Perspective

1. For examples of recent attempts to evaluate Grant's policy in terms of his Civil War and Reconstruction experience, see the following works: Kevin Buyneel, *The Third Space of Sovereignty: The Postcolonial Politics of U.S.-Indigenous Relations* (Minneapolis: University of Minnesota, 2007); Cathleen Cahill, *Federal Fathers and Mothers: A Social History of the United States Indian Agency, 1869–1933* (Chapel Hill: University of North Carolina Press, 2011); Vine Deloria Jr. and David Wilkins, *Tribes, Treaties and Constitutional Tribulations* (Austin: University of Texas Press, 1999); Greg Downs and Kate Masur, eds., *The World the Civil War Made* (Chapel Hill: University of North Carolina Press, 2015); C. Joseph Genetin-Pilawa, *Crooked Paths to Allotment: The Fight over Federal Indian Policy after the Civil War* (Chapel Hill: University of North Carolina Press, 2012); Joan Waugh, *U. S. Grant: American Hero, American Myth* (Chapel Hill: University of North Carolina Press, 2009); David Wilkins and K. Tsianina Loawaima, *Uneven Ground: American Indian Sovereignty and Federal Law* (Norman: University of Oklahoma Press, 2002).

Prelude

1. William S. McFeely, *Grant: A Biography* (New York: W. W. Norton, 1981), 286–89; Jean Edward Smith, *Grant* (New York: Simon and Schuster, 2001), 404–406.

2. "Second Inaugural Address of Abraham Lincoln," March 4, 1865, The Avalon Project, Yale Law School, Lillian Goldman Law Library, accessed January 4, 2018, http://avalon.law.yale.edu/19th_century/lincoln2.asp.

3. Ulysses Grant to Joseph H. Hawley, May 29, 1868, in *The Papers of Ulysses S. Grant*, ed. John Y. Simon (Carbondale: Southern Illinois University Press, 1991), 19:263–64; in his draft of the letter, also dated May 29, 1868, he wrote the more memorable phrase "Let us have peace," ibid., 19:264.

4. Ulysses Grant, "Inaugural Address," March 4, 1869, ibid., 19:139–42.

5. Ibid., 142.

6. Sheridan's exact words on meeting Tochaway, a Comanche who claimed to be a good Indian, were "The only good Indians I ever met were dead ones"; see Joseph Wheelan, *Terrible Swift Sword: The Life of General Philip H. Sheridan* (New York: Da Capo Press, 2013), 253. However, Sheridan denied saying this; see Paul Andrew Hutton, *Phil Sheridan and His Army* (Lincoln: University of Nebraska Press, 1985), 180.

7. Henry Knox to George Washington, June 15, 1789, *American State Papers: Indian Affairs*, 1:12–14.

8. For an analysis of Tecumseh and the Prophet, see R. David Edmunds, *Tecumseh and the Quest for Indian Leadership* (New York: HarperCollins, 1984) and *The Shawnee Prophet* (Lincoln: University of Nebraska Press, 1983).

9. Reginald Horsman, *The War of 1812* (New York: Alfred A. Knopf, 1969), 17–18; Reginald Horsman, *The Causes of the War of 1812* (New York: A. S. Barnes, 1961), 229–32.

10. Treaty of Ghent, December 24, 1814, *American State Papers: Foreign Relations* 3:745–53; copies of the treaties signed at Portage des Sioux can be found in the *American State Papers: Indian Affairs* 2:3–5; Treaty of Springwells, September 8, 1815, in *Indian Affairs: Laws and Treaties*, ed. Charles J. Kappler (Washington, DC: Government Printing Office, 1904), 2:117–19.

11. A good example of Monroe's new policy of placing Indians on specific reserves in their surrendered territory can be found in the Treaty at the Foot of the Rapids, September 19, 1817, *Indian Affairs: Laws and Treaties*, 2:145–55; the Senate's changes to Monroe's original plan for allotments on these reserves can be found in Amendments Proposed to the Treaty with the Wyandots, Senecas, Delawares, Shawanees, Pattawatomies, Ottowas, and Chippewas, December 29, 1817, *American State Papers: Indian Affairs* 2:148–50; Civilization Fund Act, March 3, 1819, *Documents of United States Indian Policy*, 3rd ed., ed. Francis Paul Prucha (Lincoln: University of Nebraska Press, 2000), 33.

12. James Monroe, "Address to the Senate," January 27, 1825, *A Compilation of the Messages and Papers of the Presidents*, ed. James D. Richardson (Washington, DC: Government Printing Office, 1897), 2:280–83; Charles D. Lowery, *James Barbour: A Jeffersonian Republican* (Tuscaloosa: University of Alabama Press, 1984), 153–67.

13. Andrew Jackson, "First Inaugural Address," March 4, 1829, *Compilation of the Messages and Papers of the Presidents*, 2:436–38; for examples of Jackson's attitudes toward removal, see his "First Annual Message," December 8, 1829, ibid., 2:442–62 and "Third Annual Message," December 6, 1831, ibid., 2:544–58.

14. The "one big reservation" policy served as the foundation of the Trade and Intercourse Act, June 30, 1834, *Documents of United States Indian Policy*, 63–68. The law designated all the land belonging to the United States west of the Mississippi, and not within Missouri, Louisiana, or the Arkansas Territory, as the "Indian country."

15. Francis Paul Prucha, *The Great Father: The United States Government and the American Indians*, abridged ed. (Lincoln: University of Nebraska Press, 1986), 108–35.

16. "Indian Commissioner Lea on Reservation Policy," November 27, 1850, *Documents of United States Indian Policy*, 81–83; Treaty of Fort Laramie with Sioux, etc., September 17, 1871, *Indian Affairs: Laws and Treaties*, 2:594–96.

17. Treaty with the Comanche, Kiowa, and Apache, July 27, 1853, *Indian Affairs: Laws and Treaties*, 2:600–602.

18. "Report of the Doolittle Commission," January 26, 1867, *Documents of United States Indian Policy*, 101–4.

19. Treaty with the Kiowa and Comanche, October 21, 1867, and Treaty with the Kiowa, Comanche, and Apache, October 21, 1867, *Indian Affairs: Laws and Treaties*, 2:977–84; "Creation of an Indian Peace Commission," July 20, 1867, *Documents of United States Indian Policy*, 104–5; "Report of the Indian Peace Commission," January 7, 1868, ibid., 105–9; "Resolutions of the Indian Peace Commission," October 9, 1868, ibid., 115–17.

20. Homer, *The Odyssey*, trans. Robert Fagles (New York: Penguin Books, 1976), bk. 5, lines 228–31.

1. One Man's Journey

1. Ulysses Grant, "Personal Memoirs of U. S. Grant," vol. 1, in *Ulysses S. Grant: Memoirs and Selected Letters; Personal Memoirs of U. S. Grant; Selected Letters 1839–1865*, ed. Mary Drake McFeely and William S. McFeely (New York: Library of America, 1990), 17.

2. Edward Chauncey Marshall, *The Ancestry of President Grant, and Their Contemporaries* (New York: Sheldon, 1869), 6–8.

3. William Brandon, *The American Heritage Book of the Indians* (New York: American Heritage, 1961), 171.

4. Marshall, *Ancestry of President Grant*, 4–8, 10–13, 18–19.

5. Alfred Cave, *The Pequot War* (Amherst: University of Massachusetts Press, 1996), 69–167; Marshall, *Ancestry of President Grant*, 18–22.

6. Fundamental Orders of 1639, The Avalon Project, Yale Law School, Lillian Goldman Law Library, accessed January 4, 2018, http://avalon.law.yale.edu/17th_century/order.asp; Albert E. Van Dusen, *Connecticut* (New York:

Random House, 1961), 80–83, 111–16; Charter of Connecticut, 1662, The Avalon Project, Yale Law School, Lillian Goldman Law Library, accessed January 4, 2018, http://avalon.law.yale.edu/17th_century/ct03.asp.

7. "The Last Will and Testament of Mathew Grant of Windsor," Marshall, *Ancestry of President Grant*, 153–55; the population reached 91,000 by 1700; see Alan Taylor, *American Colonies* (New York: Penguin Books, 2001), 177.

8. Alvin M. Josephy Jr., *500 Nations* (New York; Gramercy Books, 1994), 213–15.

9. Ibid., 215; Daniel R. Mandell, *King Philip's War: Colonial Expansion, Native Resistance, and the End of Indian Sovereignty (Witness to History)* (Baltimore: Johns Hopkins University Press, 2010), 134–35; Marshall, *Ancestry of President Grant*, 23–24.

10. The Second Charter of Virginia, May 23, 1609, The Avalon Project, Yale Law School, Lillian Goldman Law Library, accessed January 4, 2018, http://avalon.law.yale.edu/17th_century/va02.asp.

11. Marshall, *Ancestry of President Grant*, 31–32.

12. Ibid., 33.

13. Fred Anderson, *Crucible of War: The Seven Years' War and the Fate of Empire in British North America, 1754–1766* (2000; repr., New York: Vintage, 2007), 64–73.

14. The Royal Proclamation, October 7, 1763, The Avalon Project, Yale Law School, Lillian Goldman Law Library, accessed January 4, 2018, http://avalon.law.yale.edu/18th_century/proc1763.asp.

15. Robert Middlekauff, *The Glorious Cause: The American Revolution, 1763–1789* (New York: Oxford University Press, 2005), 240–58.

16. Van Dusen, *Connecticut*, 158–60; Marshall, *Ancestry of President Grant*, 44–51, 170–71; Leonard Richards, *Shays's Rebellion: The American Revolution's Final Battle* (Philadelphia: University of Pennsylvania Press, 2002), 4–22.

17. George W. Knepper, *Ohio and Its People*, 3rd ed. (Kent, OH: Kent State University Press, 2013), 35–36, 53–54, 57–59, 60–62; W. E. Peters, *Ohio Lands and Their Subdivision* (Athens, OH: printed by the author, 1918), 26–54.

18. Treaty with the Wyandot, Etc. [Treaty of Greeneville], 1795, *Indian Affairs: Laws and Treaties*, 2:39–45; The Jay Treaty, November 19, 1794, The Avalon Project, Yale Law School, Lillian Goldman Law Library, accessed January 4, 2018, http://avalon.law.yale.edu/18th_century/jay.asp.

19. Marshall, *Ancestry of President Grant*, 56–62.

20. Ibid., 61.

21. Knepper, *Ohio and Its People*, 102–12.

22. Mary Stockwell, *The Other Trail of Tears: The Removal of the Ohio Indians* (Yardley, PA: Westholme, 2015), 72–73.

23. Grant, *Personal Memoirs*, 28–29.

24. Stockwell, *Other Trail of Tears*, 189–90.

25. Treaty with the Wyandot, Etc., *Indian Affairs: Laws and Treaties*, 2:145–55.

26. Stockwell, *Other Trail of Tears*, 100–114.

27. Grant's mother was a lifelong Democrat; his father voted twice for Jackson for president but was an admirer of Henry Clay and later became a Whig; see Grant, *Personal Memoirs*, 19–20; Stockwell, *Other Trail of Tears*, 199–200.

28. Stockwell, *Other Trail of Tears*, 202, 207–12, 222–24, 226, 236–50, 263–65, 271–72.

29. Ibid., 275–79; Geoffrey Perret, *Ulysses S. Grant: Soldier & President* (New York: Random House, 1997), 30; James Fennimore Cooper, *The Wept of Wish-Ton-Wish: A Tale*, new ed. (New York: Stringer and Townsend, 1856); James Fennimore Cooper, *The Last of the Mohicans: A Narrative of 1757* (New York: Macmillan, 1900).

30. Stockwell, *Other Trails of Tears*, 307–8, 314–19; Ulysses Grant to Julia Dent, July 6, 1845, *Grant Papers*, 1:47–49; Ulysses Grant to Julia Dent, September 14, 1845, ibid., 1:53–55; Ulysses Grant to Julia Grant, January 2, 1846, ibid., 1:66–68.

31. Ulysses Grant to Julia Grant, May 24, 1846, *Grant Papers*, 1:87–89; Grant, *Personal Memoirs*, 41–42.

32. Brandon, *American Heritage Book of the Indians*, 304–6; Josephy, *500 Nations*, 346–49; Ulysses Grant to Julia Dent Grant, June 28, 1853, *Grant Papers*, 1:303–5; Ulysses Grant to Julia Dent Grant, August 30, 1852, ibid., 1:258–60; Ulysses Grant to Major Osborn Cross, July 15, 1853, ibid., 308–10.

33. Perret, *Ulysses S. Grant*, 102–13.

34. For Ely Parker's quotes, see William H. Armstrong, *Warrior in Two Camps: Ely S. Parker, Union General and Seneca Chief* (Syracuse, NY: Syracuse University Press, 1978), 73–74.

2. Parallel Lives

1. The interior secretaries and commissioners of Indian affairs estimated the total number of Indians and tribes as between 300,000 and 350,000. See "Extract from the Report of the Secretary of the Interior Relative to the Report of the Commissioner of Indian Affairs," *Annual Report of the Commissioner of Indian Affairs for the Year 1865* (Washington, DC: Government Printing Office, 1866), iii as an example.

2. Stephen Douglas, "Speech to the United States Senate, March 13–14, 1850," *Congressional Globe*, 31st. Cong., 1st Sess., Appendix, 364–75 (1850); Abraham Lincoln, "The 'House Divided' Speech," ca. 1857–58, Gilder Lehrman Institute of American History, https://ap.gilderlehrman.org/node/2211.

3. McFeely, *Grant*, 70; Armstrong, *Warrior in Two Camps*, 30.

4. Ulysses Grant to Frederick Dent, April 19, 1861, *Grant Papers*, 2:3–4. Grant purchased a slave named William Jones, whom he freed, while living in Missouri; Julia Grant owned four slaves. Parker's quotes are taken from an undated letter written to Harriet Maxwell Converse after the Civil War; see Arthur C. Parker, *The Life of General Ely S. Parker: Last Grand Sachem of the Iroquois and General Grant's Military Secretary* (Buffalo, NY: Buffalo Historical Society, 1919), 132.

5. McFeely, *Grant*, 90–110.

6. H. W. Brands, *The Man Who Saved the Union: Ulysses Grant in War and Peace* (New York: Anchor Books, 2012), 228–54.

7. Armstrong, *Warrior in Two Camps*, 77.

8. Ibid., ix, 14–15.

9. Ibid., 17–24.

10. Agreement with the Seneca, September 15, 1797, *Indian Affairs: Laws and Treaties*, 2:1027–30; Treaty with the Menominee, February 8, 1831, ibid., 2:319–23; Treaty with the New York Indians, January 15, 1838, ibid., 2:502–16; Treaty with the Seneca, May 20, 1842, ibid., 2:537–42.

11. The Judiciary Act, September 24, 1789, The Avalon Project, Yale Law School, Lillian Goldman Law Library, accessed January 4, 2018, http://avalon.law.yale.edu/18th_century/judiciary_act.asp.

12. Armstrong, *Warrior in Two Camps*, 32, 38.

13. *Joseph Fellows, Survivor of Robert Kendle, Plaintiff in Error v. Susan Blacksmith and Ely S. Parker, Administrators of John Blacksmith, Deceased*, 60 U.S. 366 (1856), Justia, US Supreme Court, accessed January 4, 2018, https://supreme.justia.com/cases/federal/us/60/366/case.html.

14. Armstrong, *Warrior in Two Camps*, 56–59, 65–66, 341–43; Treaty with the Seneca, Tonawanda Band, November 5, 1857, *Indian Affairs: Laws and Treaties*, 2:767–71.

15. Armstrong, *Warrior in Two Camps*, 82–83, 86, 90, 96; Ulysses Grant to Brigadier General Lorenzo Thomas, June 25, 1863," *Grant Papers*, 8:414; Parker, *Life of Ely Parker*, 86–87, 106–28, 328–29.

16. Treaty with the Sioux—Sisseton and Wahpeton Bands, July 23, 1851, and Treaty with the Sioux—Mdewakanton and Wahpakoota Bands, August 5, 1851, *Indian Affairs: Laws and Treaties*, 2:588–91; Kenneth Carley, *The Dakota*

War of 1862: Minnesota's Other War, 2nd ed. (St. Paul: Minnesota Historical Society Press, 2001), 1–14.

17. See Scott Berg, *38 Nooses: Lincoln, Little Crow, and the Beginning of the Frontier's End* (New York: Vintage, 2012), on the Santee Sioux War and Lincoln's pardon of condemned warriors.

18. Hampton Sides, *Blood and Thunder: The Epic Story of Kit Carson and Conquest of the American West* (New York: Doubleday, 2006), 332–38. See James Henry Carleton, *To the People of New Mexico. This Paper Sets Forth Some of the Principal Reasons Why the Navajo Indians Have Been Located upon a Reservation at the Bosque Redondo* (n.p., 1864), 1–13 for a defense of his actions.

19. Peter Iverson, *The Diné: A History of the Navajo* (Albuquerque: University of New Mexico Press, 2002), 35–65.

20. Treaty of Fort Laramie, with Sioux, Etc., September 17, 1781, *Indian Affairs: Laws and Treaties*, 2:594–96; Treaty with the Arapaho and Cheyenne, February 15, 1861, ibid., 2:807–11.

21. Jerome A. Greene, *Washita: The U.S. Army and the Southern Cheyennes, 1867–1869*, Campaigns and Commanders, vol. 3 (Norman: University of Oklahoma Press, 2004), 12–27; Stan Hoig, *The Peace Chiefs of the Cheyennes* (Norman: University of Oklahoma Press, 1980), 61–63.

22. Stan Hoig, *The Sand Creek Massacre* (Norman: University of Oklahoma Press, 1974), 145–62; Dee Brown, *Bury My Heart at Wounded Knee: An Indian History of the American West*, 30th anniv. ed. (New York: Henry Holt, 2001), 67–102.

23. Benjamin Capps, *The Indians* (New York: Time-Life Books, 1973), 187.

24. Quotes are from "Proceedings of a Military Commission Convened by Special Orders No 23, Headquarters District of Colorado, Denver, Colorado Territory, Dated February 1, 1865, in the Case of Colonel J. M. Chivington, First Colorado Cavalry," Senate Executive Document 26, 39th Cong., 2nd Sess., 2–228 (1865); see also "Massacre of the Cheyenne Indians," Report of the Joint Committee on the Conduct of the War, 38th Congr., 2nd Sess., vol. 3 (Washington, DC: Government Printing Office, 1865): i–vi, 3–108.

25. *Worcester v. Georgia*, 31 U.S. 515 (1832), Justia, US Supreme Court, accessed January 4, 2018, https://supreme.justia.com/cases/federal/us/31/515/case.html.

26. See *Annual Reports of the Secretary of the Interior* and *Annual Reports of the Commissioner of Indian Affairs* (Washington, DC: Government Printing Office, 1862–66) for the years 1861 through 1865.

27. Armstrong, *Warrior in Two Camps*, 108–11; Parker, *Life of Ely Parker*, 131–34.

28. Ulysses Grant to William Tecumseh Sherman, January 15, 1867, *Grant Papers*, 17:23–24; Hutton, *Phil Sheridan and His Army*, 180–86.

29. Ulysses Grant to Edwin Stanton, January 15, 1867 (including portions of Sherman's report to Grant dated November 21, 1866), *Grant Papers*, 17:21–22.

30. John Pope to Ulysses Grant, May 8, 1865 (telegram), ibid., 15:41n; John Pope to Ulysses Grant, May 17, 1865, ibid., 15:40–41. See also Richard N. Ellis, *General Pope and U.S. Indian Policy* (Albuquerque: University of New Mexico Press, 1970), for an excellent overview of Pope's views.

31. John Pope to Ulysses Grant, May 17, 1865, *Grant Papers*, 15:42.

32. John Pope to Ulysses Grant, June 19, 20, and 1865 (telegrams), ibid., 15:161n–162n.

33. Ulysses Grant to John Pope, May 17, 1865, ibid., 15:40–41.

34. Armstrong, *Warrior in Two Camps*, 29–30

35. The best sources on the Indian Territory during the Civil War are the *Annual Reports of the Secretary of the Interior*, the *Annual Reports of the Commissioner of Indian Affairs*, and the *Annual Reports of the Superintendents of the Central Superintendency* (Washington, DC: Government Printing Office, 1863–66) from 1862 through 1865.

36. Agreement with the Cherokee and Other Tribes in the Indian Territory, September 13, 1865, *Indian Affairs: Laws and Treaties*, 2:1050–52. For a detailed account of the negotiations, see Barbara Krauthamer, "Indian Territory and the Treaties of 1866: A Long History of Emancipation," in Downs and Masur, *World the Civil War Made*, 226–48.

37. Ely Parker to Ulysses Grant (telegram), January 20, 1866, *Grant Papers*, 16:454n; Ely Parker to Ulysses Grant, January 27, 1866," ibid., 16:458n–46ın (enclosed in Ulysses Grant to President Andrew Johnson, February 14, 1866, ibid., 16:458n); Armstrong, *Warrior in Two Camps*, 118; Treaty with the Seminole, March 21, 1866, *Indian Affairs: Laws and Treaties*, 2:910–15; Treaty with the Choctaw and Chickasaw, April 28, 1866, ibid., 2:918–31; Treaty with the Creeks, June 14, 1866, ibid., 2:931–37.

38. Ely Parker to Ulysses Grant, October 15, 1866, *Grant Papers*, 16:320n–321n.

39. Ely Parker to Ulysses Grant, January 24, 1867, ibid., 17:23n; "Transmitting a Report by Col. Parker on Affairs between the United States and the Various Indian Tribes U.S. Congress," House Misc. Doc. 37, 39th Cong., 2nd Sess. (1867). For an analysis of the development of Grant's new Indian policy primarily from Parker's point of view, see C. Joseph Genetin-Pilawa: "Ely S. Parker and the Paradox of Reconstruction Politics in Indian Country," in Downs and Masur, *World the Civil War Made*, 183–205.

40. Staunton forwarded Parker's recommendations to the Military Affairs Committees of the House of Representatives and the Senate; the report to the

House is referenced in the previous endnote; for the report to the Senate, see Senate 39A-E7, Committee on Military Affairs, in Record Group 46, *Records of the United States Senate* (Washington, DC: National Archives); the report to the Senate is also mentioned in *Grant Papers*, 17:23n; Ulysses Grant to William Tecumseh Sherman, May 29, 1867, ibid., 17:171–73.

3. A Better World Ahead

1. Roy Miller Meyer, *A History of the Santee Sioux: United States Indian Policy on Trial*, rev. ed. (Lincoln: University of Nebraska Press, 1993), 21–23; Royal B. Hasrick, *The Sioux: Life and Customs of a Warrior Society*, Civilization of the American Indian Series (Norman: University of Oklahoma, 1964), ix, 3–31.

2. "Treaty of Fort Laramie with Sioux, Etc., September 17, 1851," *Indian Affairs: Laws and Treaties*, 2:594–96.

3. Robert M. Utley, *The Indian Frontier, 1846–1890* (Albuquerque: University of New Mexico Press, 1984), 99–102.

4. Bob Drury and Tom Clavin, *The Heart of Everything That Is: The Untold Story of Red Cloud, An American Legend* (New York: Simon and Schuster, 2013), 244–45.

5. Dee Brown, *The Fetterman Massacre* (Lincoln: University of Nebraska Press, 1962), 147–89.

6. James Doolittle, et al., *Conditions of the Indians: Report of the Joint Special Committee Appointed under Joint Resolution March 3, 1865, with an Appendix* (Washington, DC: Government Printing Office, 1867), 1–4.

7. William Tecumseh Sherman to Ulysses Grant, January 14, 1867, *Grant Papers*, 17:16n; Ulysses Grant to Edwin Stanton, February 2, 1867, ibid., 17:17n; Armstrong, *Warrior in Two Camps*, 123.

8. Ulysses Grant to Edwin M. Stanton, May 25, 1865 (Endorsement of John Pope to Ulysses Grant, May 16, 1865), *Grant Papers*, 15:486n–88n; Ulysses Grant to William Tecumseh Sherman, April 18, 1866, ibid., 16:164; Ulysses Grant to William Tecumseh Sherman, May 29, 1867, ibid., 17:172.

9. Armstrong, *Warrior in Two Camps*, 123–26. For Parker's views on the situation in the West, see Ely Parker to John Rawlins, March 14, 1867, *Grant Papers*, 17:57n–58n.

10. "Report to the President by the Indian Peace Commission," January 7, 1868, *Annual Report of the Commissioner of Indian Affairs for the Year 1868* (Washington, DC: Government Printing Office, 1869), 1–90; Prucha, *Great Father*, 1:489–90.

11. "Report to the President by the Indian Peace Commission," 14.

12. Ibid., 16.

13. Ulysses Grant to William Tecumseh Sherman, May 29, 1867, *Grant Papers*, 17:171–73.

14. "Report to the President by the Indian Peace Commission," 17.

15. William Y. Chalfant, *Hancock's War: Conflict on the Southern Plains* (Norman, OK: Arthur H. Clark, 2010), 9–10; Ulysses Grant to Winfield Scott Hancock, May 23, 1867, *Grant Papers*, 17:162.

16. Treaty with the Kiowa and Comanche, October 21, 1867, *Indian Affairs: Laws and Treaties*, 2:984–89; Treaty with the Kiowa, Comanche, and Apache, October 21, 1867, ibid., 982–984; Treaty with the Cheyenne and Arapaho, October 28, 1867, ibid., 2:984–89.

17. "Report to the President by the Indian Peace Commission," 26.

18. Ibid., 7–8.

19. Ibid., 83.

20. Ibid., 1–90.

21. Ibid., 91–120.

22. William Tecumseh Sherman to Ulysses Grant, May 29, 1867, *Grant Papers*, 17:171–73; William Tecumseh Sherman to Ulysses Grant, June 10, 1867, ibid., 173n–78n.

23. For an example of the many letters and telegrams between Grant and Sherman regarding the Peace Commission, see William Tecumseh Sherman to Ulysses Grant, July 19, 1867, *Grant Papers*, 17:241n–42n.

24. McFeely, *Grant*, 276–84. For the details of the Medicine Lodge treaties, see Treaty with the Kiowa and Comanche, October 21, 1867, *Indian Affairs: Laws and Treaties*, 2:977–82; Treaty with the Kiowa, Comanche, and Apache, October 21, 1867, ibid., 2:982–84; Treaty with the Cheyenne and Arapaho, October 28, 1867, ibid., 2:984–89.

25. Treaty with the Sioux—Brule, Oglala, Miniconjou, Yanktonai, Hunkpapa, Blackfeet, Cuthead, Two Kettle, Sans Arcs, and Santee—and Arapaho, April 29, 1868, *Indian Affairs: Laws and Treaties*, 2:998.

26. Ibid., 2:999–1007.

27. Treaty with the Navaho, June 1, 1868, *Indian Affairs: Laws and Treaties*, 2:1015–20.

28. Ulysses Grant to Edwin Stanton, March 10, 1868, *Grant Papers*, 18:187–88.

29. "Political Party Platforms: Republican Party Platform of 1868," May 20, 1868, *The American Presidency Project*, compiled by Gerhard Peters and John T. Woolley, accessed January 4, 2018, http://www.presidency.ucsb.edu/ws/?pid=29622; "Political Party Platforms: Democratic Party Platform of 1868," July 4, 1868, *The American Presidency Project*, compiled by Gerhard Peters and

Notes to Pages 63–68

John T. Woolley, accessed January 4, 2018, http://www.presidency.ucsb.edu/ws/?pid=29579.

30. Ulysses Grant to William Tecumseh Sherman, May 19, 1868, *Grant Papers*, 18:257–58.

31. For examples of Grant's developing policy, see Ulysses Grant to William Tecumseh Sherman, March 14, 1866, ibid., 16:116–17, and Ulysses Grant to Edwin M. Stanton, May 16, 1866, ibid., 199–200.

32. Evan S. Connell, *Son of the Morning Star: Custer and the Little Bighorn* (New York: North Point Press, 1984), 182–97.

33. Brown, *Bury My Heart at Wounded Knee*, 168.

34. George A. Custer to Philip Sheridan, November 28, 1868, *Documents Submitted by the Secretary of War in Compliance with a Resolution of December 14, 1868 in Relation to the Late Indian Battle on the Washita River*, 40th Cong., 3rd Sess., Senate Executive Papers 1360, Senate Executive Document No. 18 (1869).

35. Ulysses Grant, "Inaugural Address," March 4, 1869, *Grant Papers*, 18:139–42.

36. Bishops Edward R. Ames, Matthew Simpson, and Other Methodist Clergy, March 1, 1868," *Grant Papers*, 18:197n; John B. Henderson, William S. Harney, Brevet Major General Alfred H. Terry, and General William Tecumseh Sherman, March 9, 1869, ibid., 18:198n.

37. Civil Rights Act, April 9, 1866, 14 Stat. 27–30 (1866); Treaty with the Wyandot, January 31, 1955, *Indian Affairs: Laws and Treaties*, 2:677–81; Fourteenth Amendment 14 Stat. 358; Armstrong, *Warrior in Two Camps*, 135–36; Ebenezer R. Hoar to Ulysses Grant, April 12, 1869, *Grant Papers*, 19:197n; Senator John M. Thayer to Ulysses Grant, March 6, 1869, *Grant Papers*, 19:197n.

38. Armstrong, *Warrior in Two Camps*, 137–40. See *Annual Report of the Commissioner of Indian Affairs, for the Year 1869* (Washington, DC: Government Printing Office, 1870), 3–42 for a summary of Indian service activities during Parker's first year of supervision.

39. Rayner Wickersham Kelsey, *Friends and the Indians, 1655–1917* (Philadelphia: Associated Executive Committee of Friends on Indian Affairs, 1917), 167–69, 187; Ely Parker to Benjamin Hallowell, February 15, 1869, *Grant Papers*, 18:193n.

40. Ely Parker, Circular Letter to Superintendent and Agents of the Indian Department, June 12, 1869, Records of the Central Superintendency of Indian Affairs, 1813–78, Letters Received from the Commissioner of Indian Affairs, Record Group 75, *Records of the Office of Indian Affairs* (Washington, DC: National Archives). See Ely Parker, "Report of the Commissioner of Indian Affairs," December 23, 1869 *Annual Report of the Commissioner of Indian Affairs, for the Year 1869*, 3–42 for a summation of Parker's hopes after ten months in office.

4. The Dawn of a Revolt

1. Ely Parker, "Report of the Commissioner of Indian Affairs," December 23, 1869, *Annual Report of the Commissioner of Indian Affairs, for the Year 1869*, 3–42.

2. John Ayers to Vincent Colyer, March 21, 1870, *Records of the Board of Indian Commissioners*, Letters Received, 1870–72, box 1, in Record Group (RG) 75.22 of the Records of the Office of Indian Affairs, RG 75 (Washington, DC: National Archives).

3. Paul R. Wylie, *Blood on the Marias: The Baker Massacre* (Norman: University of Oklahoma Press, 2016), 139, 145, 169.

4. Ibid., 181–201.

5. For an example of press coverage, see *New York Times*, February 24, March 10 and 12, 1870.

6. Appendix 23, *Second Annual Report of the Board of Indian Commissioners to the President of the United States, 1870* (Washington, DC: Government Printing Office, 1871), 89–93; Hutton, *Phil Sheridan and His Army*, 192–96.

7. For an example of Grant's leniency toward commanders, see his discussion of James Carleton in Ulysses Grant to William Tecumseh Sherman, April 18, 1866, *Grant Papers*, 16:164; "Commissioner Parker Requests the Board to Investigate the Piegan Massacre" and "Transferring the Indian Department to the War Department Prevented," *Second Annual Report of the Board of Indian Commissioners, 1870*, 89–90.

8. Ely Parker, "Report of the Commissioner of Indian Affairs," October 31, 1870, 3–12.

9. Eugene D. Schmiel, *Citizen-General: Jacob Dolson Cox and the Civil War Era* (Athens: Ohio University Press, 2014), 1–28, 57–98, 121–41, 176–232.

10. *New York Times*, June 7, 8, 9, 12, 15, 17, 1870; *New York Herald*, June 17, 1870.

11. James C. Olson, *Red Cloud and the Sioux Problem* (Lincoln: University of Nebraska Press, 1965), 100–113.

12. Armstrong, *Warrior in Two Camps*, 149–51.

13. "Authorization of the Board of Indian Commissioners," April 10, 1869, *Documents of United States Indian Policy*, 125–26.

14. Ely Parker, "Instructions to the Board of Indian Commissioners," May 26, 1869, ibid., 126.

15. Ulysses Grant, Executive Order, June 3, 1869, ibid.

16. For an example of Grant's call to civilize and Christianize the Indians, see Ulysses Grant, "Draft Annual Message," December 5, 1870, *Grant Papers*, 21:41; Prucha, *Great Father*, 1:506–7; Charles Lewis Slattery, *Felix Reville Brunot, 1820–1898: A Civilian in the War for the Union; President of the First Board of Indian Commissioners* (New York: Longmans, Green, 1901), 82–101.

17. Henry Whipple, *Lights and Shadows of a Long Episcopate; Being Reminiscences and Recollections of the Right Reverend Henry Benjamin Whipple, D.D., LL.D., Bishop of Minnesota* (New York: Macmillan, 1899), 1–32.

18. Ibid., 33–34; Henry Whipple, *An Appeal for the Red Man* (Faribault, MN: Cultural Republican, 1862), 1–10; Henry Whipple, "My Life among the Indians," *North American Review* 150 (April 1, 1890): 432–39.

19. William Welsh, *Taopi and His Friends; or, The Indians' Wrongs and Rights* (Philadelphia: Claxton, Remsen and Haffelfinger, 1869), i–xviii, 56–63, 85–87; Slattery, *Felix Reville Brunot*, 149–60.

5. Interrupted Odyssey

1. Parker, "Report of the Commissioner of Indian Affairs," October 31, 1870, *Annual Report of the Commissioner of Indian Affairs, for the Year 1870*, 5.

2. Ibid., 5.

3. *Congressional Globe*, 41st Cong., 2d Sess., pt. V, 1089–91, 4042–61, 5007–8, 5606–10, 5638.

4. Armstrong, *Warrior in Two Camps*, 149–50.

5. The prohibition is in Article 18 of An Act Making Appropriations for the Support of the Army, Etc., July 15, 1870, 40th Cong., 2nd Sess., chap. 294, 315–21; An Act Making Appropriations for the Naval Service, Etc., July 15, 1870, 40th Cong., 2nd Sess., chap. 295, 321–35.

6. An Act Making Appropriations for the Current and Contingent Expenses of the Indian Department, Etc., July 15, 1870, 40th Cong., 2nd Sess., chap. 296, 335–65.

7. Ulysses Grant, "Annual Message," December 6, 1869, *Grant Papers*, 20:38–39.

8. Ely Parker to Jacob Cox, October 31, 1870, *Annual Report of the Commissioner of Indian Affairs, for the Year 1870*, 10.

9. Grant, Annual Message, December 6, 1869, 20:39.

10. Brevet Colonel Samuel Ross to Ely S. Parker (Washington Superintendency Report), *Annual Report of the Commissioner of Indian Affairs, for the Year 1870*, 16–30.

11. Alfred Benjamin Meacham, *Wigwam and War-path; or, The Royal Chief in Chains* (Boston: John P. Dale, 1875), 1–74.

12. "Alfred Meacham to Ely Parker, September 21, 1870 (Oregon Superintendency Report)" *Annual Report of the Commissioner of Indian Affairs, for the Year 1870*, 48–55.

13. William Tecumseh Sherman, *Memoirs of General William T. Sherman*, 2nd ed. (New York: D. Appleton, 1904), 2:436–37.

14. President Benjamin Harrison applied the first civil service classifications in the Indian service to physicians, school superintendents and assistant superintendents, schoolteachers, and matrons; see Benjamin Harrison to John W. Noble (Secretary of the Interior), April 13, 1891, *Compilation of the Messages and Papers of the Presidents*, 9:173; "Report of the Board of Indian Commissioners," November 23, 1869, *Annual Report of the Commissioner of Indian Affairs, for the Year 1869*, 46; Armstrong, *Warrior in Two Camps*, 143–44; "Minutes of the November 17, 1869, Meeting of the Board of Indian Commissioners," *Records of the Board of Indian Commissioners, Papers of the Office of Indian Affairs*, Record Group 75.22 (Washington, DC: National Archives), 12–14.

15. Lawrie Tatum to Enoch Hoag, August 12, 1870, *Annual Report of the Commissioner of Indian Affairs, for the Year 1870*, 260–65; Lawrie Tatum, *Our Red Brothers and the Peace Policy of President Ulysses S. Grant* (Philadelphia: John P. Winston, 1899), 21–55.

16. Ely Parker to Jacob Cox, October 31, 1870, 3–12.

17. *Memorial and Affidavits Showing Outrages Perpetrated by the Apache Indians, in the Territory of Arizona, for the Years 1869 and 1870* (San Francisco: Francis and Valentine, 1871), 3–4.

18. Ely Parker, "Report of the Commissioner of Indian Affairs," October 31, 1870, 7–8.

19. Armstrong, *Warrior in Two Camps*, 151; "Journal of the General Council of the Indian Territory," *Chronicles of Oklahoma* 3, no. 1 (March 1925): 33–44; "Journal of the Adjourned Session of the First General Council of the Indian Territory," *Chronicles of Oklahoma* 3, no. 2 (June 1925): 120–36.

20. "Okmulgee Constitution," *Chronicles of Oklahoma* 3, no. 3 (September 1925): 120–36.

21. Columbus Delano to Ulysses Grant, January 25, 1871 (including a summation of Ely S. Parker to Columbus Delano, January 4, 1871), *Grant Papers*, 21:153n–56n; Armstrong, *Warrior in Two Camps*, 151.

22. William Welsh to Columbus Delano, November 21, 1870, *Investigation into Indian Affairs, before the Committee on Appropriations of the House of Representatives. Argument of N. P. Chipman, on Behalf of Hon. E. S. Parker, Commissioner of Indian Affairs* (Washington, DC: Powell, Ginck, 1871), 120; William Welsh's Letter Dated December 7, 1870, ibid., 111–22.

23. Letter of William Welsh, December 7, 1870, ibid., 111–15; House Resolution, December 12, 1870, ibid., 111.

24. Ely Parker to Columbus Delano, January 12, 1871, ibid., 123–25.

25. "Aaron Sargent," "William Lawrence," and "James Beck," *Biographical Directory of the United States Congress: 1774–Present*, accessed January 4, 2018,

http://bioguide.congress.gov; William Welsh, "Statement of Misconduct in the Indian Office," January 9, 1871, *Investigation into Indian Affairs*, 127.

26. Ely Parker to Honorable A. A. Sargent, January 13, 1871, *Investigation into Indian Affairs*, 128–29.

27. House Resolution, December 12, 1870, ibid., 111; Testimony of Thomas T. Buckley, January 27, 1871, ibid., 40–43.

28. N. P. Chipman, *The Tragedy of Andersonville: Trial of Captain Henry Wirz, the Prison Keeper*, 2nd ed. (Sacramento, CA: printed by the author, 1911), 32–50; "Norton P. Chipman," *Biographical Directory*.

29. For Chipman's opening cross-examinations, see Testimony of Vincent Colyer, Felix Brunot, S. E. Ward, January 17 and 24, 1871, *Investigation into Indian Affairs*, 7–18.

30. Testimony of Ely S. Parker, January 24, 1871, ibid., 18–36.

31. Testimony of William Meyers, L. H. Roberts, Thomas T. Buckley, Edward H. Amdon, Major B. DuBarry, and General M. C. Meigs, January 25 and 27, 1870, ibid., 38–50.

32. Testimony of James G. Blunt, January 31, 1871, ibid., 51–58.

33. Testimony of James W. Bosler, January 31, 1871, ibid., 58–62.

34. Ibid., 62–63.

35. Ulysses Grant to Congress, January 31, 1871, including Ely Parker to Columbus Delano, January 25, 1871; Columbus Delano to Ulysses Grant, January 25, 1871; and Ocmulgee Constitution, *Grant Papers*, 21:152–53, 153n–55n.

36. Testimony of Jacob Cox, February 1, 1871, *Investigation into Indian Affairs*, 74–80.

37. Testimony of Charles D. Woolworth, Walter A. Burleigh, William Nicolson, Joseph Williamson, Ely S. Parker, A. T. Huntington, General M. C Meigs, William Meyers, Major B. DuBarry, John Finn, Robert McBratney, Thomas J. Buckley, Henry C. Fahnestock, John T. Baldwin, Captain DeWitt Clinton Poole, Thomas E. McGraw, James W. Bosler, and Alvin C. Leighton, February 1, 3, 6, and 8, 1871, ibid., 81–110.

38. Argument of Mr. Welsh, February 15, 1871, ibid., 225–40.

39. Letter of Mr. Parker to Honorable A. A. Sargent (n.d.), ibid., 240–41.

40. For information on Vincent Colyer, see David Silkenat, "'A Typical Negro': Gordon, Peter Vincent Colyer, and the Story behind Slavery's Most Famous Photograph," *American Nineteenth Century History*, 15 (2014), No. 2, 176–179.

41. Remarks of Mr. Chipman (n.d.), *Investigation into Indian Affairs*, 241–86.

42. The Committee on Appropriations, "Report, February 25, 1871," ibid., i–vi.

43. Proposed Amendment to House Appropriations Bill, ibid., vii.

44. An Act Making Appropriations for the Current and Contingent Expenses of the Indian Department, Etc., March 3, 1871, 41st Cong., 3rd Sess., chap. 1479, 544–71; H.R. Rep. No. 41-39, i–vii, 32–33; Additional Act of Congress, March 3, 1871, *Second Annual Report of the Board of Indian Commissioners*, i.

45. *Congressional Globe*, 41st Cong., 3rd Sess., part 3, 1811–12, 1822–25. See also Buyneel, *Third Space of Sovereignty*, 65–96.

46. William H. Smith, "Opinion of the Assistant Attorney General," January 31, 1873, *Records of the Board of Indian Commissioners*.

47. For contemporary scholarship on issues related to tribal sovereignty, see Wilkins and Loawaima, *Uneven Ground*; for examples of the more complex ways that Grant's contemporaries applied citizenship, specifically as defined in the Constitution, to the Indians, see Stacey S. Smith, "Emancipating Peons, Excluding Coolies: —Reconstructing Coercion in the American West," in Downs Masur, *World the Civil War Made*, 46–74; for a discussion of equating civilization and citizenship in Reconstruction politics, see Stephen Kantrowitz, "'Not Quite Constitutionalized': The Meanings of 'Civilization' and the Limits of Native American Citizenship," ibid., 75–105.

48. Executive Orders Related to Indian Reservations from May 14, 1855, to July 1, 1912 (Washington, DC: Government Printing Office, 1902), 5–11, 23–24, 33–35, 38–39, 43, 59–62, 66–67, 77, 89–92, 94–97, 110–11, 114–15, 117–18, 120–22, 128–29, 133–35, 138–40, 157–60, 162–63, 196–97, 205–8.

49. "Grant's Meeting with Cherokee Delegation," January 20, 1872, *Grant Papers*, 21:156n. For a detailed account of Cherokee governance, see Julie Reed, *Serving the Nation: Cherokee Sovereignty and Social Welfare, 1800–1907* (Norman: University of Oklahoma Press, 2016); for insights into how the major Southern tribes defined citizenship, see Mikaela Adams, *Who Belongs: Race, Resources, and Tribal Citizenship in the Native South* (Oxford: Oxford University Press, 2016).

50. James R. Hastings, "The Tragedy at Camp Grant in 1871," *Arizona and the West*, 1, no. 2 (1959): 146–60; Appendix A b, nos. 1–27, *Third Annual Report of the Board of Indian Commissioners to the President of the United States, 1871* (Washington, DC: Government Printing Office, 1872), 13–86.

51. *Papago* is a term used in the primary sources from the period, but today the tribe refers to itself as the Tohono O'odham, or "Desert People."

52. The Treaty of Washington, *The Treaty of Washington with Correspondence, Etc.* (Ottawa: Times Steam, 1871), 13–33

53. See *Grant Papers*, 21:28–34 for charges against Fred Grant.

54. Opinion of the Assistant Attorney General, Vincent Colyer to William Welsh, March 1, May 27, and June 23, 1871, *Records of the Board of Indian*

Commissioners; Ely Parker to Ulysses Grant, June 29, 1871, *Grant Papers*, 22:71n; Ulysses Grant to Ely Parker, July 13, 1871, June 29, 1871, *Grant Papers*, 22:71; *New York Herald*, June 30, 1871.

55. Armstrong, *Warrior in Two Camps*, 160–62; William Welsh to Jacob Cox, September 13, 1871, *Grant Papers*, 22:84.

6. A Sea of Change

1. Appendix A *a*, "Report of a Visit to Red Cloud and Chiefs of the Oglalla Sioux, by Commissioner Felix R. Brunot," June 14, 1871, *Third Annual Report of the Board of Indian Commissioners*, 13–14; Ulysses Grant to Major General John M. Schofield, March 6, 1872, *Grant Papers*, 23:40–41; Ulysses Grant to George H. Stuart, October 26, 1872, *Grant Papers*, 23:270.

2. Ulysses Grant, "Draft of Annual Message," December 4, 1871, *Grant Papers*, 22:259; Ulysses Grant to George H. Stuart, October 26, 1872, ibid., 23:270.

3. H. R. Clum, "Report of the Commissioner of Indian Affairs," November 15, 1871, *Report of the Commissioner of Indian Affairs to the Secretary of the Interior, for the Year 1871* (Washington, DC: Government Printing Office, 1872), 1–8.

4. Francis A. Walker, "Report of the Commissioner of Indian Affairs," *Report of the Commissioner of Indian Affairs to the Secretary of the Interior, for the Year 1872* (Washington, DC: Government Printing Office, 1873), 3–14.

5. Ibid., 15–74.

6. Francis A. Walker, *The Indian Question* (Boston: J. R. Osgood, 1874), 5–147.

7. S. G. Arnold, "President Grant's Indian Policy," *Methodist Quarterly Review* 37 (July 1877), 409–30.

8. *Third Annual Report of the Board of Indian Commissioners*, 11–12.

9. *Second Annual Report of the Board of Indian Commissioners*, 7.

10. Board of Indian Commissioners, *Journal of the Second Annual Conference of the Board of Indian Commissioners with the Representatives of the Religious Societies Cooperating with the Government, and Reports of Their Work among the Indians* (Washington, DC: Government Printing Office, 1873), 3–22.

11. Peter J. Rahill, *The Catholic Indian Missions and Grant's Peace Policy, 1870–1884* (Washington, DC: Catholic University of America Press, 1953), 33.

12. *Second Annual Report of the Board of Indian Commissioners*, 4, 111–12.

13. E. Laveille, *The Life of Father de Smet, S.J., 1801–1873* (New York: P. J. Kennedy and Sons, 1915), 1–201; Pierre-Jean de Smet, "Indian Symbolic Catechism, 1843," Bureau of Catholic Indian Missions Records 08-1 G-01 (Milwaukee: Marquette University), accessed January 4, 2018, http://cdm16280.contentdm.oclc.org/cdm/ref/collection/p128701coll4/id/45.

14. Laveille, *Life of Father De Smet*, 229–252, 347–358.

15. "Father De Smet to Archbishop Blanchet, 1870," in *Life, Letters and Travels of Father Pierre-Jean de Smet, S.J., 1801–1873*, edited by Hiram Martin Chittenden and Alfred Talbot Richardson (New York: Francis P. Harper, 1905), 1:124n.

16. Ibid., 1:115–20.

17. Ibid., 1:120–26.

18. Father De Smet to Archbishop Blanchet, September 1866, ibid., 3:1062–77.

19. Ibid., 1:119.

20. Ibid., 1:119–20.

21. Walker, "Report of the Commissioner of Indian Affairs," 72–74.

22. *Second Annual Report of the Board of Indian Commissioners*, 33–36; Rahill, *Catholic Indian Missions*, 37.

23. Board of Indian Commissioners, *Journal of the Second Annual Conference*, 3–22.

24. Ibid., 3–5.

25. Ibid., 4, 22.

26. William Wright, *History of the Big Bonanza* (Hartford, CT: American, 1876), 47–60, 133–42; Eliot Lord, *Comstock Mining and Miners* (Washington, DC: Government Printing Office, 1883), 35–55, 301–21; Ray Allen Billington and Martin Ridge, *Westward Expansion: A History of the American Frontier*, 6th ed. (Albuquerque: University of New Mexico Press, 2006), 259–78.

27. Granville M. Dodge, "How We Built the Union Pacific Railroad," 61st Cong., 2nd Sess., Senate Document No. 477 (Washington, DC: Government Printing Office, 1910), 23–24; Sidney Dillon, "Historic Moment: Driving the Last Spike," *Scribner's Magazine* 12 (August 1892): 258–59; *Guide to the Union Pacific Railroad Lands* (Omaha: Land Department of the Union Pacific Railroad, 1870), 3–19; Billington and Ridge, *Westward Expansion*, 279–98.

28. Joseph G. McCoy, *Historic Sketches of the Cattle Trade of the West and Southwest* (Kansas City, MO: Ramsey, Millett and Hudson, 1874), 1–427; Billington and Ridge, *Westward Expansion*, 321–40.

29. Frederick Luebke, "Ethnic Group Settlement on the Great Plains," *Western Historical Quarterly* 8, no. 4 (October 1977): 405–30; Billington and Ridge, *Westward Expansion*, 341–76.

30. Larry Barsness, *Heads, Hides and Horns: The Compleat Buffalo Book* (Fort Worth: Texas Christian University Press, 1985), 128; Billington and Ridge, *Westward Expansion*, 48–49, 316–17.

31. "The Buffalo Go," in *American Indian Myths and Legends*, edited by Richard Erdoes and Alfonzo Ortiz (New York: Pantheon Books, 1984), 490–91.

32. Billington and Ridge, *Westward Expansion*, 262–68, 350–51.

33. Ulysses Grant, "Fourth Annual Message," December 2, 1872, *Messages and Letters of the Presidents*, 9:4154.

34. Ulysses Grant, "Second Inaugural Address," March 4, 1873, ibid., 9:4175–77.

35. Ibid.

36. Columbus Delano to the Acting Commissioner of Indian Affairs, January 29, 1873, Adjutant-General's Office, War Department, *Official Copies of Correspondence Relative to the War with Modoc Indians in 1872–'73, Prepared under Resolution of the United States House of Representatives, Dated January 7, 1874* (Washington, DC: Government Printing Office, 1874), 66.

7. War on the Far Horizon

1. S. A. Barrett, *The Material Culture of the Klamath Lake and Modoc Indians of Northeastern California and Southern Oregon* (Berkeley, CA: University Press, 1910), 1–56.

2. Jeff C. Riddle, *The Indian History of the Modoc War and the Causes That Led to It* (San Francisco, 1914), 17–27.

3. Treaty with the Klamath, Etc., October 14, 1864, *Indian Affairs: Laws and Treaties*, 2:865–88.

4. Alfred Meacham, "The Tragedy of the Lava Beds," in *Life of Alfred B. Meacham: Together with His Lecture, The Tragedy of the Lava Beds*, by T. A. Bland (Washington, DC: T. A. and M. C. Bland, 1883), 7–12.

5. F. B. Odeneal to Frank Wheaton, November 25, 1872, Adjutant-General's Office, *Correspondence Relative to the Modoc War*, 38; John Q. Adams to the Commanding Officer at Fort Klamath (Major John Green), December 1, 1872, ibid., 40.

6. James Jackson to John Green, December 2, 1872, ibid., 42–44; Riddle, *Indian History of the Modoc War*, 41–49.

7. James Wheaton to Edward Canby, January 19, 1873, Adjutant-General's Office, *Correspondence Relative to the Modoc War*, 50–51; James Wheaton to General Edward Canby, Third Field Order (January 1873), ibid., 54–58; John Green to the Assistant Adjutant General, January 25, 1873, ibid., 58–61; Edwin Mason to John Green, January 21, 1873, ibid., 61–62; R. F. Bernard to John Green, January 25, 1873, ibid., 62–63; Riddle, *Indian History of the Modoc War*, 50–57.

8. Cora Du Bois, *The 1870 Ghost Dance* (Lincoln: University of Nebraska Press, 1939), 1–56.

9. For the Modoc Peace Commission's organization, see Adjutant-General's Office, *Correspondence Relative to the Modoc War*, 241–64. Another important source is Record Group 48, *Records of the Indian Division of the Office of the*

Secretary of the Interior, Special Files, 1848–1907, Record Group 48, reel 4, folders 1–18, and reel 5, folders 19–51 (Washington, DC: National Archives).

10. Edward Canby to William Tecumseh Sherman, January 30, 1873 (telegram), Adjutant-General's Office, *Correspondence Relative to the Modoc War*, 64.

11. E. D. Townshend to William T. Sherman, January 30, 1873, ibid., 63; William T. Sherman to Edward Canby, January 30, 1873, ibid., 64; Columbus Delano to William Belknap, January 29, 1863, ibid., 65–66.

12. Riddle, *Indian History of the Modoc War*, 76–97; Meacham, "Tragedy of the Lava Beds," 25–43; Appendix C, "Report of A. B. Meacham, Special Commissioner to the Modocs, upon the Late Modoc War," *Annual Report of the Commissioner of Indian Affairs, for the Year 1873*, 74–82.

13. *New York Times*, April 13, 1873; newspaper clippings, 2 vols., *Records of the Board of Indian Commissioners*; Robert Winston Mardock, *The Reformers and the American Indian* (Columbia: University of Missouri Press, 1971), 117–18. A detailed account of press coverage of the Modoc War can be found in Boyd Cothran, *Remembering the Modoc War: Redemptive Violence and the Making of American Innocence* (Chapel Hill: University of North Carolina Press, 2014).

14. Meacham, "Tragedy of the Lava Beds," 4–7; Riddle, *Indian History of the Modoc War*, 188–94; George Williams to Ulysses Grant, June 7, 1873, *Grant Papers*, 24:200n–201n; "Proceedings of a Military Commission Convened at Fort Klamath, Oregon, for the Trial of Modoc Prisoners," Adjutant-General's Office, *Correspondence Relative to the Modoc War*, 133–83; Ulysses Grant, Executive Order, August 22, 1873, *Grant Papers*, 24:196; Ulysses Grant, Executive Order, September 10, 1873, Adjutant-General's Office, *Correspondence Relative to the Modoc War*, 203; Appendix C.2., "Report of Captain M. C. Wilkinson, United States Army, Special Commissioner for Removing the Modocs into the Indian Territory," December 12, 1873, *Annual Report of the Commissioner of Indian Affairs, for the Year 1873*, 82.

15. "Secretary Columbus Delano's Report," October 31, 1873, Adjutant-General's Office, *Correspondence Relative to the Modoc War*, 329.

16. Columbus Delano, *Speech of Hon. Columbus Delano, Delivered at Raleigh, North Carolina, July 24, 1872* (Washington, DC: YA Pamphlet Collection, Library of Congress, 1872), 5–10.

17. For a detailed account of the Kiowa on their Indian Territory reservation, see Jacki Thompson Rand, *Kiowa Humanity and the Invasion of the State* (Lincoln: University of Nebraska Press, 2008); for the most recent account of Parker's life, see S. C. Gwynne, *Empire of the Summer Moon: Quanah Parker and the Rise and Fall of the Comanches, the Most Powerful Indian Tribe in American History* (New York: Simon and Schuster, 2010); Clyde Jackson and Grace

Jackson, *Quanah Parker, Last Chief of the Comanches: A Study in Southwestern Frontier History* (New York: Exposition Press, 1963), 83–89; Billy Dixon, *Life and Adventures of "Billy" Dixon* (Guthrie, OK: Co-operative, 1914), 209–17; Charles Henry Sommers, *"Quanah Parker": Last Chief of the Comanches* (St. Louis: printed by the author, 1943), 22–53.

18. For military correspondence in the Red River War, see "Letters Sent and Received, Division of the Missouri," *Records of United States Army*, Record Group 393 (Washington, DC: National Archives); Hutton, *Phil Sheridan and His Army*, 248; James L. Haley, *The Buffalo War: The History of the Red River Indian Uprising of 1874* (Garden City, NY: Doubleday, 1976), 106.

19. *Annual Report of the Secretary of War, 1874* (Washington, DC: Government Printing Office, 1875), 1:25, 27; Hutton, *Phil Sheridan and His Army*, 248–49; Haley, *Buffalo War*, 105.

20. Haley, *Buffalo War*, 114–20.

21. Nelson Miles, *Personal Recollections and Observations of General Nelson A. Miles, Embracing a Brief View of the Civil War; or, From New England to the Golden Gate and the Story of His Indian Campaigns, with Comments on the Exploration, Development, and Progress of Our Great Western Empire* (Chicago: Werner, 1896), 167–68.

22. Nelson Miles to the Adjutant General, October 1, 1874, in Dixon, *Life and Adventures of "Billy" Dixon*, 275–78; Miles, *Personal Recollections*, 172–73. For Grant's release of the two chiefs, see Columbus Delano to Orville Babcock, April 18, 1873, *Grant Papers*, 24:110n–11n.

23. Haley, *Buffalo War*, 175–83; Robert Goldthwaite Carter, *On the Border with Mackenzie; or, Winning West Texas from the Comanches* (Washington, DC: Eynon Printing Company, 1935), 481–96.

24. Jackson and Jackson, *Quanah Parker*, 107–9; Sommers, *"Quanah Parker,"* 33–48; "Stumbling Bear and Twenty-Three Others," June 23, 1875, *Grant Papers*, 26:70n–71n.

25. Newspaper clippings, *Records of the Board of Indian Commissioners*.

26. "Obituary: Edward Parmelee Smith," *New York Times*, August 16, 1876.

27. Edward Parmelee Smith, "Report of the Commissioner of Indian Affairs," November 1, 1874, *Annual Reports of the Commissioner of Indian Affairs, for the Year 1874*, 10.

28. Ibid., 11.

29. Ibid., 16.

30. Edward Parmelee Smith, "Report of the Commissioner of Indian Affairs," November 1, 1875, *Annual Report of the Commissioner of Indian Affairs, for the Year 1875*, 6–9.

8. The Web of Corruption

1. Samuel B. Axtell et al., "Petition to President Grant, March 1874," *Grant Papers*, 25:362n–63n; Philip Sheridan to Edward D. Townsend, March 9, 15, 1874, ibid., 25n; Louis Rough to Ulysses Grant, February 8, 1874, ibid., 25n; Augustus Captin et al. to Ulysses Grant, December 14, 1874, ibid., 359n. For an in-depth discussion of the relationship between the Choctaw and Chickasaw tribes and their African and African American slaves, see Barbara Krauthamer, *Black Slaves, Indian Masters: Slavery, Emancipation, and Citizenship in the Native American South* (Chapel Hill: University of North Carolina Press, 2013); for insights into how the major Southern tribes defined citizenship, see Adams, *Who Belongs*.

2. For examples, see Oliver W. Barnes (Union League Club) to Ulysses Grant, March 15, 1875, *Grant Papers*, 26:85n; William Belknap to Ulysses Grant, March 17, 1875, ibid., 84n; and Ely Adams et al. to Ulysses Grant, March 17, 1875, ibid., 85n; Hutton, *Phil Sheridan and His Army*, 167–68; William Ludlow, "Extract from Report of the Chief Engineer, Dakota Territory," in *The Black Hills; or, The Last Hunting Ground of the Dakotahs: A Complete History of the Black Hills of Dakota, from Their First Invasion in 1874 to the Present Time*, by Annie D. Tallent (St. Louis: Nixon-Jones, 1899), 13–14.

3. Doane Robinson, *History of South Dakota* (Logansport, IN: B. F. Bowen, 1904), 1:260–73; Thomas Buecker, ed., "'Distance Lends Enchantment to the View': The 1874 Black Hills Expedition Diary of Fred W. Power," *South Dakota History* 27, no. 4 (1997), 197–260.

4. Custer's report is quoted in Tallent, *Black Hills*, 15.

5. Robinson, *History of South Dakota*, 1:260; quote is from Custer's report in Tallent, *Black Hills*, 15.

6. Robinson, *History of South Dakota*, 1:270–72.

7. Thomas M. Vincent to William Tecumseh Sherman, July 12, 1875, *Grant Papers*, 26, 163n; Robinson, *History of South Dakota*, 1:261.

8. Ulysses Grant, "Speech (to the Cherokee Nation)," October 11, 1874, "Speech (to the Choctaw Nation)," October 12, 1874, "Speech (to the Creek Nation)," October 12, 1874, *Grant Papers*, 25:253–54, 257.

9. Ulysses Grant, "Speech (to the Cherokee Nation)," October 11, 1874, "Speech (to the Choctaw Nation)," October 12, 1874, "Speech (to the Creek Nation)," October 12, 1874, ibid., 25:253–54, 257.

10. Ulysses Grant, "Draft Annual Message," December 7, 1874, ibid., 25:282.

11. Columbus Delano to William Belknap, March 22, 1875, *Grant Papers*, 26:113–14; Henry Newton and Walter Jenney, *Report on the Geology and Resources*

of the Black Hills of Dakota, with Atlas (Washington, DC: Government Printing Office, 1880), 2; Columbus Delano to Ulysses Grant, June 9, 1875, *Grant Papers*, 26:86n.

12. Olson, *Red Cloud and the Sioux Problem*, 171–98; Othniel C. Marsh to Ulysses Grant, July 10, 1875, *Grant Papers*, 26:208n–14n: Ulysses Grant to Othniel Marsh, July 16, 1875, ibid., 208.

13. Ulysses Grant, "Speech to the Sioux Delegation," May 26, 1875, *Grant Papers*, 26:119–20.

14. Ulysses Grant, "Council with the Sioux," June 2, 1875, ibid., 26:138–43; "Speech of Secretary Delano," June 2, 1875, ibid., 26:146n–47n; Olson, *Red Cloud and the Sioux Problem*, 187; *New York Times*, June 6, 1875; *New York Herald*, June 11, 1875.

15. "End of the Big Talk at Washington," *Frank Leslie's Illustrated Newspaper*, June 19, 1875.

16. Newton and Jenney, *Geology and Resources of the Black Hills*, 2, 5, 300.

17. Henry T. Crosby to Orville Babcock, July 5, 1875, *Grant Papers*, 26:162n–63n.

18. "Exonerated," *Washington Weekly Chronicle*, February 17, 1874, *Records of the Board of Indian Commissioners, Papers of the Office of Indian Affairs*, Record Group 75.

19. Felix Brunot to Ulysses Grant, May 8, 1870, *Grant Papers*, 25:375n–76n; Levi P. Luckey to Felix Brunot, May 18, 1874, ibid., 25:376n; Slattery, *Felix Reville Brunot*, 222–24; Felix Brunot and the Board of Indian Commissioners to Ulysses Grant, May 27, 1874, *Records of the Board of Indian Commissioners*.

20. *Report of the Special Commission Appointed to Investigate the Affairs of the Red Cloud Indian Agency, July 1875, Together with the Testimony and Accompanying Documents* (Washington, DC: Government Printing Office, 1875), iii–lxxv; *Sixth Annual Report of the Board of Indian Commissioners to the President of the United States, 1874* (Washington, DC: Government Printing Office, 1875), 3–14.

21. "Certain Surveying Frauds: Special Dispatches to the New York Times," *New York Times*, April 11, 1876.

22. For Grant's choices and subsequent changes, see "Ulysses Grant to Columbus Delano, June 16, 1875, *Grant Papers* 26:159–60n; "Frank Wayland Palmer," *Annals of Iowa* 8 (1908): 316–17; "Abram Comingo," *Biographical Directory*; William Joseph Barnds, "The Ministry of the Reverend Samuel Dutton Hinman, among the Sioux," *Historical Magazine of the Protestant Episcopal Church* 38, no. 4 (December 1969), 393–401.

23. W. B. Allison et al., *Report of the Commission Appointed to Treat with the Sioux Indians for the Relinquishment of the Black Hills* (Washington, DC: Government Printing Office, 1875), 3–19.

24. Columbus Delano to Ulysses Grant, July 5, 1875, *Grant Papers*, 26:330n–31n; Ulysses Grant to Columbus Delano, September 22, 1875, ibid., 26:329.

25. Arthur T. Pierson, *Zachariah Chandler: An Outline Sketch of His Life and Public Services* (Detroit: Post and Tribune, 1880), 337–55.

26. John Q. Smith, "Report of the Commissioner of Indian Affairs," October 30, 1876, *Annual Report of the Commissioner of Indian Affairs, for the Year 1876* (Washington: Government Printing Office, 1877), iii–xxv.

27. "Chronology," November 3, 1875, *Grant Papers*, 26:xxvi; Philip Sheridan to Alfred Terry, November 9, 1875, ibid., 26:163n; Hutton, *Phil Sheridan and His Army*, 298–99.

28. Robinson, *History of South Dakota*, 1:282–84; Billington and Ridge, *Westward Expansion*, 276–77.

29. Hutton, *Phil Sheridan and His Army*, 301–4; James H. Bradley, *The March of the Montana Column: A Prelude to the Custer Disaster*, ed. Edgar I. Stewart (Norman: University of Oklahoma Press, 1961), 7–68; John Gibbon, *Gibbon on the Sioux Campaign of 1876* (Bellevue, NV: Old Army Press, 1970), 4–17; J. W. Vaughn, *The Reynolds Campaign on Powder River* (Norman: University of Oklahoma Press, 1961), 43–163.

30. "Extravagance and Corruption in the War Department," *New York Herald*, February 10, 1876; Edward S. Cooper, *William Worth Belknap: An American Disgrace* (Madison, NJ: Fairleigh Dickinson University Press, 2003), 17–39, 233; William Belknap to Ulysses Grant, March 2, 1875, *Grant Papers*, 27:54n; Ulysses Grant to William Belknap, March 2, 1875, ibid., 27:53.

31. George Armstrong Custer, *My Life on the Plains; or, Personal Experiences with Indians* (New York: Sheldon, 1874), 120–23; Hutton, *Phil Sheridan and His Army*, 310.

32. William Tecumseh Sherman to Philip Sheridan, April 28, 1875, *Grant Papers*, 27:71n; Philip Sheridan to William Tecumseh Sherman, April 29, 1875, ibid., 27:71n; George Armstrong Custer to Ulysses Grant, May 1, 1876, ibid., 27:72n; Ulysses Grant Jr. to William Tecumseh Sherman, May 4, 1876, ibid., 27:72n (with clipping from the *New York World*); William Tecumseh Sherman to Alfred Terry, May 8, 1875, ibid., 27:72n; Hutton, *Phil Sheridan and His Army*, 310–13.

33. Ernie LaPointe, *Sitting Bull: His Life and Legacy* (Salt Lake City: Gibbs-Smith, 2009), 64–65: Robert M. Utley, *Sitting Bull: The Life and Times of an American Patriot* (New York: Henry Holt, 1993), 138; Connell, *Son of the Morning Star*, 264–332, 373–411; James Donovan, *A Terrible Glory: The Last Great Battle of the American West* (New York: Little, Brown, 2008), 204–314; Ulysses Grant

to the Senate, July 8, 1876, *Grant Papers*, 27:169; William Tecumseh Sherman to Ulysses Grant, July 8, 1875, ibid., 27:170n–72n.

34. Ulysses Grant, "Interview at Long Branch," September 1, 1876, *Grant Papers*, 27:250n.

35. "The Career of G. W. Manypenny," *Wisconsin Magazine of History* 1, no. 3 (March 1918): 324–25.

36. George Manypenny, et al., "Report of the Sioux Commission Appointed to Obtain Certain Concessions from the Sioux," Senate Executive Document 9, 44th Cong., 2nd Sess., 330–57 (1876).

37. An Act to Ratify an Agreement with Certain Bands of the Sioux Nation of Indians and also with the Northern Arapaho and Cheyenne Indians, 44th Cong., 2nd Sess., chap. 72, February 28, 1877.

38. Ulysses Grant, "Draft Annual Message," December 3, 1876, *Grant Papers*, 28:65.

9. A Forgotten Legacy

1. Brown, *Bury My Heart at Wounded Knee*, 315–66, 415–50.

2. Helen Hunt Jackson, *A Century of Dishonor: A Sketch of the United States Government's Dealings with Some of the Indian Tribes* (New York: Harper and Brothers, 1881), viii, 359. For criticism of Grant's "Peace Policy," see Robert Utley, "The Celebrated Peace Policy of General Grant," *North Dakota History* 20 (July 1953): 121–42; see also Henry G. Waltmann, "Circumstantial Reformer: President Grant & the Indian Problem," *Arizona and the West* 13, no. 4 (Winter 1971): 323–42. Recent works that evaluate Grant's Indian policy in light of his Reconstruction experience but continue to characterize it as a "peace" or "Quaker" policy include Deloria and Wilkins, *Tribes, Treaties and Constitutional Tribulations*, Cahill, *Federal Fathers and Mothers*, and Genetin-Pilawa, *Crooked Paths to Allotment*.

3. General William Tecumseh Sherman to Congressman W. A. J. Sparks, January 19, 1876, *Documents of American Indian Policy*, 145–46; John Schofield, *Annual Report of the Secretary of War 1868*, House Executive Document 1, 40th Cong., 3rd Sess., Ser. 1367, xvii–xviii; Nelson A. Miles, "The Indian Question," *North American Review* 128 (March 1879): 309–11.

4. Clinton Fisk, et al., *Tenth Annual Report of the Board of Indian Commissioners, for the Year 1878* (Washington, DC: Government Printing Office, 1878), 9–13.

5. Henry Whipple, Preface, in Jackson, *A Century of Dishonor*, v–x.

6. Jackson, *Century of Dishonor*, 32–297.

7. Ibid., 337–42.

8. Mardock, *Reformers and the American Indian*, 198–202.

9. Chester Alan Arthur, "State of the Union Address," December 6, 1881, *Compilation of the Messages and Papers of the Presidents*, 8:55–56.

10. An Act to Provide for the Allotment of Lands in Severalty to Indians on the Various Reservations, *Indian Affairs: Laws and Treaties*, 1:33–36.

11. An Act to Amend and Further Extend the Benefits of the Act Approved February Eighth, Eighteen Hundred and Eighty-Seven, 26 Stat. 794; Amendments to the Dawes Act, February 28, 1891, 26 Stat. 794; Burke Act (Forced Fee Patenting Act), May 8, 1906, 34 Stat. 182; Indian Citizenship Act, June 2, 1924, 43 Stat. 253.

12. See Janet A. McDonnell, *The Dispossession of the American Indian, 1877–1934* (Bloomington: Indiana University Press, 1991), for an analysis of allotment's impact.

13. Charles Eastman, *The Soul of the Indian* (Boston: Houghton, 1911); Luther Standing Bear, *My Indian Boyhood* (Boston: Houghton Mifflin, 1931); John Neihardt, *Black Elk Speaks: Being the Life Story of a Holy Man of the Sioux* (New York: William Morrow, 1932).

14. Lewis H. Morgan, *The League of the Ho-dé-no-sau-nee or Iroquois* (Rochester, NY: Sage and Brother, 1851), xi.

15. Armstrong, *Warrior in Two Camps*, 172–73.

16. Ibid., 173.

17. Lewis Merriam, et al., *The Problem of Indian Administration: Report of a Survey Made at the Request of Honorable Hubert Work, Secretary of the Interior, and Submitted to Him, February 21, 1928* (Baltimore: Johns Hopkins Press, 1928).

18. The board's efforts to eradicate Indian culture are clearly seen in the *Records of the Board of Indian Commissioners* from the late 1870s through the early 1930s in the National Archives. Two excellent studies on John Collier are Lawrence Kelly, *The Assault on Assimilation: John Collier and the Origins of Indian Policy Reform* (Albuquerque: University of New Mexico Press, 1983), and Kenneth R. Philip, *John Collier's Crusade for Indian Reform* (Tucson: University of Arizona Press, 1970). See also Mary Stockwell, "Native Americans: Experiences and Culture," in *A Companion to Warren G. Harding, Calvin Coolidge, and Herbert Hoover*, ed. Katherine A. S. Sibley (Malden, MA: Wiley Blackwell, 2014), 251–69; Wheeler-Howard Act (Indian Reorganization Act), June 18, 1934, 48 Stat. 984.

19. Neihardt, *Black Elk Speaks*, 250.

Bibliography

Primary Sources

An Act to Amend and Further Extend the Benefits of the Act Approved February Eighth, Eighteen Hundred and Eighty-Seven. 26 Stat. 794 (1891).

"The Adjourned Session of the First General Council of the Indian Territory." *Chronicles of Oklahoma* 3, no. 2 (June 1925): 120–36.

Adjutant-General's Office, War Department. *Official Copies of Correspondence Relative to the War with Modoc Indians in 1872–'73, Prepared under Resolution of the United States House of Representatives, Dated January 7, 1784.* Washington, DC: Government Printing Office, 1874.

Allison, William, et al. *Report of the Commission Appointed to Treat with the Sioux Indians for the Relinquishment of the Black Hills.* Washington, DC: Government Printing Office, 1875.

Amendments to the Dawes Act. 26 Stat. 794 (1891).

American State Papers: Foreign Relations 3:745–53.

American State Papers: Indian Affairs 1:12–14; 2:3–5, 148–50.

Annual Reports of the Board of Indian Commissioners to the President, 1869–1878. Washington, DC: Government Printing Office, 1870–79.

Annual Reports of the Commissioner of Indian Affairs, for the Years 1865–1878. Washington, DC: Government Printing Office, 1866–79.

Annual Reports of the Secretary of Interior, for the Years 1869–1878. Washington, DC: Government Printing Office, 1870–79.

Annual Reports of the Superintendents of the Central Superintendency, for the Years 1862–1865. Washington, DC: Government Printing Office, 1863–66.

Arnold, S. G. "President Grant's Indian Policy." *Methodist Quarterly Review* 37 (July 1877): 409–30.

Bland, T. A. *Life of Alfred B. Meacham: Together with His Lecture, The Tragedy of the Lava Beds.* Washington, DC: T. A. and M. C. Bland, 1883.

Board of Indian Commissioners. *Journal of the Second Annual Conference of the Board of Indian Commissioners with the Representatives of the Religious*

Societies Cooperating with the Government, and Reports of Their Work among the Indians. Washington, DC: Government Printing Office, 1873.

Bradley, James H. *The March of the Montana Column: A Prelude to the Custer Disaster*. Edited by Edgar I. Stewart. Norman: University of Oklahoma Press, 1961.

Buecker, Thomas, ed. "'Distance Lends Enchantment to the View': The 1874 Black Hills Expedition Diary of Fred W. Power." *South Dakota History* 27, no. 4 (1997): 197–260.

Burke Act (Forced Fee Patenting Act). 34 Stat. 182 (1906).

Carleton, James Henry. *To the People of New Mexico. This Paper Sets Forth Some of the Principal Reasons Why the Navajo Indians Have Been Located upon a Reservation at the Bosque Redondo*. N.p., 1864.

"Certain Surveying Frauds: Special Dispatches to the *New York Times*." *New York Times*, April 11, 1876.

Charter of Connecticut, 1862. The Avalon Project, Yale Law School, Lillian Goldman Law Library. Accessed January 4, 2018. http://avalon.law.yale.edu/17th_century/ct03.asp.

Chipman, N. P. *The Tragedy of Andersonville: Trial of Captain Henry Wirz, the Prison Keeper*. 2nd ed. Sacramento, CA: printed by the author, 1911.

Chittenden, Hiram Martin, and Alfred Talbot Richardson, eds. *Life, Letters and Travels of Father Pierre-Jean de Smet, S.J., 1801–1873*. Vols. 1–4. New York: Francis P. Harper, 1905.

Circular of the Catholic Commissioner of Indian Missions, the Catholics of the United States. Baltimore: John Murphy, 1874.

Civil Rights Act. 14 Stat. 27–30 (1866).

Congressional Globe. 41st Cong., 3rd Sess. 3 (1811–12, 1822–25).

Cooper, James Fennimore. *The Last of the Mohicans: A Narrative of 1757*. New York: Macmillan, 1900.

———. *The Wept of Wish-Ton-Wish: A Tale*. New ed. New York: Stringer and Townsend, 1856.

Custer, George Armstrong. *My Life on the Plains; or, Personal Experiences with Indians*. New York: Sheldon, 1874.

Delano, Columbus. *Speech of Hon. Columbus Delano, Delivered at Raleigh, North Carolina, July 24, 1872*. Washington, DC: YA Pamphlet Collection, Library of Congress, 1872.

de Smet, Pierre-Jean. "Indian Symbolic Catechism, 1843." Bureau of Catholic Indian Missions Records 08-1 G-01. Milwaukee: Marquette University. Accessed January 4, 2018. http://cdm16280.contentdm.oclc.org/cdm/ref/collection/p128701coll4/id/45

Dillon, Sidney. "Historic Moment: Driving the Last Spike." *Scribner's Magazine* 12 (August 1892): 258–59.

Dixon, Billy. *Life and Adventures of "Billy" Dixon.* Guthrie, OK: Co-operative, 1914.

Documents Submitted by the Secretary of War in Compliance with a Resolution of December 14, 1868, in Relation to the Late Indian Battle on the Washita River. 40th Cong., 3rd Sess., Senate Executive Papers 1360, Senate Executive Document No. 18 (1869).

Dodge, Granville M. "How We Built the Union Pacific Railroad." 61st Cong., 2nd Sess., Senate Document No. 477. Washington, DC: Government Printing Office, 1910.

Doolittle, James, et al. *Conditions of the Indians: Report of the Joint Special Committee Appointed under Joint Resolution March 3, 1865, with an Appendix.* Washington, DC: Government Printing Office, 1867.

Douglas, Stephen. Speech to the United States Senate, March 13–14, 1850. *Congressional Globe.* 31st Cong., 1st Sess., Appendix, 364–75 (1850).

Executive Orders Related to Indian Reservations from May 14, 1855, to July 1, 1912. Washington, DC: Government Printing Office, 1912.

Frank Leslie's Illustrated Newspaper.

"Frank Wayland Palmer." *Annals of Iowa* 8 (1908): 316–17.

Fundamental Orders of 1639. The Avalon Project, Yale Law School, Lillian Goldman Law Library. Accessed January 4, 2018. http://avalon.law.yale.edu/17th_century/order.asp.

Gibbon, John. *Gibbon on the Sioux Campaign of 1876.* Bellevue, NV: Old Army Press, 1970.

Grant, Ulysses S. *Ulysses S. Grant: Memoirs and Selected Letters; Personal Memoirs of U.S. Grant; Selected Letters 1839–1865.* Edited by Mary Drake McFeely and William S. McFeely. New York: Library of America, 1990.

Guide to the Union Pacific Railroad Lands. Omaha: Land Department of the Union Pacific Railroad, 1870.

Homer. *The Odyssey.* Translated by Robert Fagles. New York: Penguin Books, 1976.

Indian Citizenship Act. 43 Stat. 253 (1924).

Investigation into Indian Affairs, before the Committee on Appropriations of the House of Representatives. Argument of N. P. Chipman, on Behalf of Hon. E. S. Parker, Commissioner of Indian Affairs. Washington, DC: Powell, Ginck, 1871.

Jackson, Helen Hunt. *A Century of Dishonor: A Sketch of the United States Government's Dealings with Some of the Indian Tribes.* New York: Harper and Brothers, 1881.

Bibliography

The Jay Treaty, November 19, 1794. The Avalon Project, Yale Law School, Lillian Goldman Law Library. Accessed January 4, 2018. http://avalon.law.yale.edu/18th_century/jay.asp.

Jones, Landon, ed. *The Essential Lewis and Clark*. New York: HarperCollins, 2002.

Joseph Fellows, Survivor of Robert Kendle, Plaintiff in Error v. Susan Blacksmith and Ely S. Parker, Administrators of John Blacksmith, Deceased. 60 U.S. 366 (1856). Justia, US Supreme Court. Accessed January 4, 2018. https://supreme.justia.com/cases/federal/us/60/366/case.html.

"Journal of the Adjourned Session of the First General Council of the Indian Territory." *Chronicles of Oklahoma* 3, no. 2 (June 1925): 120–36.

"Journal of the General Council of the Indian Territory." *Chronicles of Oklahoma* 3, no. 1 (March 1925): 33–44.

The Judiciary Act, September 24, 1789. The Avalon Project, Yale Law School, Lillian Goldman Law Library. Accessed January 4, 2018. http://avalon.law.yale.edu/18th_century/judiciary_act.asp.

Kappler, Charles J., ed. *Indian Affairs: Laws and Treaties*. 7 vols. Washington, DC: Government Printing Office, 1904.

"Letters Sent and Received, Division of the Missouri." *Records of United States Army*. Record Group 393. Washington, DC: National Archives.

Lincoln, Abraham. "The 'House Divided' Speech," ca. 1857–58. Gilder Lehrman Institute of American History. https://ap.gilderlehrman.org/node/2211.

Lord, Eliot. *Comstock Mining and Miners*. Washington, DC: Government Printing Office, 1883.

Lowe, Charles. "The President's New Indian Policy." *Old and New*, 3 (April 1871): 497–504.

Manypenny, George, et al. "Report of the Sioux Commission Appointed to Obtain Certain Concessions from the Sioux." Senate Executive Document 9, 44th Cong., 2nd Sess., 330–57 (1876).

"Massacre of the Cheyenne Indians." Report of the Joint Committee on the Conduct of the War, 38th Cong., 2nd Sess., vol. 3 (Washington, DC: Government Printing Office, 1865): i–vi, 3–108.

McCoy, Joseph G. *Historic Sketches of the Cattle Trade of the West and Southwest*. Kansas City, MO: Ramsey, Millett and Hudson, 1874.

Meacham, Alfred. *Wigwam and War-path; or, The Royal Chief in Chains*. Boston: J. P. Dale, 1875.

———. *Wi-ne-ma (the Woman Chief) and Her People*. Hartford, CT: American, 1876.

Memorial and Affidavits Showing Outrages Perpetrated by the Apache Indians, in the Territory of Arizona, for the Years 1869 and 1870. San Francisco: Francis and Valentine, 1871.

Merriam, Lewis, et al. *The Problem of Indian Administration: Report of a Survey Made at the Request of Honorable Hubert Work, Secretary of the Interior, and Submitted to Him, February 21, 1928.* Baltimore: Johns Hopkins Press, 1928.

Miles, Nelson A. "The Indian Question." *North American Review* 128 (March 1879): 309–11.

———. *Personal Recollections and Observations of General Nelson A. Miles, Embracing a Brief View of the Civil War; or, From New England to the Golden Gate and the Story of His Indian Campaigns, with Comments on the Exploration, Development and Progress of Our Great Western Empire.* Chicago: Werner, 1896.

Morgan, Lewis H. *The League of the Ho-dé-no-sau-nee or Iroquois.* Rochester, NY: Sage and Brother, 1851.

Newton, Henry, and Walter Jenney. *Report on the Geology and Resources of the Black Hills of Dakota, with Atlas.* Washington, DC: Government Printing Office, 1880.

New York Herald.

New York Times.

"Okmulgee Constitution." *Chronicles of Oklahoma* 3, no. 3 (September 1925): 120–36.

Parker, Ely S. Circular Letter to Superintendent and Agents of the Indian Department, June 12, 1869. Records of the Central Superintendency of Indian Affairs, 1813–78, Letters Received from the Commissioner of Indian Affairs, Record Group 75, *Records of the Office of Indian Affairs.* Washington, DC: National Archives.

Paul, R. Eli, ed. *Autobiography of Red Cloud: War Leader of the Oglalas.* Helena: Montana Historical Society Press, 1977.

"Political Party Platforms: Democratic Party Platform of 1868," July 4, 1868. *The American Presidency Project.* Compiled by Gerhard Peters and John T. Woolley. Accessed January 4, 2018. http://www.presidency.ucsb.edu/ws/?pid=29579.

"Political Party Platforms: Republican Party Platform of 1868," May 20, 1868. *The American Presidency Project.* Compiled by Gerhard Peters and John T. Woolley. Accessed January 4, 2018. http://www.presidency.ucsb.edu/ws/?pid=29622.

Bibliography

"Proceedings of a Military Commission Convened by Special Orders No 23, Headquarters District of Colorado, Denver, Colorado Territory, Dated February 1, 1865, in the Case of Colonel J. M. Chivington, First Colorado Cavalry." Senate Executive Document 26, 39th Cong., 2nd Sess., 2–228 (1865).

Prucha, Francis Paul, ed. *Documents of United States Indian Policy*. 3rd ed. Lincoln: University of Nebraska Press, 2000.

Records of the Board of Indian Commissioners, Records of the Office of Indian Affairs. Record Group 75.22. Washington, DC: National Archives.

Records of the Indian Division of the Office of the Secretary of the Interior, Special Files, 1848–1907. Record Group 48, reel 4, folders 1–18, and reel 5, folders 19–51. Washington, DC: National Archives.

Records of the Office of Indian Affairs. Record Group 75. Washington, DC: National Archives.

Records of the United States Senate. Record Group 46. Washington, DC: National Archives.

Report of the Special Commission Appointed to Investigate the Affairs of the Red Cloud Indian Agency, July 1875, Together with the Testimony and Accompanying Documents. Washington, DC: Government Printing Office, 1875.

Richardson, James D., ed. *A Compilation of the Messages and Papers of the Presidents*. 10 vols. Washington, DC: Government Printing Office, 1897.

Ridge, Martin, ed. *America's Frontier Story: A Documentary History of Westward Experience*. New York: Holt, Rinehart and Winston, 1969.

The Royal Proclamation, October 7, 1763. The Avalon Project, Yale Law School, Lillian Goldman Law Library. Accessed January 4, 2018. http://avalon.law.yale.edu/18th_century/proc1763.asp.

Schofield, John. *Annual Report of the Secretary of War 1868.* House Executive Document 1, 40th Cong., 3rd Sess., Ser. 1367, xvii–xviii.

The Second Charter of Virginia, May 23, 1609. The Avalon Project, Yale Law School, Lillian Goldman Law Library. Accessed January 4, 2018. http://avalon.law.yale.edu/17th_century/va02.asp.

"Second Inaugural Address of Abraham Lincoln," March 4, 1865. The Avalon Project, Yale Law School, Lillian Goldman Law Library. Accessed January 4, 2018. http://avalon.law.yale.edu/19th_century/lincoln2.asp.

"'Secret' Journal on Negotiations of the Chickasaw Treaty of 1818." The Avalon Project, Yale Law School, Lillian Goldman Law Library. Accessed January 4, 2018. http://avalon.law.yale.edu/19th_century/nt005.asp.

Sherman, William Tecumseh. *Memoirs of General William T. Sherman*. 2nd ed. 2 vols. New York: D. Appleton, 1904.

Simon, John Y., ed. *The Papers of Ulysses S. Grant.* 31 vols. Carbondale: Southern Illinois University Press, 1967–2009.

Standing Bear, Luther. *My Indian Boyhood.* Boston: Houghton Mifflin, 1931.

Tatum, Lawrie. *Our Red Brothers and the Peace Policy of President Ulysses S. Grant.* Philadelphia: John C. Winston, 1899.

"Transmitting a Report by Col. Parker on Affairs between the United States and the Various Indian Tribes U.S. Congress." House Misc. Doc. 37, 39th Cong., 2nd Sess. (1867).

The Treaty of Washington with Correspondence, Etc. Ottawa: Times Steam, 1871.

Walker, Francis A. *The Indian Question.* Boston: J. R. Osgood, 1874.

Welsh, William. *Taopi and His Friends; or, The Indians' Wrongs and Rights.* Philadelphia: Claxton, Remsen and Haffelfinger, 1869.

Wheeler-Howard Act (Indian Reorganization Act). 48 Stat. 984 (1934).

Whipple, Henry. *An Appeal for the Red Man.* Faribault, MN: Cultural Republican, 1862.

———. *Lights and Shadows of a Long Episcopate; Being Reminiscences and Recollections of the Right Reverend Henry Benjamin Whipple, D.D., LL.D., Bishop of Minnesota.* New York: Macmillan, 1899.

———. "My Life among the Indians." *North American Review* 150 (April 1, 1890): 432–39.

Worcester v. Georgia. 31 U.S. 515 (1832). Justia, US Supreme Court. Accessed January 4, 2018. https://supreme.justia.com/cases/federal/us/31/515/case.html.

Wright, William. *History of the Big Bonanza.* Hartford, CT: American, 1876.

Secondary Sources

Adams, Mikaela. *Who Belongs: Race, Resources, and Tribal Citizenship in the Native South.* Oxford: Oxford University Press, 2016.

Anderson, Fred. *Crucible of War: The Seven Years' War and the Fate of Empire in British North America, 1754–1766.* 2000. Reprint, New York: Vintage, 2007.

Armstrong, William H. *Warrior in Two Camps: Ely S. Parker, Union General and Seneca Chief.* Syracuse, NY: Syracuse University Press, 1978.

Barnds, William Joseph. "The Ministry of the Reverend Samuel Dutton Hinman, among the Sioux." *Historical Magazine of the Protestant Episcopal Church* 38, no. 4 (December 1969): 393–401.

Barrett, S. A. *The Material Culture of the Klamath Lake and Modoc Indians of Northeastern California and Southern Oregon.* Berkeley, CA: University Press, 1910.

Bibliography

Barsness, Larry. *Heads, Hides and Horns: The Compleat Buffalo Book* (Fort Worth: Texas Christian University Press, 1985.

Berg, Scott. *38 Nooses: Lincoln, Little Crow, and the Beginning of the Frontier's End.* New York: Vintage, 2012.

Billington, Ray Allen, and Martin Ridge. *Westward Expansion: A History of the American Frontier.* 6th ed. Albuquerque: University of New Mexico Press, 2001.

Biographical Directory of the United States Congress: 1774–Present. Accessed January 4, 2018. http://bioguide.congress.gov.

Brandon, William. *The American Heritage Book of the Indians.* New York: American Heritage, 1961.

Brands, H. W. *The Man Who Saved the Union: Ulysses Grant in War and Peace.* New York: Anchor Books, 2012.

Brown, Dee. *Bury My Heart at Wounded Knee: An Indian History of the American West.* 30th anniv. ed. New York: Henry Holt, 2001.

———. *The Fetterman Massacre.* Lincoln: University of Nebraska Press, 1962.

Buyneel, Kevin. *The Third Space of Sovereignty: The Postcolonial Politics of U.S.–Indigenous Relations.* Minneapolis: University of Minnesota, 2007.

Cahill, Cathleen. *Federal Fathers and Mothers: A Social History of the United States Indian Agency, 1869–1933.* Chapel Hill: University of North Carolina Press, 2011.

Capps, Benjamin. *The Indians.* New York: Time-Life Books, 1973.

"The Career of G. W. Manypenny." *Wisconsin Magazine of History* 1, no. 3 (March 1918): 324–25.

Carley, Kenneth. *The Dakota War of 1862: Minnesota's Other War.* 2nd ed. St. Paul: Minnesota Historical Society Press, 2001.

Carter, Robert Goldthwaite. *On the Border with Mackenzie; or, Winning West Texas from the Comanches.* Washington, DC: Eynon, 1935.

Cave, Alfred. *The Pequot War.* Amherst: University of Massachusetts Press, 1996.

Chalfant, William Y. *Hancock's War: Conflict on the Southern Plains.* Norman, OK: Arthur H. Clark, 2010.

Connell, Evan S. *Son of the Morning Star: Custer and the Little Bighorn.* New York: North Point Press, 1984.

Cooper, Edward S. *William Worth Belknap: An American Disgrace.* Madison, NJ: Fairleigh Dickinson University Press, 2003.

Cothran, Boyd. *Remembering the Modoc War: Redemptive Violence and the Making of American Innocence.* Chapel Hill: University of North Carolina Press, 2014.

Deloria, Vine, Jr., and David Wilkins. *Tribes, Treaties and Constitutional Tribulations*. Austin: University of Texas Press, 1999.

Donovan, James. *A Terrible Glory: The Last Great Battle of the American West*. New York: Little, Brown, 2008.

Dowd, Gregory Evans. *War under Heaven: Pontiac, the Indian Nations, and the British Empire*. Baltimore: Johns Hopkins University Press, 2004.

Downs, Greg, and Kate Masur, eds. *The World the Civil War Made*. Chapel Hill: University of North Carolina Press, 2015.

Drury, Bob, and Tom Clavin. *The Heart of Everything That Is: The Untold Story of Red Cloud, an American Hero*. New York: Simon and Schuster, 2013.

Du Bois, Cora. *The 1870 Ghost Dance*. Lincoln: University of Nebraska Press, 1939.

Eastman, Charles. *The Soul of the Indian*. Boston: Houghton, 1911.

Edmunds, R. David. *The Shawnee Prophet*. Lincoln: University of Nebraska Press, 1983.

———. *Tecumseh and the Quest for Indian Leadership*. New York: HarperCollins, 1984.

Ellis, Richard N. *General Pope and U.S. Indian Policy*. Albuquerque: University of New Mexico Press, 1970.

Erdoes, Richard, and Alfonzo Ortiz, eds. *American Indian Myths and Legends*. New York: Pantheon Books, 1984.

Fellman, Michael. *Citizen Sherman: A Life of William Tecumseh Sherman*. New York: Random House, 1995.

Genetin-Pilawa, C. Joseph. *Crooked Paths to Allotment: The Fight over Federal Indian Policy after the Civil War*. Chapel Hill: University of North Carolina Press, 2012.

Greene, Jerome A. *Washita: The U.S. Army and the Southern Cheyennes, 1867–1869*. Campaigns and Commanders, vol. 3. Norman: University of Oklahoma Press, 2004.

Gwynne, S. C. *Empire of the Summer Moon: Quanah Parker and the Rise and Fall of the Comanches, the Most Powerful Indian Tribe in American History*. New York: Simon and Schuster, 2010.

Haley, James L. *The Buffalo War: The History of the Red River Indian Uprising of 1874*. Garden City, NY: Doubleday, 1976.

Hasrick, Royal B. *The Sioux: Life and Customs of a Warrior Society*. Civilization of the American Indian Series. Norman: University of Oklahoma, 1964.

Hastings, James R. "The Tragedy at Camp Grant in 1871." *Arizona and the West* 1, no. 2 (1959): 146–60.

Hoig, Stan. *The Peace Chiefs of the Cheyennes*. Norman: University of Oklahoma Press, 1980.

Bibliography

———. *The Sand Creek Massacre.* Norman: University of Oklahoma Press, 1974.
Horsman, Reginald. *The Causes of the War of 1812.* New York: A. S. Barnes, 1961.
———. *The War of 1812.* New York: Alfred A. Knopf, 1969.
Hurt, R. Douglas. *The Ohio Frontier: Crucible of the Old Northwest, 1720–1830.* 2nd ed. Bloomington: Indiana University Press, 1998.
Hutton, Paul Andrew. *Phil Sheridan and His Army.* Lincoln: University of Nebraska Press, 1985.
Iverson, Peter. *The Diné: A History of the Navajo.* Albuquerque: University of New Mexico Press, 2002.
Jackson, Clyde, and Grace Jackson. *Quanah Parker, Last Chief of the Comanches: A Study in Southwestern Frontier History.* New York: Exposition Press, 1963.
Jones, Lewis T. *The Quakers of Iowa.* Iowa City: State Historical Society of Iowa, 1904.
Josephy, Alvin M., Jr. *500 Nations.* New York; Gramercy Books, 1994.
Kelly, Lawrence. *The Assault on Assimilation: John Collier and the Origins of Indian Policy Reform.* Albuquerque: University of New Mexico Press, 1983.
Kelsey, Marie Ellen, comp. *Ulysses S. Grant: A Bibliography.* Westport, CT: Praeger, 2005.
Kelsey, Rayner Wickersham. *Friends and the Indians, 1655–1917.* Philadelphia: Associated Executive Committee of Friends on Indian Affairs, 1917.
Knepper, George W. *Ohio and Its People.* 3rd ed. Kent, OH: Kent State University Press, 2013.
Krauthamer, Barbara. *Black Slaves, Indian Masters: Slavery, Emancipation, and Citizenship in the Native American South.* Chapel Hill: University of North Carolina Press, 2013.
Kvasnicka, Robert M., and Herman J. Viola, eds. *The Commissioners of Indian Affairs, 1824–1977.* Lincoln: University of Nebraska Press, 1979.
LaPointe, Ernie. *Sitting Bull: His Life and Legacy.* Salt Lake City: Gibbs-Smith, 2009.
Laveille, E. *The Life of Father de Smet, S.J., 1801–1873.* New York: P. J. Kennedy and Sons, 1915.
Lewis, Lloyd. *Sherman: Fighting Prophet.* New York: Harcourt, Brace, 1932.
Lowery, Charles D. *James Barbour: A Jeffersonian Republican.* Tuscaloosa: University of Alabama Press, 1984.
Lowery, Melinda. *Lumbee Indians in the Jim Crow South: Race, Identity, and the Making of a Nation.* Chapel Hill: University of North Carolina Press, 2010.

Luebke, Frederick. "Ethnic Group Settlement on the Great Plains." *Western Historical Quarterly* 8, no. 4 (October 1977): 405–30.

Mandell, Daniel R. *King Philip's War: Colonial Expansion, Native Resistance, and the End of Indian Sovereignty (Witness to History)*. Baltimore: Johns Hopkins University Press, 2010.

Mardock, Robert Winston. *The Reformers and the American Indian*. Columbia: University of Missouri Press, 1971.

Marshall, Edward Chauncey. *The Ancestry of President Grant, and Their Contemporaries*. New York: Sheldon, 1869.

McDonnell, Janet A. *The Dispossession of the American Indian, 1887–1934*. Bloomington: Indiana University Press, 1991.

McFeely, William S. *Grant: A Biography*. New York: W. W. Norton, 1981.

Meyer, Roy Miller. *A History of the Santee Sioux: United States Indian Policy on Trial*. Rev. ed. Lincoln: University of Nebraska Press, 1993.

Middlekauff, Robert. *The Glorious Cause: The American Revolution, 1763–1789*. New York: Oxford University Press, 2005.

Morris, Charles, ed. *Makers of Philadelphia: An Historical Work Giving Sketches of the Most Eminent Citizens of Philadelphia from the Time of William Penn to the Present Day*. Philadelphia: L. R. Hamersley, 1894.

Neihardt, John. *Black Elk Speaks: Being the Life Story of a Holy Man of the Sioux*. New York: William Morrow, 1932.

Olson, James C. *Red Cloud and the Sioux Problem*. Lincoln: University of Nebraska, 1965.

Parker, Arthur. *The Life of General Ely S. Parker: Last Sachem of the Iroquois and General Grant's Military Secretary*. Buffalo, NY: Buffalo Historical Society, 1919.

Perret, Geoffrey. *Ulysses S. Grant: Soldier & President*. New York: Random House, 1997.

Peters, W. E. *Ohio Lands and Their Subdivision*. Athens, OH: printed by the author, 1918.

Philip, Kenneth R. *John Collier's Crusade for Indian Reform*. Tucson: University of Arizona Press, 1970.

Pierce, Michael D. *The Most Promising Young Officer: A Life of Ranald Slidell Mackenzie*. Norman: University of Oklahoma Press, 1993.

Pierson, Arthur T. *Zachariah Chandler: An Outline Sketch of His Life and Public Services*. Detroit: Post and Tribune, 1880.

Prucha, Francis Paul. *American Indian Policy in Crisis: Christian Reformers and the Indian, 1865–1900*. Norman: University of Oklahoma Press, 1976.

———. *The Great Father: The United States Government and the American Indians.* Abridged ed. Lincoln: University of Nebraska Press, 1986.

———. *The Indians in American Society: From the Revolutionary War to the Present.* Berkeley: University of California Press, 1985.

———. *United States Indian Policy: A Critical Bibliography.* Bloomington: Indiana University Press, 1977.

Rahill, Peter J. *The Catholic Indian Missions and Grant's Peace Policy, 1870–1884.* Washington, DC: Catholic University of America Press, 1953.

Rand, Jacki Thompson. *Kiowa Humanity and the Invasion of the State.* Lincoln: University of Nebraska Press, 2008.

Reed, Julie. *Serving the Nation: Cherokee Sovereignty and Social Welfare, 1800–1907.* Norman: University of Oklahoma Press, 2016.

Richards, Leonard. *Shays's Rebellion: The American Revolution's Final Battle.* Philadelphia: University of Pennsylvania Press, 2002.

Riddle, Jeff C. *The Indian History of the Modoc War and the Causes That Led to It.* San Francisco, 1914.

Robinson, Doane. "A Comprehensive History of the Dakota or Sioux Indians." *South Dakota Historical Collections.* vol. 2. Aberdeen: State Historical Society, 1904.

———. *History of South Dakota.* 2 vols. Logansport, IN: B. F. Bowen, 1904.

Rushmore, Elsie Mitchell. *The Indian Policy during Grant's Administration.* Jamaica, NY: Marion Press, 1914.

Schmiel, Eugene D. *Citizen-General: Jacob Dolson Cox and the Civil War Era.* Athens: Ohio University Press, 2014.

Sides, Hampton. *Blood and Thunder: The Epic Story of Kit Carson and the Conquest of the American West.* New York: Doubleday, 2006.

Silkenat, David. "'A Typical Negro': Gordon, Peter, Vincent Colyer, and the Story behind Slavery's Most Famous Photograph." *American Nineteenth Century History* 15, no. 2 (2014): 169–86.

Slattery, Charles Lewis. *Felix Reville Brunot, 1820–1898: A Civilian in the War for the Union; President of the First Board of Indian Commissioners.* New York: Longmans, Green, 1901.

Smith, Jean Edward. *Grant.* New York: Simon and Schuster, 2001.

Soderland, Arthur E. *Connecticut.* Nashville: Thomas Nelson, 1976.

Sommers, Charles Henry. *"Quanah Parker": Last Chief of the Comanches.* St. Louis: printed by the author, 1943.

Stabler, Scott L. "Ulysses S. Grant and the 'Indian Problem.'" *Journal of Illinois History* 6 (Winter 2003): 297–316.

Stockwell, Mary. "Native Americans: Experiences and Culture." In *A Companion to Warren G. Harding, Calvin Coolidge, and Herbert Hoover*, edited by Katherine A. S. Sibley. Malden, MA: Wiley Blackwell, 2014, 251–69.

———. *The Other Trail of Tears: The Removal of the Ohio Indians*. Yardley, PA: Westholme, 2015.

Sully, Langdon. *No Tears for the General: A Life of Alfred Sully, 1821–1879*. Palo Alto, CA: American West, 1974.

Tallent, Annie D. *The Black Hills; or, The Last Hunting Ground of the Dakotahs: A Complete History of the Black Hills of Dakota, from Their First Invasion in 1874 to the Present Time*. St. Louis: Nixon-Jones, 1899.

Taylor, Alan. *American Colonies*. New York: Penguin Books, 2001.

Utley, Robert M. "The Celebrated Peace Policy of General Grant." *North Dakota History* 20 (July 1953): 121–42.

———. *The Indian Frontier, 1846–1890*. Albuquerque: University of New Mexico Press, 1984.

———. *Sitting Bull: The Life and Times of an American Patriot*. New York: Henry Holt, 1993.

Van Dusen, Albert E. *Connecticut*. New York: Random House, 1961.

Vaughn, J. W. *The Reynolds Campaign on Powder River*. Norman: University of Oklahoma Press, 1961.

Wallace, Ernest, and E. Adamson Hoebel. *The Comanches: Lords of the South Plains*. Norman: University of Oklahoma Press, 1952.

Waltmann, Henry G. "Circumstantial Reformer: President Grant & the Indian Problem." *Arizona and the West* 13, no. 4 (Winter 1971): 323–42.

Waugh, Joan. *U.S. Grant: American Hero, American Myth*. Chapel Hill: University of North Carolina Press, 2009.

Wheelan, Joseph. *Terrible Swift Sword: The Life of General Philip H. Sheridan*. New York: Da Capo Press, 2013.

Wilkins, David, and K. Tsianina Loawaima. *Uneven Ground: American Indian Sovereignty and Federal Law*. Norman: University of Oklahoma Press, 2002.

Wright, Richard. *The Middle Ground: Indians, Empires, and Republics in the Great Lakes Region, 1650–1815*. Cambridge: Cambridge University Press, 1991.

Wylie, Paul R. *Blood on the Marias: The Baker Massacre*. Norman: University of Oklahoma Press, 2016.

Index

Page numbers in italics indicate illustrations.

Adams, John Quincy, 10–11, 24, 48
Adobe Walls (Texas), 146, 148–49, 152, 181
Alabama claims, 113
Alice Park, 157
Allison, William, 166
allotment, 185–87, 189–91
American Episcopal Church, 120
Anadarko Agency, 148
Andrews, George, 93, 198
Angel, William P., 34
Apache Indians: agencies, 198, 203; Camp Grant Massacre, 112–13; Carleton's campaign, 38; Cochise, 92, 132; Parker's plans for, 49–50; resistance to Grant's policy by, 69, 73–74, 91, 93; treaties, 12, 54, 56–57, 61, 63; Walker's defense of Grant's policy toward, 115–17, 132, 155, 180–81
Appalachian Mountains, 17–20, 22
Applegate, Jesse, 139–40
Arapaho Indians: actions by, during Civil War, 8; agency, 200; buffalo hunters, 128, 130; Grant's attitude toward, 132, 181–82; Great Sioux War, 172, 174–75; life of, in Indian Territory, 73; meeting with Brunot, 83; meeting with Peace Commission, 54–57; Parker's plans, 50; Sand Creek Massacre, 40; Sherman's recommendations, 44; treaties, 12, 38–39, 51–52, 61, 63, 99; Walker's description of, 117
Arikaree Indians, 12
Arpaiva Apache, 111
Arthur, Chester Allen, 185
Ashby, William H., 166
Assiniboine Indians 12, 117
Astor, Mrs. John Jacob, 184
Atchison, Topeka, and Santa Fe Railroad, 126–27
Augur, Christopher C., 54

Babcock, Orville, 173
Baker, Eugene, 71–72
Bannock Indians, 58, 180, 199
Baptist Church, 120, 124, 203, 206
Barbour, James, 10–11, 48
Battle of the Little Bighorn, 174–76, 187
Bear Butte, 157
Bear Chief, 72
Beauvais, Geminien, 166
Beck, James, 98, 101, 105, 107
Belknap, Carrie, 173
Belknap, William, 75; appointment as secretary of war, 139; Black Hills strategy, 160; corruption scandal, 172–73, 176, 189; Red River War strategy, 146; resignation, 173
Benteen, Frederick, 174, 176
Big Bonanza, 126
Big Red Meat (Pearuaakupakup), 148

247

Index

Bishop, Nathan, 79–80, 82, 119
Black Elk, 187, 189, 191
Black Elk Speaks, 187
Blackfeet Confederation, 70
Blackfeet Indians: agency, 204; buffalo, 129–30; description, 50; Grant's plans for, 49; Piegan Massacre, 72–73; treaty (1876), 178; Walker's defense of "feeding system," 121
Black Hills: Allison's commission, 166–69; Custer's exploration, 156–57; description, 50; final treaty to purchase, 176–79; Fort Laramie treaty (1868), 59; gold rush into Black Hills, 157–59; Grant's negotiations to purchase, 154, 156, 160–64; Jenney's exploration, 160; map, 177; Red Cloud's demands (1870), 77; role in Great Sioux War, 171–72, 182, 184; rumors of gold in, 126
Black Jim, 141–42
Black Kettle: Custer's attack on Washita River, 63–64, 183; death, 64; Fort Wise treaty, 39–40; move to Washita River, 63–64; Sand Creek Massacre, 40
Blacksmith, John, 33–34
Blanchet, Francois, 122–23
Blood Indians, 70, 72
Bloody Point, 135
Blunt, James G., 102–3, 105, 107, 170
Board of Indian Commissioners: actions after Grant's presidency, 190; assignment of missionaries to Indian service, 91, 120, 124–35; attitude toward Grant's policy, 85, 88–89, 118–20; attitude toward Indians, 80–85; attitude toward Parker, 86; board's understanding of duties, 79–80; creation of, 78; dismissal of, 190–91; first members, 79–80; Grant's understanding of duties of, 79; new members, 165; Parker's understanding of duties of, 78–79; resignation of original members, 164–65: role in Parker's trial, 99–101; supervisors of Indian service, 109
Bogus Charley, 141
Bogy, Lewis 41, 166
Bosque Redondo, 7, 38, 58
Bosler, James W.: accusation against Welsh, 104; congressional testimony, 103; contract with Parker, 87; Welsh's accusation of fraud, 95, 97–99, 101
Boston Charley, 141–42
Boston Indian Citizenship Association, 184
Bowers, Joe, 43
Bozeman (Montana), 51
Bozeman Trail, 51–52, 54, 58–59, 62, 86, 156, 160
Brancho, 142–43
Browning, Orville, 41, 55
Brunot, Felix R.: appointment to Board of Indian Commissioners, 79; attitude toward Indians, 83; chairmanship of board, 82; congressional testimony, 99–101; demands for further reforms, 164; first western tour, 82–83; opposition to Grant's Indian policy, 83–85; opposition to treaties, 110; philanthropy, 80; resignation, 164–65
Buell, George, 148
buffalo, 129; disappearance of, 128–30; Grant's attitude toward, 130
Bureau of Indian Affairs, 191
Burke Act (Forced Patenting Act), 186
Burnet, Jacob, 24

Cady, W. F., 120
Calhoun, John C., 9, 34
Campbell, Robert, 79, 93
Campbell, Thomas, 156
Camp Grant Massacre, 111–12
Camp Supply 83, 150
Canby, Edward, 142: appointment as peace commissioner, 139; attitudes toward Modoc, 139–40; background,

248

139; death, 141, 155, 167, 181; negotiations with Modoc, 140–41
Canyon de Chilly 38, 61
Captain Jack (Kintpuach), 144; assassination of Canby, 141; capture, 141–42; leadership in Modoc War, 136–40; Modoc chief, 136; negotiations with Canby, 140–41; trial and execution, 143
Carleton, James, 38, 61
Carrington, Henry, 51–54
Case, Samuel, 139–40
Cass, Lewis, 25
Catholic Church, 120, 124–25, 168, 203, 206
Catholic priests, 74, 73, 121–22, 124
cattle drive, 126
cattle ranching, 127
Central Pacific Railroad, 126
Century of Dishonor, A, 183–85
Chandler, Zechariah, 170–71
Chase, Salmon P., 6, 35
Cherokee Indians: agencies, 201–3; life in Indian Territory, 46, 93–94, 109–12, 118, 152–53, 158–59, 184, 186; removal from Georgia, 10, 24, 41
Cheyenne Indians: agency, 200–201; description, 50–51; Fort Laramie Treaty (1851), 12, 38–39; Great Sioux War, 172, 174–75, 178, 180–82, 184; Parker's plans, 49; Peace Commission, 54, 56, 57; Red Cloud's War, 52; Red River War, 146, 151–52, 156; Sand Creek Massacre, 39–40; Sherman's recommendations, 44
Chickasaw Indians, 46, 74, 93, 109, 152, 186, 201, 203
Chief Joseph, 180, 183
Chipman, Norton, 100; background, 99; defense of Parker, 99–100; cross-examination of witnesses, 101–4; final summation, 106–8; Welsh's attack on, 114
Chivington, John, 40

Choctaw Indians, 25, 46, 93, 109, 152, 158–59, 186, 201, 203
Civil Rights Act of 1866, 65
Civilization Act, 10
"civilize and Christianize," 79, 83, 92, 118, 120, 125, 189
Clarke, Horace, 11
Clarke, Malcolm, 70–71
Clay, Henry, 9, 34
Cleveland, Grover, 185
Clickitat Indians, 27
Clum, Henry R., 116
Cobell, Joseph, 71
Cochise, 92, 132
Coeur d'Alene Indians, 121
Colfax, Schuyler, 5
Collier, John, 190
Collins, John, 166
Columbia Barracks, 27
Colyer, Vincent: appointment of missionaries to Indian service, 120, 124–25; background and appointment to Board of Indian Commissioners, 82; emissary to Apache, 112–14; support for Welsh, 99–100, 102, 108, 112
Comanche Indians: agencies, 91, 200; description, 12, 49–50, 69, 116–17, 128, 132, 181; Grant in Texas, 26; meeting with Peace Commission, 54, 56–57; Parker's plans for Comanche, 49; Parker's pre–Civil War meeting with, 45; post–Civil War in Texas, 47; Red River War, 146–52, 156; treaties, 12, 61, 73; Washita River Massacre, 8, 63
Comingo, Abram, 166
Commissioner of Indian Affairs: origin of post, 12. See also commissioners' entries (Clum, Henry R.; Parker, Ely S.; Smith, Edward Parmelee; Smith, John Quincy; Walker, Francis A.)
Committee on Indian Affairs (House of Representatives), 35
Committee on Indian Affairs (Senate), 54, 66, 120

Index

Comstock Lode, 126, 156
concentration (Indian policy), 12–13, 38–39, 51
Confederation Congress, 49, 69
Congregational Church, 120, 125, 204, 206
Connecticut Indian Citizenship Association, 184
Connecticut Western Reserve, 20–21
Cooke, Jay, 105, 108, 157
Cooley, Dennis, 41, 46
Coolidge, Calvin, 190
Cooper, James Fennimore, 25
Cornplanter, 32
Cothecocona, 71
Cox, Jacob, 74, 76–77, 91, 93, 104–5, 108, 120
Crazy Horse, 52, 167, 171, 173–74, 176
Creek Indians, 46, 93–94, 109, 158–159, 186, 200–201, 203
Crook, George, 112, 171–72, 174, 176
Crow Indians, 12, 56, 121, 130, 174, 204
Crowley, W. C. C., 112
Curtis, Charles, 186
Custer, George Armstrong: accusations against Grant's administration, 172–74; Black Hills expedition, 156–57, 162; death, 176; role in Great Sioux War, 172, 174–76, 187; Washita River Massacre, 63–64, 69, 183
Custer's Last Stand, 175; description, 174–76

Dalles Indians, 27
Dana, Charles, 36
Davidson, "Black Jack," 148
Dawes, Henry, 185
Dawes Act, 185–86
Delano, Columbus: appointment as interior secretary, 93; Colyer's charges against Parker, 112–13; corruption charges, 165–166, 172,189; defense of Grant's Indian policy, 139, 143–46; resignation, 166, 169–70; role in appointing Christian missionaries, 120–21; strategy in Black Hills, 160, 162, 164; strategy in Red River War, 146; Welsh's charges against Parker, 95–96, 106
Delano, John, 165
Delaware Indians, 21, 23, 25, 184, 200
Democratic Party platform (1868), 62
Dent, Frederick (Grant's father-in-law), 31
Dent, Frederick, Jr. (Grant's brother-in-law), 26
Desert Land Act, 130
de Smet, Pierre-Jean, 121–24
Digger Indians, 27
Dodge, William, 79–80, 82
Dog Soldiers, 39
Doolittle, James, 40, 52
Doolittle Commission, 40, 52–53
Dorchester (Massachusetts), 15–16
Douglas, Stephen, 12, 29–31, 35
Dutch Reformed Church, 120, 124, 204, 206
Dyer, Leroy, 140–41, 204

Eastern Cherokee, 46
Eastern Niantic Indians, 17
Eastman, Charles (Ohiyesa), 187, 189
Episcopal Church, 120, 124, 204, 206
Evans, John (governor), 40
Evans, John (trader), 173

Fallen Timbers (battle) 9, 11, 21
Farwell, John V., 79–80, 93
Fellows, Joseph, 33–34
Fellows v. Blacksmith, 34–35
Fetterman, William, 13, 52–54
Fetterman's Massacre, 13, 52–53
Fifteenth Amendment, 7
Fillmore, Millard, 12
Fisk, Clinton B., 165
Fitzpatrick, Thomas, 12
Five Civilized Tribes, 186
Flathead Indians, 121, 123–24, 129, 203

Fort: Abraham Lincoln, 156, 158, 172, 174; Benson, 72; C. F. Smith, 51, 62; Cobb, 63; Concho, 148; Dodge, 148; Ellis, 172; Fetterman, 62, 77, 172; Griffin, 148; Humboldt, 27; Larned, 54; Laramie, 39, 51, 54–56, 59, 61, 121–22, 161, 179; Phil Kearney, 51–53, 62; Reno, 51; Shaw, 72, 172; Sill, 91, 148, 151, 173; Smith, 45–46; Sumner, 38, 61, 63; Sumter, 31, 127
Fort, Greenburg, 129
Fourteenth Amendment, 5, 65
Freedmen, 2, 4–5, 43, 47, 128, 152, 155, 182
Freedmen's Bureau, 62, 112, 165
French and Indian War (Seven Years' War), 18–19
French Creek, 156–59, 162, 171
Fundamental Orders, 17

Galena (Illinois), 28–29, 35–36
Garfield, James A., 87
Grant, Fred (Grant's son), 28, 113, 158, 189
Grant, Hannah Simpson (Grant's mother), 22–23, 31
Grant, Jesse (Grant's father), 21–23, 28
Grant, Julia Dent (Grant's wife), 26–28, 158
Grant, Matthew (Grant's first American ancestor), 15–16, 18
Grant, Nellie (Grant's daughter), 6–7, 28
Grant, Noah, III (Grant's grandfather), 19–21
Grant, Rachel (Grant's grandmother), 19, 21
Grant, Ulysses, Jr. (Grant's son), 28
Grant, Ulysses S., 6; analysis of Indian policy, 179–82; ancestry, 15–21; appointment of army officers to Indian service, 64–65, 197–201; appointment of missionaries to Indian service, 89–91, 202–6; attitude toward western settlement, 126–30; Belknap scandal, 172–73; Civil War service, 31–32, 36, 37, 38, 42–43; congressional opposition to Indian policy, 86–89; Custer's charges of corruption, 173–74; Custer's dismissal, 174; Delano scandal, 165–66, 169–70; early life, 23–24; early military career, 26–28; early political opinions, 29, 31; education, 23; end of treaty system, 109–11; final Indian wars, 179; first impression of Indians, 26–27; first inauguration, 4–8; first meeting with Red Cloud, 74, 75, 76–77; formation of Indian policy, 1–3, 47–49; Fred Dent's behavior at West Point, 113; friendship with Parker, 25; general of the army, 43–47; Great Sioux War, 171–72, 174–76; importance of Indian Territory, 131, 159; Lee's surrender at Appomattox, 4–5; loss of faith in original Indian policy, 155–56; Manypenny's Peace Commission, 176–79; parents, 21–23; Parker's resignation, 113–14; peace commission to Modoc, 139; plans for Black Hills, 166–69; plans for Modoc, 134–36; presidential candidate (1868), 58–59, 61–62; relationship with Board of Indian Commissioners, 79, 84–85; resignation of Board of Indian commissioners, 184–85; response to Battle of Little Bighorn, 176; response to Camp Grant Massacre, 111–12; response to Canby's death, 141–43; response to Piegan Massacre, 72–73; response to Welsh's accusations against Parker, 104; second inauguration, 131–32; second meeting with Red Cloud, 161–62, 163; settlement of *Alabama* claims, 113; strategy in Red River War, 146–47; West Point, 25, 26
Great American Desert, 23, 127
Great Migration, 22
Great Plains, 29, 43, 50, 74, 79, 82–83, 122, 126–28, 134

Index

Great Sioux War, description, 171–72, 174–78; map, 177
Green, John, 138, 141
Gros Ventre Indians, 12, 121, 199

Hammond, Charles G., 165
Hancock, Winfield Scott, 56
Handcock's War, 56
Handsome Lake, 24, 32
Harding, Warren G., 190
Harney, William S., 46, 54
Harrison, William Henry, 9, 22
Haudenosaunee (Iroquois), 18, 121, 187, 188
Hazen, William, 63, 201
Heavy Runner, 71–72
Henderson, John B., 54
Henry, Joseph, 160
Hinman, Samuel Dutton, 166
Hoar, Ebenezer, 65–66
Homestead Act, 127–28, 159
Hooker, Jim, 141

Indian Citizenship Act, 186
Indian policy: Adams administration, 10–11; allotment, 185–87; Board of Indian Commissioners' opposition to Grant's policy, 83–85; concentration, 12; Confederation Congress, 49, 69; formation of Grant's policy, 45–47; Franklin D. Roosevelt administration, 190–91; Harding administration, 190; Hoover administration, 190; Jackson administration, 11, 59, 191; Monroe administration, 9–10; one big reservation, 11–12; Parker's role in implementing Grant's, 66–68; Washington administration, 8–9, 49, 59, 66, 69
Indian Removal Act, 11, 178
Indian Reorganization Act, 190–91
Indian Rights Association, 184
Indian Ring, 25, 164

Indian service: appropriations for Indian service, 18, 66, 87–89, 97, 107, 110; battle for control of Indian service, 2, 82, 85, 88, 98, 100–101, 108–10, 113, 190; charges of corruption, 48, 79, 81, 84, 95, 102, 106, 125–26, 154, 164, 170, 173; military in Indian service, 1, 18, 67, 90–91, 182, 197–201; missionaries in Indian service, 2, 183, 189, 202–6
Indian Territory: agencies, 124, 202–3; Grant's plans for Indian Territory, 131–34, 158–60; Grant's visit (1874), 158; Indian Territory during Civil War, 45–46; reservations in Indian Territory, 25, 42, 44
Indians. *See individual tribes*
Interior Department: creation of, 12; Hoover administration, 190; New Deal, 191. *See also Grant's Interior secretaries* (Chandler, Zechariah; Cox, Jacob; Delano, Columbus)
Inyan Kara, 156

Jackson, Andrew: Battle of New Orleans, 22; Grant family support, 31; Indian policy, 1, 3, 8, 62, 66, 84, 178, 191; Indian removal, 11, 13–14, 23–25, 33, 42, 46, 59, 73
Jackson, Helen Hunt, 183–85
Jay Cooke and Company, 105, 108
Jefferson, Thomas, 9, 16, 62
Jenney, Walter P., 160
Johnson, Andrew, 5, 7, 41, 46–48, 51, 53–55, 59, 62, 166
Judiciary Act (1789), 34

Kansas-Nebraska Act, 12, 29
Kansas Pacific Railroad, 126–29, 129
Kendle, Robert, 33
King Philip (Metacomet), 17–18
King Philip's War, 18, 25
Kiowa Indians: agencies, 91. 202; description, 50, 117, 128; meeting

with Brunot, 83; meeting with Peace Commission, 54, 56–57; Parker's plans for Kiowa, 47; Red River War, 146–48, 150–52, 156; treaties, 12, 56, 61, 68, 73; Washita River Massacre, 69
Klamath Indians, 132, 135–36, 137, 181, 187, 204
Klamath Reservation, 136, 137

Lakota Sioux, 50–52, 54, 57–58, 62, 74, 76–77, 86, 130
Lane, Henry S., 79–80
Lawrence, Albert G., 166
Lawrence, William, 98, 105, 107
Lea, Luke, 12
League of the Ho-dé-no-sau-nee or Iroquois, The, 187–88
Lee, Robert E., 42–43
Lights and Shadows of a Long Episcopate, The, 80
Lincoln, Abraham, 5–7, 30–31, 35, 37, 41, 48, 80, 136, 141
Little Crow, 36–37
Long Walk, 7, 38, 58
Lost River Valley, 136, 138, 140
Luther Standing Bear, 187, 189
Lutheran Church, 125, 205–6
Lyman, Wyllys, 150

Mackenzie, Ranald, 148, 150–51
Madison, James, 9–10
Mandan Indians, 12
Manypenny, George, 176, 178
Marias Massacre, 70–74
Maricopa Indians, 112, 124, 204
Marsh, Othniel, 160
Marshall, John, 41
Marshall, Samuel, 18
Martindale, John H., 33–34
Massasoit, 16–17
Meacham, Alfred Benjamin, 90, 136, 139, 141, 197

Merriam, Lewis, 190
Merriam Report (*The Problem of Indian Administration*), 190
Mescalero Apache, 38
Mescalero Reservation, 155, 198, 203
Methodist Church, 24, 40, 120, 124, 204, 206
Mexican War, 11, 27, 31
Miami Indians, 21
Miles, Nelson, 148
mining, impact on tribes, 126
Modoc Indians, 134–36
Modoc War, 137, 138–43
Mohegan Indians, 17
Monroe, James, 9–10
Morgan, Lewis Henry, 187–88
Morris, Robert, 33
Mountain Chief, 71–72
My Indian Boyhood, 187

Narragansett Indians, 17
Navajo Indians (Diné), 7, 12, 38, 58–59, 61, 124, 181, 198, 203
Newton, Henry, 160
Nez Perce Indians, 121, 128, 180, 183–84, 199, 203
Niobrara River, 158
Northern Pacific Railroad, 96, 127, 157

Ocmulgee Constitution, 93–95
Odeneal, Thomas B., 136, 138
Office of Indian Affairs: creation of, 11. *See also commissioners' entries* (Clum, Henry R.; Parker, Ely S.; Smith, Edward Parmelee; Smith, John Quincy; Walker, Francis A.)
Ogden, Robert, 33–34, 45
Ohio Country, 9, 19–22
one big reservation (Indian policy), 11
Oregon Territory, 27, 31
Oregon Trail, 29, 51, 90
Osage Indians: agencies, 190, 200, 202; controversy over blankets, 99–100,

Index

Osage Indians (*continued*) 102–3, 106–7, 124, 155; description, 46, 94, 99
Ottawa Indians, 19, 21, 23–25, 94
Owl Child, 70–71

Paiute Indians, 138–39, 198, 203
Palmer, Frank Weyland, 166
Palo Duro Canyon, 150
Papago Indians, 111–12
Parker, Cynthia Ann, 146
Parker, Ely S.: analysis of Grant's Indian policy, 189; ancestry, 32; appointment as commissioner of Indian Affairs, 65–66; council in Ocmulgee, 93–95; defender of Tonawanda Seneca, 33–35; early political opinions, 29–31; education, 33–34; emergency on Upper Missouri (1870), 77–78, 82, 85; engineering career, 35; failure to win Union Army commission, 32, 35; first meeting with Grant, 28–29; formation of Grant's Indian policy, 1–2, 14, 47–49, 64; Grant's military secretary, 5, 35–36, 37, 39, 42; implementation of Grant's Indian policy, 67–68, 197–201; initial response to Welsh's charges, 97–99; later life, 114, 188–89; meeting with Red Cloud, 74–77; post–Civil War Indian service, 45–49, 53–54; reaction to Indian service changes, 112–13; reaction to Piegan Massacre, 72–73; relationship with Board of Indian Commissioners, 78–79; resignation as commissioner of Indian Affairs, 113–14; role in *Fellows v. Blacksmith*, 34–35; scholar of the Haudenosaunee, 187–88; Seneca head chief, 34; trial in Congress, 99–110; Welsh's accusations, 95–97
Parker, Quanah, 146, 147, 148, 151
Pawnee Indians, 77, 118, 198, 203
Peace Commission, 13–14, 54–57, 59, 63, 122
Peace Policy, 1–2, 115, 143, 159, 179

Pease, William B., 72, 199
Pequot War, 16–17
Peta Nocona, 146
Piegan Indians, 70
Piegan Massacre, 70–74
Pierre (Dakota Territory), 45, 158
Pima Indians, 112, 124, 198, 204
Pinal Apache Indians, 111
Pine Ridge Reservation, 187
Polk, James K., 27, 31, 34, 45
Ponca Indians, 180, 183–84, 199, 205
Pontiac, 19
Pope, John, 37, 44–45
Powder River Valley, 51–52, 55, 86, 115
Power, Fred, 156
Presbyterian Church, 24, 80, 120, 125, 203, 206
Price, William, 148
Proclamation of 1763, 19
Promontory Point, 126

Quaker Policy, 1–2, 173, 181
Quakers (Hicksite), 67, 202, 206
Quakers (Orthodox), 67, 202, 206
Quapaw Indians: agency, 202; controversy over payment to General Blunt, 99, 102–3, 105, 107, 170; description, 46

Ramsey, Alexander, 37
Rawlins, John, 5, 36, 39, 139
Red Cloud: agency, 205; background, 51, 74; Fort Laramie Treaty (1868), 59; meeting with de Smet, 122; meeting with Grant administration (1870), 74, 75, 76–77; meeting with Grant administration (1875), 160–62, *163*, 164; negotiations for the Black Hills, 167–69, 171, 178; opposition to Bozeman Trail, 51–52, 55; Parker's aid in 1870 emergency, 115
Red Cloud's War, 55, 57, 86
Red Jacket, 32
Red River War: description, 146–51; map, 150

Reed, Silas, 166
Reno, Marcus, 174–76
Republican Party Platform (1868), 62
Riddle, Frank, 139, 141
River Tribes, 16
Robeson, George, 173–74
Rogers, Robert, 18–19
Roosevelt, Franklin D., 3, 190–91
Roseborough, A. M., 139
Ross, Samuel, 139
Ruggles, Benjamin, 24
Ruggles, George, 157

Sackett, Minnie, 66, 114
Sanborn, John B., 54, 65
Sand Creek Massacre, 7, 40–42, 52, 54
Santee Sioux Indians, 50, 80, 95, 118, 157, 200, 202
Santee Sioux War, 7, 36–37, 40, 151
Sargent, Aaron, 96, 98, 105, 107
Saville, John, 160, 165
Schofield, John, 115
Schonchin John, 141–42
Sells, Elijah, 46
Seminole Indians, 21, 23–25
Seneca Indians (Ohio), 21, 23–25
Seventh Cavalry, 64, 69, 156, 171–72, 174, 176
Seward, William, 32, 35
Sheridan, Philip: attitude toward Indians, 8, 43–44; defense of Major Baker, 72; headquarters in Chicago, 146; meeting with Grant (1875), 158; plan for Black Hills exploration, 156; role in Piegan Massacre, 71; role in Washita River Massacre, 63–64; strategy for Great Sioux War, 171, 174, 176; strategy for Red River War, 147, 149, 151
Sherman, William Tecumseh: advice to Grant on Indians, 43–44. 47–48, 57–58; defense of Major Baker, 72; Grant's use of missionaries, 90–91; role in Modoc War, 139; role in Peace Commission, 62–63; role in Piegan Massacre, 71–72; role in Washita River Massacre, 63; strategy for Great Sioux War, 146; strategy in Red River War, 146–47, 151
Shoshone Indians, 174, 199, 205
Sibley, Henry Hasting, 165
Sioux City (Iowa), 158
Sioux Indians: agencies, 101, 124, 200; defense of Sioux culture, 183, 187; description, 12–13, 49–51; emergency on Upper Missouri (1870), 86–87, 97; Fetterman's massacre, 52–53; gold in Sioux country, 126, 156, 158; Grant's fight for the Black Hills, 158, 160–64, 167–68; Great Sioux War, 2, 171–72, 174, 182; Peace Commission findings, 52; Red Cloud's War, 8, 49; Santee Sioux War, 7, 36–37, 44–45; Sherman's recommendations, 44; Sioux Country (map), 60; treaties, 12, 51, 58–61, 69, 76
Sioux Reservation: description, 156–57, 161–63, 176, 178, 187; Fort Laramie treaty map, 60; Great Sioux War map, 177
Sitting Bull, 167, 168, 171–73, 175–76
Slolux, 142–43
small reservation (Indian policy), 13, 39, 42
Smith, Edward Parmelee, 146, 151–55, 160, 164, 166, 170–71
Smith, James Webster, 113
Smith, John E., 35–36
Smith, John Quincy, 170–71
Snake Indians, 58, 136
Soul of the Indian, The, 187
Southern Pacific Railroad, 127
Spotted Tail, 74, 75, 160, 162, 165, 167, 169, 171, 174
Stickney, William, 165
Stowe, Harriet Beecher, 184
Stuart, George H., 79–80, 114, 116, 119
Sully, Alfred, 72, 199
Swift Bear, 55, 74, 75

Index

Taney, Roger B., 34–35
Tappan, Samuel Forster, 54
Tatum, Lawrie, 91–92, 190, 200, 202
Taylor, Nathaniel, 41, 54, 59, 65
Taylor, Zachary, 12
Tecumseh, 9, 11, 22
Tenskwatawa (the Prophet), 9–10, 22
Terry, Alfred, 54, 158, 166, 172, 174, 176
Teton Sioux, 50
Thayer, John, 66
Thomas, Eleazer, 140–41, 143, 155–56
Timber Culture Act, 130
Tippecanoe, Battle of, 9, 12
Tobey, Edward S., 79–80, 119
Tod, George, 21
Tonawanda reserve, 32–35, 66
Tonawanda Seneca, 45–46, 188–89
Transcontinental Railroad, 44, 53, 61, 74, 76, 126
Treaty of Fort Laramie (1851), 51
Treaty of Fort Laramie (1868), 60, 61–63, 74, 76, 115, 152, 154, 156, 160–62, 167, 178–79
Treaty of Ghent, 9–10
Treaty of Greenville, 21–22
Treaty of Guadalupe Hidalgo, 11, 47
Treaty of Medicine Lodge, 55–57, 59, 61–63, 73, 146, 152
Treaty of Washington, 113
Tule Lake, 135–136, 137, 138

Union Pacific Railroad, 77
Unitarian Church, 125, 205–6
Upper Creek Indians, 9
Ute Indians, 73, 180

Walker, Francis A., 116–18, 151
Wallowa Valley, 180, 184
Wampanoag Indians, 16–18
War Department, debate over return of Office of Indian Affairs, 14, 47–48, 53, 58, 64, 73, 84, 182–83

War Hawks, 9, 22
War of 1812, 9, 11, 22–23
Washita River Massacre, 63–64, 69, 183–84
Wayne, Anthony, 21
Webster, Daniel, 34
Welsh, Herbert, 184
Welsh, William: accusations against Commissioner Smith, 164; accusations against Parker, 2, 95–98; actions at Parker's trial, 99–106, 109; appointment to Board of Indian Commissioners, 79–80; background, 79–80; continuing criticism of Parker, 114; goals for Board of Indian Commissioners, 82; portrait, 97; relationship with board, 85–86, 88; resignation from board, 82
Western Cherokee, 46
West Point, 23, 25–28, 31, 113, 139
Wheaton, Frank, 138
Whipple, Henry, 80–81, 84, 88, 110, 178, 183–84
Whiskey Ring, 173
White Antelope, 40
Whitman, Royal, 111
Williamson, Joseph, 105
Windsor (Connecticut), 16–18, 25
Winema, 139, 141
Wirz, Henry, 99–100, 143
Wister, Thomas, 46
Wodziwab, 138–39
Women's National Indian Association, 184
Woodall, Zechariah, 150
Worcester v. Georgia, 41
Wounded Knee Massacre, 180, 187
Wyandot Indians, 21, 23–26, 65, 84

Yankton Sioux, 50, 130
Yates, Richard, 31

Mary Stockwell was a professor of history and the department chair at Lourdes University, where she won numerous awards for her teaching, before becoming a full-time writer. She has also been a Gilder Lehrman Fellow at the New York Public Library and an Earhart Foundation Fellow at the William L. Clements Library at the University of Michigan. Her most recent works include *The Other Trail of Tears: The Removal of the Ohio Indians*, a finalist for the Ohio Library's Association's 2016 Best Book Award, and *Unlikely General: "Mad" Anthony Wayne and the Battle for America*, for Yale University Press in 2018. Her history books used by young people throughout the United States include *The Ohio Adventure*, *A Journey through Maine*, and *Massachusetts: Our Home*, the 2005 winner of the Golden Lamp Award from the Association of Educational Publishers for Best Book.

THE WORLD OF  ULYSSES S. GRANT

Edited by John F. Marszalek & Timothy B. Smith

After the assassination of Abraham Lincoln, Ulysses S. Grant became the most popular American alive. He symbolized the Federal victory, the destruction of slavery, and the preservation of the Union. Grant remained a popular topic among historians who have written about those years, but over time scholars and the public removed Grant from his place in the pantheon of leading Americans. As the decades passed and attitudes toward the Civil War and war itself changed, the public's perception of Grant devolved: no longer a national idol, Grant was instead written off as a heartless general and corrupt president. In the early twenty-first century, however, Grant's place in history is being reinterpreted. Now he is increasingly seen as a success on the battlefield, a leading proponent of African American civil rights, and the first of the modern American presidents.

To further an understanding of Ulysses S. Grant through a close analysis of his life and work, this innovative book series provides a thorough examination of particular events and periods of Grant's life in order to present important insights into his generalship, presidency, influence, and reputation. Books in the series explore Grant's character as well as his role in American history. By delving into the deeper detail and context of what Grant did and saw, this series aims to break new ground and provide the historical profession and the general reading public with accurate, readable perspectives showing Grant's significant contributions to the world he lived in and to the years that followed.

OTHER BOOKS IN
The World of Ulysses S. Grant

Citizen of a Wider Commonwealth: Ulysses S.
Grant's Postpresidential Diplomacy
Edwina S. Campbell

The Best Writings of Ulysses S. Grant
Edited by John F. Marszalek

The Decision Was Always My Own:
Ulysses S. Grant and the Vicksburg Campaign
Timothy B. Smith